CITY
ON THE
EDGE

CITY
ON THE
EDGE

The Transformation of Miami

ALEJANDRO PORTES
AND
ALEX STEPICK

UNIVERSITY OF CALIFORNIA PRESS
BERKELEY   LOS ANGELES   LONDON

University of California Press
Berkeley and Los Angeles, California

University of California Press, Ltd.
London, England

© 1993 by
The Regents of the University of California

Library of Congress Cataloging-in-Publication Data
Portes, Alejandro, 1944–
    City on the edge : the transformation of Miami /
Alejandro Portes and Alex Stepick.
        p.   cm.
    Includes bibliographical references and index.
    ISBN 0-520-08217-6 (alk. paper)
    1. Miami (Fla.)—Race relations.   2. Miami (Fla.)—Ethnic
relations.   3. Miami (Fla.)—Social conditions.   4.
Minorities—Florida—Miami.   I. Stepick, Alex.   II. Title.
    F319.M6P68   1993
    305.8′009759′381—dc20   92-39417
                                                             CIP

Printed in the United States of America
9 8 7 6 5 4 3 2 1

For Maria Patricia and Carol,
with thanks

Contents

List of Illustrations   viii

List of Tables   x

Preface   xi

Acknowledgments   xv

1.   Change Without a Blueprint   1

2.   A Year to Remember: Mariel   18

3.   A Year to Remember: The Riot and the Haitians   38

4.   The Early Years   61

5.   Enter the Cubans   89

6.   How the Enclave Was Built   123

7.   A Repeat Performance? The Nicaraguan Exodus   150

8.   Lost in the Fray: Miami's Black Minorities   176

9.   Reprise   203

Postscript: In the Eye of the Storm   223

Notes   229

Bibliography   259

Index   275

Illustrations

Photographs

Following page 107

1. The Miami skyline
2. Sign in Miami
3. Chapel of Our Lady of Charity, Biscayne Bay
4. Bay of Pigs Memorial, Woodlawn Cemetery
5. Flags in Woodlawn Cemetery
6. Domino players in Little Havana
7. Funeral home in Miami
8. Street scene, Little Havana
9. Billboard in Miami
10. Downtown Little Haiti, Miami
11. Haitian street vendors, Little Haiti
12. Street scene, Little Haiti
13. Haitian boat and captain, Miami River
14. Haitian dock worker, Miami River
15. Haitian agricultural workers, southwest of Miami
16. Haitian bean picker, southwest Dade County
17. Haitian shoppers in a Cuban-owned market
18. Religious college in Miami Beach
19. Students at Talmudic University, Miami Beach
20. Hasidic Jews, Miami Beach

21. Monument to Carl Fisher, founder of Miami Beach
22. Mural in northwest Miami
23. Cubans protesting Nelson Mandela's visit to Miami, 1990
24. Anti-Mandela protester, 1990
25. Protester arguing with Mandela supporter, 1990
26. Tent city for people made homeless by Hurricane Andrew
27. Store destroyed by hurricane
28. Home destroyed by hurricane

Figures

1. Extent of subordination and speed of assimilation 7
2. Population of the Miami metropolitan area, 1980 20
3. Weekly Mariel arrivals and negative *Miami Herald* articles on the inflow, 1980 28
4. Professionals, executives, and laborers, Dade County, 1970 and 1980 42
5. Income, affluence, and poverty, Dade County, 1980 44
6. Unemployment rates by race and origin, Dade County, 1980–90 45
7. Black professionals and administrators working for Dade County government, 1982–90 181

Maps

1. The Miami metropolitan area, 1980 19
2. Black population, Miami metropolitan area, 1990 186
3. Spanish-origin population, Miami metropolitan area, 1990 187

Tables

1. Attitudes Toward American Ethnic Groups Held by the American Public, 1982   31

2. Perceptions and Experiences of Discrimination of Mariel Refugees, 1983 and 1986   33

3. Ethnic Groups' Employment by Sector, Dade County, 1960–80   41

4. Characteristics of Haitian Entrants in South Florida, 1983   57

5. Growth of Miami's Black Businesses, 1977–87   180

6. Black- and Cuban-owned Firms, 1987   182

7. Employment and Business Establishments in the Miami Metropolitan Area, 1950–87   209

8. Ethnic Composition of Metropolitan Miami, 1950–90   211

Preface

Miami is not a microcosm of the American city. It never was. From its very beginnings a century ago, the Biscayne Bay metropolis possessed an air of unreality, a playground divorced from its natural habitat by the deeds of Yankee developers. For a while it seemed that no fantasy, no matter how farfetched, could not be enacted here. The thin strip of land between jungle and reef hence became less an American Riviera than a compendium of the nation's foibles. During the last three decades or so Miami has evolved, shedding its light-hearted past to become a serious, some say tragic, place. The Cuban Revolution marked the beginning of this change, which was pushed along by new influxes of Caribbean migrants and by native reactions to the presence of so many outsiders. Cubans, of course, played a pivotal role in the transformation, for their actions and dreams, while inspiring the Cuban community, also affected the character and identity of other groups. And thereby the entire community changed.

Our interest in this city dates back to the early seventies when we began studying the arrival and resettlement of new immigrant groups in the area. As sociologists, our principal focus was the adaptation of foreign-born minorities to their new environment. As time passed, however, it became clear that the environment itself was changing in ways that we could not have anticipated. The immigrants were transforming not only themselves, but also the city around them. Unwittingly, Miami had become the nation's first full-fledged experiment in bicultural living in the contemporary era.

Other U.S. cities, such as New York and Los Angeles, also have large Spanish-speaking and immigrant populations, but nowhere has the social and economic weight of the newcomers or their political significance been greater than in South Florida. In New York, new arrivals are promptly absorbed into the immense fabric of the city; the very diversity of nationalities in New York conspires against any single group becoming too prominent. In Miami, the regrouped Cuban bourgeoisie not only redefined the character of the city, but also prompted other ethnic communities—native Blacks and whites included—to cast their own identities in sharper relief.

Other bilingual and bicultural cities and regions have of course existed in the history of the nation. Milwaukee and St. Louis at the turn of the twentieth century were German towns; northern Wisconsin and Michigan were heavily Scandinavian; inhabitants of parishes in the Louisiana lowlands spoke Acadian French; and San Antonio, Santa Fe, and other towns in the vast territories taken from Mexico retained Spanish for a long while. But the passage of time and the growing hegemony of American culture diluted these experiences and accustomed us to the spectacle of immigrants who had been Americanized before reaching U.S. shores or who promptly shed their cultural trappings in quest of assimilation. Arising from a unique set of historical circumstances, the Miami experiment is unique and unlikely to be repeated. Yet the passions that it awoke and the social energies that it released may carry significant lessons as America becomes again, under the influence of growing immigration, a multiethnic society.

The immediate predecessor of this book was a six-year panel study of the adaptation process of Cuban and Haitian immigrants in South Florida. That study was prompted by the 1980 Mariel exodus, accompanied by a rising number of Haitian "boat people" arriving in Florida at about the same time. Our original intention was to learn how these immigrants—unwelcome by almost every sector of American society—managed to cope in their new social environment. The social reception and economic situation of Mariel Cubans and Haitians was chronicled in a series of articles, cited in the following chapters. Yet to pursue the broader goal of analyzing the transformation of Miami under the influence of these and earlier immigrant waves, we had to shift methodological gears.

To learn more about the city, we supplemented the original

panel study with a series of interviews with leaders of the communities that form its ethnic mosaic. First, leaders of the original refugee groups targeted for study—Cubans and Haitians—were contacted and interviewed in 1983. This was followed by systematic canvassing of Black, Jewish, Anglo (as native whites are called today), Cuban, and Nicaraguan leaders in 1987–88 and by supplementary interviews with the same or new informants in 1990–91.

Simultaneously, we had to delve deeper into the history of the area and gather data on present developments. Rich chronicles of the Florida peninsula and the island of Cuba written by historians such as Marjory Stoneman Douglas, Alva Moore Parks, Hugh Thomas, and Herminio Portell Vila helped us understand the long-term trends that gave rise to modern Miami. Yet most of these histories ended just as the city's unique transformation was getting under way. As we turned to the present, the data-gathering routine became less routine: scarcely a day passed without some new development taking place in the city. This was change not only without a blueprint, but at breakneck speed.

By the mid-eighties, others have begun to notice the same thing. Literary figures traveled from New York and other northern cities to record their impressions of the place. The resulting books were useful to us, not merely for their insights, but because they obviated the need to justify a serious study of what, until then, had been regarded as a fading tourist resort. For some of these authors, like T. D. Allman, events in South Florida even prefigured the future of other American cities.

In what follows, the story of Miami is told in a somewhat unconventional way that deserves explanation. The first chapter illustrates the overlap of diverse and contradictory discourses about the city that are so much part of its evolution in recent years. We look then at the proximate causes of the rise of these competing discourses in the events that took place in the pivotal year of 1980— the Mariel exodus, the arrival of the Haitian "boat people," and the violent riot in the Black sections of the city (chapters 2 and 3). Next we explore the more distant origins of contemporary events, both in the history of Florida, from colonial days to the eve of the Cuban Revolution (chapter 4), and in the peculiar relationship between Cuba and the peninsula during the first half of the twentieth century (chapter 5). This relationship led to the overwhelming preference for Miami shown by Cubans displaced from their homeland and to the subsequent construction of an ethnic enclave economy in the city (chapter 6).

Finally we examine how the latest immigrant group—the Nicaraguans—as well as the Haitians and native Blacks have fared in this new Miami and their likely prospects for the future (chapters 7 and 8). Chapter 9 then assesses the whole in terms of both past theories of urbanization and ethnic relations and practical lessons in urban policy.

Miami's story does not end with the closure of this narrative. Even as we brought it to a tentative conclusion, an unexpected event gave this remarkable transformation a new and tragic turn. Hurricanes are nothing new in South Florida, but the fury of Hurricane Andrew in August 1992 and the magnitude of the destruction left in its wake amount to a new hiatus in the history of the area. We visited the city again in the storm's aftermath, went to the most affected areas, and talked to both victims of the debacle and experts on natural disasters.

This sad inquiry in the month after the disaster offered persuasive evidence that the extent of the damage was no fleeting news item, but would mark the evolution and collective identity of the area for years to come. The Postscript summarizes what we learned in the partially destroyed city and the likely effects the event will have on its social and demographic makeup. The irruption of a natural cataclysm into what already was a complex situation may lead to unexpected outcomes, but our overall sense is that its primary effect will be to accelerate the process of change already under way, outlined in the following chapters.

A final word on the title. It was difficult to arrive at a designation that was neither ominous nor celebratory but that captured the obvious tension in the unprecedented events experienced by this city. In our view, such events signal transformation and challenge, not necessarily decline. Miami is not "in the abyss," but on a threshold. The city is several things at once: at the southern end of the land and astride two cultural worlds; about to complete its first century of existence; and, above all, on the edge of a future marked by uncertainty, but also by the promise of pathbreaking innovations in urban life. The multilingual, multicultural experiment that is Miami holds important lessons for what the American city will be about in a changed world.

Acknowledgments

The original longitudinal study of Mariel Cuban and Haitian refugees in South Florida on which this book is partially based was supported by grants from the National Science Foundation (SES-8215567) and the National Institute of Mental Health (MH 41502). Additional support for field interviews and data gathering in Miami came from a grant from the Ford Foundation. We are grateful to officials in all three institutions, and in particular to Dr. William A. Diaz of the Ford Foundation for his timely assistance and encouragement.

The original and the two follow-up surveys of Mariel refugees in Miami were conducted by Dr. Juan M. Clark of Miami-Dade Community College. We owe an immense debt to Juan for his expertise and dedication to the project. A similar stellar performance was delivered by Carol Stepick, field director of the third Haitian refugee follow-up, which focused on issues of mental health and help-seeking among this group.

The nationality of the authors (Cuban and "Anglo" in local parlance) precluded them from conducting unbiased first-person interviews with several key informants in the polarized Miami environment. The bulk of this task fell to Dr. Patricia Fernandez-Kelly, a social anthropologist by training, whose field skills and relatively "neutral" origins did wonders to open doors that otherwise would have been closed to us. Without her help and the materials that she accumulated, this book could not have been written.

We are grateful as well to all our informants, busy people who gave generously of their time, often on more than one occasion. In keeping with our covenant at the time of the interviews, their names must remain anonymous. A number of our colleagues were similarly generous in reading early versions of various chapters and providing encouragement for what, for us, was a "first"—an attempt to combine the analysis of survey data with first-person testimonies and anecdotal material. Our New York–based colleagues Richard Sennett, Aristide Zolberg, and Janet Abu-Lughod must be mentioned in this regard. Without their support and inspiration, we probably would have reverted to standard modes of data analysis.

We acknowledge with gratitude the assistance of Dr. Charles W. Blowers and Mr. Oliver Kerr of the Research Division, Metro-Dade Planning Department, who made available to us valuable data and graphics on the Miami area. We would also like to thank Steve Doig of the *Miami Herald*, Sandra Dibble of *National Geographic* and formerly the *Miami Herald*, Mike Clary of the *Los Angeles Times*, and Roland Fisch of Florida Keys Community College, all of whom provided data that we found useful.

At the University of California Press, our editor Naomi Schneider and the reviewers assigned to the manuscript gave us welcome encouragement as well as well-targeted criticisms. We can only hope that the final version reflects, at least in part, their efforts to improve the book. At Johns Hopkins, we benefited from the comments and advice of Melvin L. Kohn, Christopher Chase-Dunn, and David Kyle; at Florida International University, from those of Lisandro Perez, A. Douglas Kincaid, Max Castro, Guillermo Grenier, and Mark Rosenberg. To Mark, in particular, we owe the idea of the title. But none of them and none of the other persons named above bears any responsibility for the content, which is exclusively ours.

Last but not least, we owe a great debt of gratitude to Cristiana Camardella and Diane Berger, who transcribed each chapter, struggled with illegible longhands, and produced in the end a handsome manuscript. We commend their efforts and hope that they are pleased with the final product.

Chapter One

Change Without a Blueprint

J. Michael Quinlan, federal director of prisons, was a worried man. Eight days into a major riot, there were no signs that the situation was about to ease or that more than one hundred hostages would be released unharmed. The prisoners' cause, meanwhile, was gaining ground. They had rigged a public address system on top of the prison walls to broadcast their demands and talk to relatives. Prisoners' wives and mothers huddled in tents just outside the penitentiary, not far from the families of the hostages. Neither group wanted violence. A busload of prisoners' relatives had just arrived in Washington, D.C., to intercede with the attorney general on behalf of those inside.

More vexing to federal officials were the rioters' demands. Everyone agreed that conditions inside the prison were intolerable and that many had been detained for years without due process. Neither of these facts, however, sparked the rebellion. Rather, the prisoners revolted when they heard they would be *released,* in order to be sent out of the country. The receiving nation's government had assured U.S. authorities that no reprisals would be taken against the deportees, which made the latter's attitude even more extraordinary.

Quinlan had a trump card in his favor should the impasse turn to armed violence, and that was the solid support shown by the public for the government and against the rebellious foreigners. That support was apparent everywhere—everywhere, that is, but in one city. There the rioters' demands not to be deported struck a responsive chord. Previously dismissed as "scum," the prisoners,

1

with their sorry living conditions and their endless sentences, had elicited little concern in the past, but when they declared that they would rather die than go home, their compatriots in Miami claimed them as their own. While the rest of the country prayed for the safety of the hostages, in this one city the masses and the rosaries were performed for the sake of the captors and their plight.

For Quinlan and his men, time was running out. Public patience was wearing thin as day after fruitless day of negotiations passed, making the authorities look ever more impotent. Then the rioters voiced a new demand: they wanted to see someone who would vouch for their safety after they surrendered. They did not ask for the attorney general of the United States or any other important Washington official; rather, they requested an obscure priest from the place where the masses were being said in their behalf.

Monsignor Agustin Román, auxiliary bishop of Miami, is an unpretentious little man. White-haired, with a slight frame, he was an incongruous figure next to the burly prison officials. His presence, however, accomplished what the federal authorities had been unable to. Román's message to the rebelling Mariel prisoners in Oakdale and in Atlanta began "Dear brothers," and ended with a plea that they demonstrate to the world "Christian good will." Behind the pious rhetoric, the message said this: You belong to us and we will not abandon you. A few hours later, the 1987 Mariel prison riots were history.[1]

Appeals by the downtrodden to fellow ethnics are not uncommon—ethnic group sympathies, after all, often flow in directions contrary to those of the mainstream. Yet events after 1987 demonstrated that Miami was indeed unique in the extent to which contrasting worldviews existed and were superimposed on each other.

On January 24, 1990, former policeman William Lozano stood before a packed Miami courtroom awaiting sentence on two counts of manslaughter. A month earlier, he had been convicted of shooting and killing Black motorcyclist Clement Lloyd and his passenger in a desolate street of the Overtown ghetto. Lloyd had disobeyed an order to stop and raced in the direction of the officer, who felled him with a single shot. The event triggered two nights of arson and looting, put down only by massive police force and the mayor's promise that justice would be done. When Lozano received a seven-year sentence for manslaughter, the community breathed a sigh of relief—no rioting this time. Black Miami was reassured that police killings would no longer occur with impunity. Clement Lloyd's relatives complained about the light sentence but pronounced themselves satisfied about the verdict. As one of them put it, "At least Lozano is a known criminal now."

To protect himself from the vindictive mood of Black Miami, Lozano hired one of the city's best criminal attorneys. As his legal debts mounted, the now unemployed policeman appeared to have reached the end of the rope. He had one advantage, though. Among his fellow Colombians and much of the Latin population Lozano was seen, if not exactly as a hero, at least as a victim and scapegoat. His first public broadcast over Miami Cuban radio netted $150,000 in contributions; subsequent appeals produced substantial amounts as well. The fact that Lozano was "a known criminal" did not seem to lessen him in the eyes of his fellow Latins. Thanks to their contributions, he was able to retain a high-powered defense team.

On June 25, 1991, two and a half years after the shooting, the Third Florida District Court of Appeals threw out Lozano's sentence and ordered a new trial. The original judge had dismissed all motions for a change of venue with the argument that in this metropolitan area of two million people an impartial jury could be found. The appellate court disagreed. The people of Miami were in fact too sharply divided over Lozano's fate—some ready to lynch him, others providing financial support for his cause—to leave space for a fair trial.[2]

Since its beginnings at the start of the century, American urban sociology has focused on a few themes that repeat themselves with uncanny regularity. Stripped of their academic garb, these themes reflect the perennial preoccupations of the urban citizenry: Who really rules? How can local elites be made more accountable to their fellow citizens? What explains the plight of ethnic minorities? How can conflict be resolved? Students of urban life have attempted to provide answers to these and other questions and, in the process, have created a rich imagery of what the American city is all about. It is useful to review some of these images, for they form the backdrop against which the above events and those de-

scribed in the following pages can be understood. Their significance is not that they help account for the course of events in
Miami, but precisely that they fit the story so awkwardly.

Community Power

The question "Who rules the city?" has led to an elaborate literature and to the development of complex methods for understanding the true character of urban power. Spearheaded in the 1940s
and into the 1960s by such scholars as Floyd Hunter, Robert Dahl,
and C. Wright Mills, the basic controversy centered on whether
the "business class" was the sole arbiter of local decision-making
or whether other groups also had a say in urban affairs. Crucial
among the latter were public officials, often elected on the voting
strength of ethnic minority blocks. Were such elected officials part
of the "real" power structure, or were they merely window dress-
ing to cover the actions of the true movers and shakers? "Pluralism" and "elitism" became the accepted labels in this long-running
controversy.[3]

More recently, the elitist position has expanded to embrace
analysis of the urban "growth machine." Proponents of this view,
notably Harvey Molotch and John Logan, portray the growth machine as a confabulation of property capitalists bent on profiting
from their control of urban amenities and scarce urban space.
Techniques include manipulation of zoning ordinances and other
tricks to render empty land valuable or to redefine the use of built
spaces. Hence it is not "business" in general, but the business of
creating profits out of locational advantage, that determines the
pattern of urban growth.[4]

Locals and Cosmopolitans

In a 1946 report to the U.S. Senate, C. Wright Mills raised a related
issue, namely whether cities suffered when their economies became dominated by outside interests. Mills denounced footloose
corporate capitalism that extracted resources but provided little to
the community in return. In lieu of "branch" capitalism, Mills
proposed to the Congress a program to revitalize local business on
the theory that community-based enterprises were more egalitar-

ian and more responsive to local welfare. Critics called Mills's position retrograde; the growth of the American economy, they said, required the emergence of powerful multicentric corporations, and they produced an array of studies to demonstrate that corporate executives could be just as civic-minded as locals, and often more effectively so.[5] With variations, this debate between advocates of "cosmopolitan" versus "local" economic control endures today.

Ethnicity and Assimilation

It was ethnicity, however, that emerged as the fundamental leitmotiv of American urban sociology. Indeed, it could not have been otherwise, given a citizenry molded by successive waves of immigration, each different in many ways from earlier ones. The themes of social power and social class on which Hunter, Mills, and other classics focused became increasingly intertwined with those of race, language, and culture. The fundamental controversy about ethnicity was whether racial and cultural markers were tied to class position and hence disappear with upward mobility or whether they represent a separate and autonomous dimension of social structure. The first position was eloquently argued by W. Lloyd Warner and his associates on the basis of their massive study of "Yankee City" (Newburyport, Massachusetts). Writing in the 1940s, Warner captured the differences that he and his students observed in social prestige and social recognition in a sixfold classification of "class." Classes in Yankee City ranged from the white Protestant "upper-upper" elite and mostly white "lower-upper" professionals to the largely ethnic "upper-lower" strata of factory workers and the "lower-lower" skid row population.[6]

An "ethnic," in Warner's theory, was someone who by reason of culture or race was outside the community's mainstream and considered himself or herself or was considered by others to belong to a distinct subsociety. Ethnics concentrated in the bottom rungs of the social structure—the lower middle and lower classes—depending on their work skills and length of local residence. Climbing the social ladder required that one join the cultural mainstream, but even fully acculturated minorities might not prove acceptable to the "upper-upper" brahmins who controlled the prestige hierarchy. Warner and Leo Srole identified skin color (race), language, and religion as the fundamental criteria of elite acceptance: the more similar ethnic groups are, along these dimensions, to those occupying positions of prestige and power in the community, the faster their assimilation. Race was the most important factor, followed by language and then religion.[7] The combined operation of these factors within the urban population led to an ethnic class hierarchy that also predicted the expected speed of assimilation. Figure 1 reproduces Warner and Srole's hierarchy of ethnicity and the consequent pecking order in Yankee City.

In the 1940s and 1950s, it seemed reasonable to assume that all "ethnics" wished to and would follow the path of assimilation. By the sixties, that story had become open to doubt. Several authors pointed to the presence of "unmeltable ethnics," for whom no amount of acculturation appeared sufficient to gain them acceptance into the urban mainstream. Others noted how distinct cultural traits endured through the generations thanks to strong group institutions and the unwillingness of certain minorities to lose their identity. Often such resilient ethnicity was displayed even *after* a group had moved significantly upward in the economic hierarchy. Focusing on these exceptions, Nathan Glazer, Daniel P. Moynihan, and Andrew Greeley questioned the earlier assumptions and suggested that the American city was not really a "melting pot" where minorities would sooner or later lose their identities and join the mainstream, but rather a "social mosaic" where ethnic-based solidarities persisted across generations.[8]

With the passage of time, the intertwined themes of power, class, race, and ethnicity and the associated controversies came to define how students of urban life thought about the American city. Although the answers given by "pluralists" and "elitists," "locals" and "cosmopolitans," and "melting pot" versus "social mosaic" advocates differed, the questions remained consistent: Who really governs? How does outside business control affect civic welfare? Why are ethnic minorities outside the social mainstream? What would it take to change their situation? The search for answers gave rise over time to a methodological repertoire—a tool kit— that researchers carried from city to city and applied in a more or less standardized fashion.

Extent of Subordination	Racial Type	Cultural Type	Speed of Assimilation and Upward Mobility
	I. Light Caucasoids	1. English-speaking Protestants 2. Protestants who do not speak English 3. English-speaking Catholics and other non-Protestants 4. Catholics and other non-Protestants who do not speak English 5. English-speaking non-Christians 6. Non-Christians who do not speak English	
	II. Dark Caucasoids	Cultural types 1 to 6	
	III. Mongoloid and Caucasoid mixtures with Caucasoid appearance dominant (appearance of "dark" Mediterranean)	Cultural types 1 to 6	
	IV. Mongoloid and Caucasoid mixtures that appear Mongoloid	Cultural types 1 to 6	
	V. Negroid and all Negroid mixtures	Cultural types 1 to 6	

Figure 1. Extent of subordination and speed of assimilation. Adapted from W. Lloyd Warner and Leo Srole, *The Social Systems of American Ethnic Groups* (New Haven: Yale University Press, 1945), 288. By permission of Yale University Press.

Researchers approaching modern Miami with the same time-honored ideas and the same methodological tools, however, would be in for a shock. Although the city is in the United States, it does not resemble in the slightest the models of Yankee City and other urban classics. Nor does it fit very well more recent descriptions of a "social mosaic" composed of established ethnic groups that maintain certain elements of their culture under the hegemonic umbrella of a white Protestant elite. In Miami, the fragments of the mosaic are loose and do not come together in any familiar pattern. Consider the following reversals vis-à-vis traditional American urban life:

1. While the "business class" does exercise undisputable control in governing the city, it is composed increasingly of recent immigrants, rather than exclusively of "old" families or corporate "branch" executives. This is particularly true in the case of the "growth machine" created by foreign-born builders and developers.

2. The clash between local and outside corporate control occurs, but in Miami the proliferating local small businesses are owned mostly by immigrants, while the corporate "branch" offices are American-owned. Many of the latter are there not to produce goods for the domestic market but to sell services to other foreigners, often through the mediation of the local immigrant-owned firms.

3. There is no mainstream. The hegemony of the old "upper-uppers" has given way to parallel social structures, each complete with its own status hierarchy, civic institutions, and cultural life. As a result, economic mobility and social standing have ceased to depend on full acculturation or on pleasing the elites of the old class order.

4. The overlap of parallel social systems in the same physical space has given rise to acculturation in reverse—a process by which foreign customs, institutions, and language are diffused within the native population. As a consequence, biculturalism has emerged as an alternative adaptive project to full assimilation into American culture. Opponents of biculturalism, immigrants and natives alike, must either withdraw into their own diminished circles or exit the community.

The existence of these parallel social structures is what underlay the Mariel prisoners' call for Bishop Román rather than Attorney General Meese to act as guarantor of their fate.[9] Their move would have been inconceivable had their coethnics in Miami occupied the role assigned to them by Warner and other classic authors on community power. For that matter, the very fact that Mariel refugees were in American prisons at all is explainable only in terms of the unusual process of change that had overtaken South Florida before their arrival.

Competing Discourses

Social facts are not self-intelligible. Their interpretation depends on the cognitive frames in which they are placed, and these in turn are products of prior social interactions. Common meanings are arrived at when relevant audiences agree to stress certain aspects of a given phenomenon and interpret them on the basis of shared past experience. Existing "frames" of what American urban life is like, including those elaborated in the sociological research literature, prove to be of limited utility for rendering events in South Florida understandable. These events represent social change without a blueprint; because they led precisely to the fragmentation of previously held consensual views, it is not surprising that several competing discourses emerged to explain them, each with its own distinct shades of meaning and moral tone. Only in such a context would it be conceivable for William Lozano, convicted felon, to solicit and obtain support from a wide segment of the very city where his alleged crime was committed.

To approach developments in Miami, we first make use of W. I. Thomas's concept of "definition of the situation," a term that highlights how subjective perceptions of reality can influence reality itself.[10] In our view, definitions of the situation comprise (a) a frame of reference embodying one or more generalized ideas and (b) an "object" that is interpreted in terms of those ideas. Different objects are interrelated by reference to the common frame, giving rise to a perspective, or "discourse," in which apparently disparate aspects of reality are integrated into a meaningful interpretive whole. The difference between Miami and most communities studied by sociologists in the past is that in Miami even everyday events—not to mention more explosive conflicts between social classes and interest groups—are not necessarily assessed within a common frame of reference, but may be inserted into different, mutually unintelligible, interpretive frameworks.

At present, several perspectives sufficiently broad to provide a coherent account of life in this metropolitan area are identifiable. The most common ones may be labeled the "Anglo cultural reaffirmation," the "Cuban or pan-Latin success story," and the "Black double marginality" discourses. By way of illustration, the following excerpts of statements made by community leaders in interviews, addressing four frequent "objects" of debate in Miami, may be taken as typical of each discourse. The statements are drawn from interviews, conducted between 1983 and 1988, with approximately sixty of the most prominent business, political, and religious leaders in the city as a complement to a large survey of the recently arrived immigrant population in the area.[11] Three of these "objects"—Miami's "major problem," language, and interethnic relations—were posed as questions to all respondents; the fourth—the *Miami Herald*—emerged spontaneously in several conversations.

Miami's Major Problem

Native white business executive, former chairman of a large local corporation (interviewed in 1987):

You have two levels, one is what is going to happen to the nation as a whole over the next fifty years when the Hispanic population may become over fifty percent of the population; and the other level is the short-term impact of Hispanics in a city like this one. You deal with perceptions because you don't really know what percentage of the population is making the noise, but you hear the noise, the major noise, the dominant noise, and you are beginning to hear more and more that the Cubans are not interested in integrating into American society, and if that is the case, then that has to be the number-one problem in Miami.

That is a problem because there isn't a great deal in Caribbean and Latin American cultures that's going to add anything to democracy at all. And I think there is a good chance that it will detract from it. Cubans really value economic freedom, but there are other freedoms they don't value.

Cuban businessman, owner of a local factory, emigrated in the early 1960s (1986):

Our most serious problem in Miami is the devaluation of South American currencies because in this city there has been created a large current of business with Central and South America; many properties were built, many apartments were sold, apart from the exports. The devaluations in Venezuela, Mexico, and Brazil paralyzed economic activity in Miami. At the same time, construction of apartments for all those South Americans who wanted to own something here stopped. This is our most serious problem today. Until currencies regain their value and economic tranquility returns to those countries, Miami—which is the key link between the United States and Latin America—will continue to suffer.

Black community activist, director of a social service agency in Liberty City, the major Black area of South Florida (1987):

The real problem in 1987 is that the Blacks have not concluded that they must take control of their destiny. That's the real problem now. But that was not the real problem in 1964. Then, the problem was to remove the shackles of segregation. You had to go through that process in order to get to where we are in 1987. . . . Now, having gone through that process, the final lap is to put everything in perspective, and to ask ourselves what are we going to do about it, because all they have done since 1619 has not been in our interest, but theirs. In order to take charge of its own destiny, this community must simply, selfishly become unabatedly pro-Black.

Case in point: there is something special about Blacks and Revlon beauty care products. We find out that Blacks buy over fifty-one percent of all the beauty care products made in the country. . . . If we are the main consumers in that industry, then the appropriate response is for us to become major producers of that which we consume.

Language

Jewish lawyer, director of the regional branch of a major national Jewish organization (1986):

This is a community like a volcano. . . . A major issue concerns the tensions between native Americans and Hispanics. The focal point is language. There is a very strong "English Only" movement or variations of it. In twenty-five years, close to three hundred thousand Cubans have come here, and many have done very well. The fact is that they have taken over the city both in terms of numbers and economic presence. This has created a lot of resentment and bitterness in some circles. I think the popularized statement that typified the tension was the bumper sticker that read, "When the last American leaves Miami, please take the flag." That represents the middle- and lower-middle-class feeling about what happened here.

Native white business executive (quoted above with regard to Miami's major problem):

What happens is that in an open store there will be two or three women talking in an incomprehensible language, and people, I think, sometimes just get tired of being surrounded by Spanish. More importantly, there are many, many times when the Cubans know that the people in the room with them don't understand. Like my wife and her hairdresser: she speaks Spanish entirely while she is working on her hair. My son is an absolute linguist, he speaks Portuguese and Spanish fluently. He learned while he was in Rochester, New York, not while he lived in Miami, Florida. It is popular there to be bilingual; it isn't popular in Miami.

Cuban civic activist, head of a multiethnic community organization, emigrated in the early 1960s (1986):

Language has great importance because if an individual owns a store whose clients come from Latin America, he will need bilingual employees. During Christmastime, ninety percent of the stores advertise for bilingual employees. To a person who does not know the language, this situation represents an economic problem because he knows that, unless he knows Spanish, he would not compete successfully in the labor market. This problem is especially important in the Black community, which has the greatest number of unemployed. The young Black knows that it would be much more difficult to secure a job if he does not speak Spanish.

Black owner of a major business in Liberty City, active in the local chamber of commerce (1987):

There is also a growing number of Cuban-owned businesses in Black neighborhoods but they don't hire Blacks. For example, I was in a drug-store a couple of weeks ago and there was a black Cuban lady at one of the cash registers. I went to her and she didn't even want to talk to me. I thought to myself, "Talk to me, if I'm going to leave my money here, you ought to learn how to speak English." They come in our areas, they take our jobs, they take our dollars, and don't even have the decency to learn the language!

Interethnic Relations

Native white attorney, partner in a large local law firm (1987):

The problem of Blacks in Miami is very serious. But my feeling is that the Black population is so relatively small in number that I am not sure it's on anybody's agenda. . . . The number of Hispanics is so overwhelming that the contest is over. I mean there is competition, there is tension, there is concern in the Black community. But Cubans are so well entrenched, so large in numbers, that it's not an issue anymore.

Now, there is another big problem worth investigating: the concept of giving in the Latin community. One of the problems that FIU [Florida International University] has had is that [former president] Wolfe couldn't raise any money. So what did we do? The power structure and the Cubans said, "Let's go get ourselves a good old Cuban boy." Let's see whether old Maidique [Cuban-born, U.S.-educated president of FIU], President Mitch, can demonstrate that he can raise dollars from the Latin community. If he can't raise dollars, in my book he's failed.

There is a lot of work that needs to be done in teaching the concept of philanthropy within the Latin community. The Cubans have been here over twenty years, they have made great economic strides, the kids play football and baseball, they go to the operas, they do all these things; why not give more to the community?

Cuban businessman (quoted above with regard to Miami's major problem):

Relations between the different ethnic communities in Miami are normal as in any democratic country. Ethnic differences do not interfere at all in commercial relations. As to community activities, each one works in the place he or she prefers. There are persons who like to work in the United Way; and there is the Liga contra el cancer [League Against Cancer, a charity founded in Havana], which everyone joins to work for a good cause.

Perhaps, the most affected relations could be those between Cubans and Blacks, in the sense that Blacks are less trained as entrepreneurs, but I do not believe that there is an extraordinary friction. Our chief accountant was Black, a great Black, but right now there are no American Blacks working in our company. When we arrived from Cuba and opened our small business, the situation was like this: when a shipment arrived in customs, we would go to a corner and there would be ten, fifteen, twenty Blacks standing waiting for work. We picked them up so that they would unload our boxes, paid them, and returned them to the same place. Today, you don't see anything like this. I sincerely believe that, in Miami, the person who doesn't work is because he or she does not want to. Proof: why are so many Haitians now sewing in our factory?

Black attorney, community activist (1987):

Initially, as the Cubans began to be very competitive, as the new banks tended to be Cuban, as the Cubans began to come into the insurance and traditional financial markets where the Jews had played an important role, the issue was no longer Jews against Anglos but one of the survival of the status quo. . . .

Blacks were left behind. Miami is the only city I've ever seen where Blacks don't own a radio station, or a television station, or a car dealership, or a savings and loan, or an insurance company—anything! Blacks here have not only been manipulated out of the mainstream of the power structure, but, more importantly, they have been manipulated out of the economic mainstream of Miami, and when you're out of the economic mainstream, you're out of the political arena.

Black community activist (quoted above with regard to Miami's major problem):

In those days, I said to Cubans in a speech that there was going to be a time when white folks are going to try to treat you all like niggers. They're going to put you again in your place as they do with all minority groups. But unlike Black Americans, Cubans had no history of being kept in their place, and as a result, they responded differently. We Black folks were saying to white folks, "Let us in." Cubans were saying to white folks, "Let us in so that we can take over." Now, in 1987, you hear whites telling us that we should form an alliance with them to keep Cubans in their place. I say, "I've had my experience with you all. Don't tell me now that you and I can buddy-buddy because you're trying to keep Cubans from doing what is right for their own."

The Miami Herald

Native white executive of Knight-Ridder Corporation, parent company of the *Miami Herald* (1987):

In our business, which is the publishing business, we made a bet during the 1960s that the normal pattern of immigration that this country had seen over many years when ethnic minorities came in in large numbers and settled in different sections would not be very different here; that within a reasonable number of years, English would become the dominant language. So we made a bet in 1960 that that would occur here in Miami as a large number of Cuban refugees came in following Castro's takeover. That didn't happen as fast as we thought it would. We belatedly started in our business a Spanish edition called *El Miami Herald*. It's a very expensive proposition for us, but it has helped us gain acceptance and circulation in the Hispanic community. We think that it is important to us and important to them that the *Herald* be available in both Spanish and English. We circulate that Spanish section in conjunction with the *Miami Herald*, so that we believe that, by virtue of having the two together, we'll eventually move back toward the ultimate utilization of English as the primary language.

Cuban bank director, member of the Cuban-American National Foundation, emigrated in the early 1960s (1989):

The conflict between the Cuban community and the *Herald* reached its peak when, after the resignation of one of the directors of the Cuban-American National Foundation, the newspaper started speculating, without basis of fact, about internal divisions in the organization. We decided to write an open letter. Jorge Mas Canosa [president of the foundation] brought a writer from Washington who wrote the letter in an afternoon, and it was published, as a paid announcement, the following day. The *Herald* never expected that we Cubans would do something like that! There was a meeting in which, in fact, we considered organizing a boycott against the newspaper. Richard Capen, the editor, called to complain, but, faced with the threat of a massive boycott, the newspaper relented and has changed course one hundred and eighty degrees in recent months.

We've told Capen that it does not matter what the *Nuevo Herald* [the new revamped Spanish edition of the *Miami Herald* created in 1988 after the editors of the earlier version, *El Miami Herald*, resigned over disagreements with the newspaper's editorial line] publishes because praises to the community which appear there are for Cubans of Calle Ocho [Southwest Eighth Street, the main thoroughfare of Miami's Little Havana section]. Much more important is what is published in English, which is read nationwide. The *Herald* sometimes plays a double game, publishing articles in English that do not appear in Spanish and vice versa.

Black attorney (quoted above with reference to interethnic relations):

The *Miami Herald* runs a lot of negative stories about Miami. Initially, I think that a few personalities of the *Herald*'s senior management saw the job of the newspaper as to be truthful even if it destroyed the city. They have been extremely misguided. At the same time, they have been a very positive force in Miami. As positive as they can be, they can also be wrong. Traditionally, like all the rest of the downtown primarily old-Anglo establishment, the *Herald* assumed that the Cubans would go away; if they didn't assume it, they at least hoped they would, and so they ignored them. They must have thought, "They're here and we have to live with them, but maybe the Castro government will be overthrown and we'll send them back there." They didn't understand that the history of every group that has come to America is that *nobody* ever goes back home.

Different frames, different definitions of the situation. Discourses that do not clash directly, but rather slide past each other as if moving on different planes. Clearly, the arrival of the "three hundred thousand Cubans" over twenty-five years was the key event that ruptured the traditional worldview in this southern American city. But such an interpretation does not suffice. There are more Latins in Los Angeles and New York than in Miami, yet those cities never experienced a similar transformation. There, immigrants "know their place" and do not challenge the established social hierarchy or the fundamental shared definitions. As for Blacks, African-American communities in other cities are neither as powerless nor as militant when they revolt. It is as if the parallel social structures and definitions that were created by the arrival of the Cubans simultaneously pushed Blacks into double subordination and opened space for them to revitalize the discourse about civil and human rights.

Everywhere one turns in Miami, this fragmentation of the old standard frame produces oddities, mostly comic but at times poignant and even tragic: the young Black waitress in the airport bar serving *café cubano* to Canadian tourists; the Carnival of Miami, which is really the old Havana *Carnaval*; the city bracing itself for the next, fully expected riot as a jury debates the fate of a police officer. These everyday facts of life have gained the attention of outsiders who have written insightfully about Miami's paradoxes. While other large Latin communities in East Los Angeles or the Bronx go unsung and unnoticed, Miami has attracted the attention of several prominent American literati. Joan Didion, for example, had this to say about the native white establishment in 1987: "This set of mind, in which the local Cuban community was seen as a civic challenge to be determinedly met, was not uncommon among Anglos to whom I talked in Miami, many of whom persisted in the related illusions that the city was small, manageable, prosperous in a predictable broad-based way, southern in a progressive sunbelt way, American, and belonged to them."[12] And David Rieff highlighted one of the many local peculiarities: "At the edge of Coral Gables, I noticed a sign advertising, 'The Caballero Funeral Home, Founded 1858.' Miami, of course, did not exist in 1858 and I realized with a start that the owners meant founded *in Havana* in 1858. It is as if Cuban Miami recapitulates all the particles of prerevolutionary Havana with, of course, the exception of the left."[13]

Drug running, the periodic Black riots, Mariel, the stark beauty of the city—all have been extensively chronicled in books, articles, films, and "Miami Vice." But after each colorful snippet, the question remains: How did it happen? How could a large American city be transformed so quickly that its natives often chose to emigrate north in search of a more familiar cultural setting? How could an immigrant group, especially one coming from the Third World, reproduce its institutions so thoroughly that a parallel social structure was established? At what point did acculturation in reverse begin? And, perhaps most important, where will this process of change without a blueprint lead?

For answers, one must look back, first at 1980, a year still fresh in people's minds, and then at the deep and unappreciated roots of the city in the Caribbean.

Chapter Two

A Year to Remember

Mariel

Nineteen eighty was some year. If you were an old native, you probably still believed that nothing much had really changed in Miami, that immigrants would eventually learn English and life would go on as usual. Yet as with all major processes of change, the forces underlying the dramatic events of that year had long been at work, unknown and unforeseen by those whose lives they were about to transform. They finally irrupted in 1980. As the city reeled from one unexpected event after another, its inhabitants confronted head-on the prospect of a future without precedent in American urban history. For some, this prospect was a challenge to be "determinedly met"; for others, it was a looming threat to be escaped. Property values collapsed all over town as the city abandoned, once and for all, the image of a sunny tourist destination and faced that of an uncertain bridge between two worlds.

The Mariel Exodus

On April 1, 1980, Jose Antonio Rodriguez Gallegos, a bus driver, rammed his minibus through the gates of the Peruvian embassy in Havana in an effort to gain political asylum. During the ensuing melee, a Cuban guard was killed. Fidel Castro angrily withdrew police protection from the embassy, a move that brought over ten thousand Cubans from all parts of the island to the embassy in search of refuge. This popular demonstration of a yearning to leave Cuba was a major embarrassment to the Castro regime; it felt compelled to open the port of Mariel, declaring that anyone wishing to leave could do so. Castro then proceeded to invite Cuban

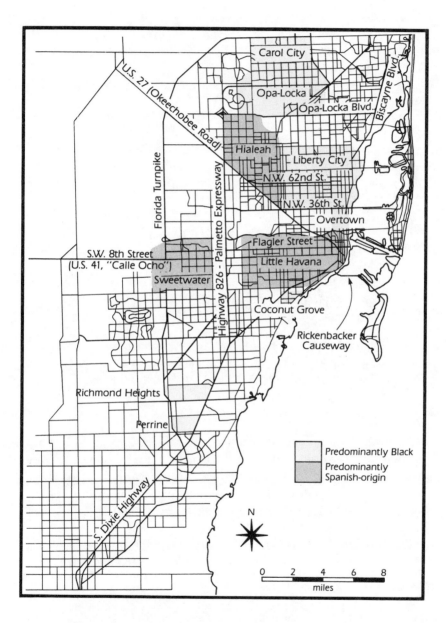

Map 1. The Miami metropolitan area, 1980.

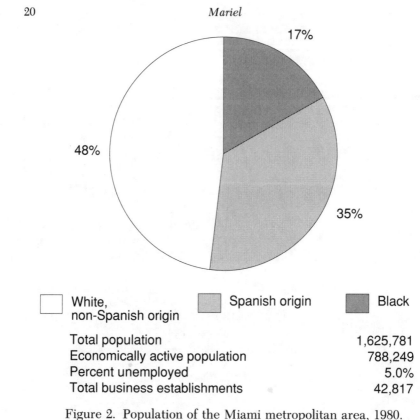

White, non-Spanish origin	Spanish origin	Black

Total population   1,625,781
Economically active population   788,249
Percent unemployed   5.0%
Total business establishments   42,817

Figure 2. Population of the Miami metropolitan area, 1980.
Metro-Dade Planning Department, Research Division, *Dade County Facts* (Miami: Metropolitan Dade County Government, 1990), 2, 6.

exiles in the United States to come pick up their relatives.[1] On April 20, two lobster boats carrying about forty Cubans arrived in Key West. The following day, Radio Havana reported that eleven more boats were leaving Mariel; meanwhile, twenty-five Miami-based boats were said to be en route to Mariel. The 1980 "Freedom Flotilla" was under way.[2]

Two Cuban researchers with the Center for the Study of the Americas in Havana later reported their view of the composition of the outflow:

We can affirm with certainty that 45.25 percent of all persons that abandoned Cuba through the port of Mariel had delinquent backgrounds as follows:

1. Crimes against property (theft, etc.) 40.1%
2. Dangerous condition° 16.4
3. Fraud and falsification 4.0
4. Crimes against the public administration 1.7
5. Possession and sale of drugs 5.5
6. Forbidden games 4.3
7. Crimes against physical integrity 4.4
8. Crimes against the normal development of sexual relations 10.8
9. Crimes against the security of the state 5.2
10. Violations of public order 4.0
11. Others 3.7

°Dangerous condition is the special likelihood that a person will commit crimes in the future, demonstrated by the conduct that he or she observes (Penal Code of Cuba, Law 21, Title 11).[3]

This account of those leaving the island in 1980 dressed in academic garb the much stronger indictment by the Supreme Leader of the Revolution himself: "Those that are leaving from Mariel are the scum of the country—antisocials, homosexuals, drug addicts, and gamblers, who are welcome to leave Cuba if any country will have them" (Fidel Castro, May Day Celebration Speech, 1980). For once, Castro's enemies in Miami did not disagree: "Mariel destroyed the image of Cubans in the United States and, in passing, destroyed the image of Miami itself for tourism. The *marielitos* are mostly Black and mulattoes of a color that I never saw or believed existed in Cuba. They don't have social networks; they roam the streets desperate to return to Cuba. There will be two hundred more airplane kidnappings" (Cuban-American official, City of Miami, August 1983).[4]

Mariel was a unique episode in American immigration history. Instead of immigrants coming on their own, they were actually brought into the country, not by government agencies, but in boats chartered by earlier immigrants.[5] Mariel was high drama in the Straits of Florida, performed by the two warring factions of Cuban society before the astonished eyes of the United States. In the end, none of the principals involved were to achieve their goals. Mariel turned out to be a losing game all around.

• By releasing 125,000 people in less than six months, the Cuban government hoped to demonstrate to the world how liberal its exit policy was and so counteract the bad publicity created when ten thousand Cubans desirous to leave occupied the Peruvian embassy in Havana. The strategy backfired. The large number of refugees, the testimony of emigrants, the deliberate placement aboard the boats of ex-convicts and mental patients in order to nail the image of exiles as "scum" simply confirmed the totalitarian nature of the Castro government.

- Cuban exiles spent millions of dollars chartering boats to rescue their relatives from the island. Some succeeded, but most ended up ferrying a cargo of unknowns across the Straits of Florida. Although subsequent research has shown that hardened criminals, mental patients, and other true undesirables represented a minority, perhaps 10 percent, of the new arrivals, their presence stigmatized the entire exodus and, in the view of many, adversely affected not only the reputation of Cubans in the United States but also Miami's allure as a tourist destination.

- The Carter administration at first attempted to control the exodus but then backed down, apparently fearful of alienating Cuban-American voters. On May 5, 1980, the president pledged that the United States would continue to provide "an open heart and open arms" for those leaving Cuba and asked Congress for supplemental aid. On May 14, Carter again reversed his policy, proposing an airlift from Cuba and ordering boats carrying refugees to be stopped and seized. This presidential order was largely ignored. The administration's indecision did not play well in the November 1980 presidential elections: among those voting against Carter was a solid majority of Cuban-Americans.[6]

- The Mariel refugees who came to the United States in search of political freedom and a better life found their path blocked at every turn by growing discrimination. The labels affixed to the exodus by the Cuban government—"scum" and "lumpen"—were picked up by the U.S. media and beamed nationwide. In November 1982, a front-page story in the *Columbus [Ohio] Dispatch* reported that "the 'Marielistas,' a society of Cuban criminals who came to this country on the 'Freedom Flotilla,' might be organizing in Columbus. The criminal syndicate whose members advertise their specialties by tattoos between thumb and forefinger have been seen around town buying handguns."[7] As late as 1987, the *Boston Herald* reported the capture of the "South

Shore Stalker," described as a "29 year-old Marielito . . . released from jail to join the Mariel boatlift, along with thousands of other convicts and mentally ill patients."[8] With such images reaching across the country, it is not surprising that they eventually altered the attitudes of the very community that had engineered the new refugees' departure, the Miami Cuban-Americans.

• To native white South Floridians, the new wave of exiles was a threat to be determinedly opposed. Their organ, the *Miami Herald*, spearheaded a campaign that aimed, to begin with, at avoiding U.S. involvement prior to the opening of the Mariel harbor, and then at having the flow of refugees diverted elsewhere, preferably to other Latin American countries. The *Herald* repeatedly castigated Cuban-Americans for their eagerness to rescue relatives left in Cuba and shrilly echoed Castro's characterization of the new refugees. This effort, too, backfired. The exodus was not diverted from Miami; moreover, the stigma of Mariel so tarnished the thus far pristine image of anti-Castro exiles that a new, reactive discourse arose.

Mariel and the *Herald*

The *Miami Herald* coverage of events related to Mariel reveals both how quickly things developed and how determined the newspaper was to stem the tide. A day-by-day account of these events was produced as part of our study of post-1980 immigration to South Florida.[9] The following summary indicates clearly the positions adopted by that news organization with respect to the unfolding events.

April 7. The *Miami Herald* reports that Cubans in the Peruvian embassy in Havana most likely will end up in the United States. Dade County officials state that they will be unable to accept the Cubans, citing a housing shortage and a depressed local economy. Miami mayor Maurice Ferre asks that, if refugees are admitted, they be sent to other parts of the country. Hialeah mayor Dale Bennett predicts that refugees will have a major impact and says that immediate federal aid will be needed.

April 12. In its editorial page, the *Herald* takes up the theme of hemispheric cooperation and calls for a "multinational sense of responsibility" regarding the resettlement of the ten thousand embassy refugees. Proposals are made to transport refugees to a temporary site on the way to Peru.

April 24. A *Miami Herald* editorial condemns the boatlift, begun three days earlier, calling it humiliating and dangerous and asserting that the "would-be rescuers from Florida are pawns in Castro's open diplomatic war." The article predicts that Castro will permit only a trickle of refugees to leave from Mariel and continue to deny permission for the airlift that would take the entire ten thousand to welcoming Costa Rica. Mayor Ferre echoes the *Herald* and calls for a ship to take all the asylum seekers to Costa Rica.

April 29. In a forceful editorial, the *Herald* states that "Carter administration officials seem to be afraid to anger Cuban-American voters by demanding an end to the influx, but they don't want to legitimize it by mobilizing Federal assistance." The paper reports that 3,200 Cubans have arrived, and 1,500 boats are waiting in Mariel to bring more. "Local resources—particularly housing— already are exhausted, and a potentially ugly backlash is building among non-Hispanics."

May 1. Florida governor Bob Graham authorizes $100,000 for basic assistance and opens the National Guard Armory in Homestead as a shelter because of the growing processing backlog. The first article on psychological problems among Mariel refugees appears in the *Herald*; it reports that some of the refugees have a prior history of severe psychopathology and questions whether they had been part of the Peruvian embassy crowd. A second, very negative article reports that 5,000 Cubans had arrived in over 100 boats the previous day, and "the strident exile community in the United States shows little inclination of winding things down." In what is described as a more sinister assessment of the refugees, the *Herald* comments that a high-ranking U.S. official surveying "the sullen, seedy looking contingent that arrived aboard the Ocean Queen said privately: 'just look at that bunch. Awfully funny that there are no women and children in the group. Something tells me we may have a bunch of criminals here.'"

May 6. President Carter declares a state of emergency in Florida. U.S. marshals and marines are sent to South Florida to manage the inflow. The Coast Guard counts 374 boats headed for Florida and 74 headed for Mariel. Over 3,500 Cubans arrive on this day alone, bringing the total to over 16,000 in fifteen days.

May 8. The processing center at Fort Chaffee in Arkansas is readied. U.S. Immigration and Naturalization Service officers in Key West claim, according to the *Herald*, that "as many as four out of five of the most recent arrivals have come from Cuban prisons," but also that only 209 refugees—less than 1 percent of arrivals to date—had been detained in Dade County after their preliminary screening suggested a criminal record.

May 11. In extensive coverage of the crisis this Sunday, the *Miami Herald* reports results of an informal poll of Miami residents. Under the headline "Dade Fears Refugee Wave," a long article reports significant negative reaction to the inflow by both native whites and Blacks, in contrast to general acceptance by Dade's Hispanics, and concludes that this "reveals potentially dangerous disagreements among Dade's non-Latin white, Latin, and black populations."

May 18. The processing center at Fort Indiantown Gap in Pennsylvania opens to take the overflow from Chaffee.

May 31. During the preceding five weeks, the boatlift is estimated to have brought over ninety thousand Cubans into the country. A *Herald* editorial calls for a coordinated program to settle the new refugees and contrasts the "new" Cubans with the old: "This is not the entrepreneurial class that moved in 15 years ago. . . . A Cuban ghetto might develop."

June 4, 5. The *Miami Herald* runs an editorial reviewing the negative impact of Mariel on Dade County and the need to safeguard against such "floods." A couple of articles claim that, as the boatlift wanes, Castro is sending hundreds of criminals to the United States.

June 17. President Carter requests that Congress appropriate $385 million for Cuban refugee programs.

June 20. A presidential order grants a special six-month "entrant" status to Haitians and Cubans who arrived before June 20, allowing them to work and qualify for Aid for Families with Dependent Children (AFDC), Supplemental Security Income (SSI), Medicaid, and other assistance programs.

June 26, 27. Legal action is taken to block refugee children from Dade public schools. A *Miami Herald* editorial strongly criticizes President Carter for yielding to fears of Cuban exile violence if the United States prevented exiles from going to Mariel: "The President consciously let the threat of mob reaction intimidate him into ignoring the law and allowing his own policies to be trampled. When the President finally ordered the boatlift halted on May 15, he did so because the Cuban-American community itself had become unhappy over the mental patients and criminals that Fidel Castro had included among the Mariel refugees."

June 30. Over 114,000 Mariel refugees have arrived.

July 7, 8. The *Miami Herald* claims that over twenty thousand homosexual Cuban refugees await sponsors; the number is denied the next day by government officials.

July 24, 25. A series of articles in the *Herald* focuses on the crime attributed to Mariel refugees. A judge reports a crime wave from boatlift juveniles; Miami Beach reports a crime increase of 34 percent since the refugees arrived; teen violence is also reported to thrive in refugee barracks.

August 16. Three passenger jets are hijacked to Cuba by Mariel entrants, making six such hijackings in one week.

August 30. Cuban exiles in Miami rally demanding that Peruvian embassy refugees now settled in Lima be allowed to enter the United States.

September 5–8. The *Miami Herald* reports two deaths in a gun battle and provides detailed accounts of Mariel refugees involved in crimes. Stories of crimes by refugees run each day for four consecutive days.

September 14. The *Herald* reports that homesick refugees are trying to start a "reverse flotilla."

September 18. White House officials announce in Miami a plan to alleviate the crisis caused by the influx of immigrants. A *Miami Herald* front-page article reports a crime wave in Little Havana, the perpetrators being Mariel criminals: 775 percent more robberies than in 1979; 284 percent more car thefts; 191 percent more burglaries; 110 percent more assaults.

September 26. Cuba officially closes Mariel harbor to U.S.-bound emigrants after 159 days and a total of 124,769 new refugees.

The Anglo Perspective

The position adopted by the *Miami Herald* was understandable. As the voice of the Anglo establishment, it considered the Mariel exodus a serious double threat: first, as an economic cataclysm, given the depressed state of local industry and the negative impact of the inflow on Miami's status as a tourist destination; and second, as a direct threat to the establishment power structure, given the addition of many thousands to an already uncomfortably large Cuban population. Hence, through editorials, letters to the editor, and the "spin" it put on news stories, the *Herald* sought initially to prevent the new wave of Cuban immigration from taking place and, when that failed, to discredit the fresh arrivals.

The development of this discourse is quite revealing. Yohel Camayd-Freixas conducted a systematic content analysis of stories about Mariel printed by the *Miami Herald* during the first fourteen weeks of the crisis, beginning on Sunday, April 6, 1980. All articles that depicted the Mariel exodus in critical terms and Mariel refugees as problematic were rated as "negative"; those that were descriptive, positive, neutral, or indifferent were grouped as "positive."[10] Figure 3 shows that, as the exodus took shape, negative coverage by the *Herald* increased following, with a short lag, the upward swing of the inflow. Despite the conservative bias of the graph, which counts as "positive" all neutral or purely descriptive articles, negative coverage reached 90 percent of all printed items pertaining to Mariel in the *Herald* in the week of May 26, and remained at between 40 and 60 percent thereafter.

In seeking to advance its policy goals, Camayd-Freixas notes, the *Miami Herald* identified the Cuban exile community as its major source of opposition and acted aggressively to counter this group's efforts to bring their relatives and the original Peruvian embassy occupants to the United States.[11] In the course of articulating these goals, the *Herald* acted with both great energy and notable ineffectiveness.

Until 1980, Cuban exile politics had focused on the idea of returning to the island. Occasional sallies into local politics were criticized by the community itself as detracting from the goal of liberating Cuba from Castro's regime. Despite the vaunted power

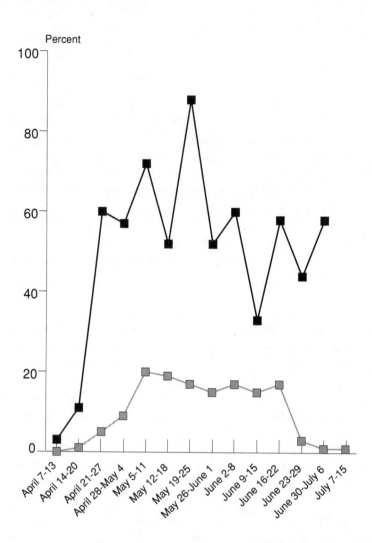

Percent

- ■ Percentage of articles and editorials in the *Miami Herald* about Mariel and its refugees published during the week that were evaluated as negative

- ▪ Percentage of the 124,799 Mariel refugees who arrived during the week indicated

Figure 3. Weekly Mariel arrivals and negative *Miami Herald* articles on the inflow, 1980. Yohel Camayd-Freixas, *Crisis in Miami* (Boston: Boston Urban Research and Development Group, 1988), III-42; Juan M. Clark, José I. Lasaga, and Rose S. Reque, *The 1980 Mariel Exodus: An Assessment and Prospect* (Washington, D.C.: Council for Inter-American Security, 1981), 5.

of Cuban-American voters, only a handful of Cubans held elec-
tive office in 1980, and those who did generally downplayed their
nationality. A few successful Cuban entrepreneurs joined the
local Chamber of Commerce and other American business organizations and tried to melt, as far as possible, into the Anglo
mainstream.[12]

As the *Herald* launched its campaign against a possible new
wave of Cubans, then, the exile community was defenseless to
confront it. So far, exile organizations had been concerned with
events in the island, not local politics in Miami. There was no
alternative Cuban "discourse" about the city, and no organ to
advance it. The *Herald* thus had the field to itself and could present
the new arrivals in any light it chose to—in this instance, consistently negative. Yet the newspaper's articulate pleas, directed
mostly to the federal government, fell on deaf ears. What most
disturbed the *Herald*'s editors and the native white establishment
was how an American president could sacrifice *them* to accommo-
date the wishes of a foreign minority. As a columnist bitterly complained years later, "Castro always seems to call the shots here."[13]
The most scathing editorials during the Mariel crisis, in fact, were
reserved not for the Cubans, but for President Carter, who in the
newspaper's view had allowed himself to "be intimidated by mob
reaction" and his own policies "to be trampled."

The South Florida native white community was concerned
largely with preserving its own life-style; it had little inclination to
go poking into the complexities of foreign policy and the singular
link between Cuban exiles and the federal government. Yet for
twenty years, the exile community had been the U.S. government's
most resolute partner in the struggle against Castro communism
and that dictator's attempts at expansion in Latin America. For
Washington, the Miami exiles were not an "ethnic" group, but an
important ally in the fight for Cuba and Latin America. Forcefully
stopping these supporters in the high seas as they attempted to
"liberate" their kin would not play well abroad, especially among
friends of the United States elsewhere in the hemisphere. Hence,
the bigger goal of preserving American global hegemony clashed
with the local goal of preserving Anglo hegemony in Miami. The
latter had to give way. It was this alternative definition of exiles as
citizens of an invaded neighboring nation, rather than as a domes-

tic ethnic minority, that enabled them to act without much concern for local matters, to the dismay of the *Herald* and its allies.

In Miami in 1980, the two major segments of the local population each felt betrayed by the federal government, but for different reasons. The exiles had long deplored the failure of the Kennedy administration to follow through with the Bay of Pigs invasion, and subsequent U.S. administrations were condemned for their efforts to prevent exile raids on Cuba. Local Anglos, in turn, felt abandoned when Washington failed to back their struggle to save Miami from the Cubans. The *Herald's* articles and editorials during the Mariel crisis faithfully reflected the latter position.

Reactive Ethnicity

The perspective articulated in 1980 by the Miami Anglo establishment, though ultimately unfruitful regarding its goals, did have several unintended effects. Two of these shaped the subsequent evolution of that group's principal contender during the Mariel episode, the Cubans; a third unintended effect changed the "mood" of the city, in particular in the third major segment of its population, the Blacks (see chapter 3). The first such effect was to stigmatize the Mariel refugees, not only nationwide but within the Cuban community itself. The *Herald* was not solely responsible for the reversal of the exiles' original support for Mariel refugees; the presence of many "undesirables" deliberately placed aboard the boats by the Cuban government played a significant role as well. Yet the newspaper's insistence on stories of criminals and mental patients, to the neglect of the majority of Mariel refugees who were not misfits, advanced the high profile of the newcomers as an undesirable addition to Miami's population.

Up to that point, the self-image of Cuban exiles had been a happy mix: they were not only America's allies in the global anti-communist struggle but also a "model" minority. Several articles in the national press during the 1960s and 1970s described the Cuban "success story" in Miami as well as the contributions exiles had made to the economic renaissance of the city.[14] With Mariel, this positive image faded quickly; Cuban-Americans now found themselves classed with the most downtrodden and discriminated-against minorities. A national Gallup poll conducted shortly after

the exodus described vividly the extent of the Cubans' un-
popularity: after Mariel, Cubans ranked dead last in the public's
view of contributions made by different ethnic groups to the national welfare (table 1). For a minority long accustomed to public
praise, such opinions came as a rude awakening.

The reaction of many older Cubans was to blame the Mariel
arrivals for the new situation and to create social distance from
them. By the time we initiated our study of immigrants in South
Florida in 1983, a highly negative stereotype of the "Mariels" had
crystallized in the established Cuban community. The following
comments exemplify the views heard in 1983 and repeated, with
notable consistency, in subsequent years:

Cuban businessman, employer of ten Mariel refugees in his
restaurant and liquor store (1983):

TABLE 1. *Attitudes Toward American Ethnic Groups
Held by the American Public, 1982*

	Has Been Good for the Country	Has Been Bad for the Country	Mixed Feelings/ Don't Know
English	66%	6%	28%
Irish	62	7	31
Jews	59	9	32
Germans	57	11	32
Italians	56	10	34
Poles	53	12	35
Japanese	47	18	35
Blacks	46	16	38
Chinese	44	19	37
Mexicans	25	34	41
Koreans	24	30	46
Vietnamese	20	38	42
Puerto Ricans	17	43	40
Haitians	10	39	51
Cubans	9	59	32

Source: Roper Organization, *Roper Reports* (1982), 84-4, 2-27.

The main problem I've had with Marielitos is their inclination to petty theft. They don't steal out of need, they earn enough for a living. It's a habit learned under communism. These people don't behave like Cubans. I don't believe that they will be able to move up economically like the old Cubans because they lack manners and education. Also they are violent, they are accustomed to solve everything with shouts and blows. Several times I've had to pack a gun to deal with drunken Mariel employees.

Cuban social worker, head of a City of Miami social service agency (1983):

The quality of Cuban refugees who arrived in the seventies is very different from those who came in 1980. About one-third of the 125,000 Marielitos are trash—delinquents, homosexuals. Their effects on Miami have been terrible. In our office, we try to find employment for them and provide them with transportation to their new jobs. However, many employers don't want Mariel refugees. The reason why the Marielitos are different is that many came alone, rather than as part of family groups. Eighty percent of those who come here asking for jobs are lone individuals. . . . And they have high expectations: they don't accept minimum wages. They say, "It's too little," and prefer to continue living on welfare and food stamps.

Mariel refugees also learned quickly about the changed views of their compatriots. In 1983, we completed a survey of the Mariel population living in the principal areas of Cuban concentration in the Miami metropolitan area (Dade County). The sample of 520 was reinterviewed three years later. On both occasions, respondents were asked if they perceived discrimination against their own group (Mariel refugees) by native whites (Anglos) and by "old" Cubans; we also asked them if they had personally experienced discrimination by either group (table 2).[15] In 1983, after three years of U.S. residence, only a minority of Mariel refugees— 25 percent—reported that Anglo-Americans discriminated against them, with roughly the same proportion stating that they had suffered such experiences personally. Three times as many, however—almost 75 percent—reported that older Cubans discriminated against them, and over 50 percent had been directly affected. Three years later, personal experiences of discrimination had declined somewhat, but the perception that such discrimina-

TABLE 2. *Perceptions and Experiences of Discrimination*
of Mariel Refugees, 1983 and 1986

	Three Years after Arrival (1983)	Six Years after Arrival (1986–87)
Believe that Mariel Cubans are discriminated against by Anglos	26%	32%
Believe that Mariel Cubans are discriminated against by older-established Cubans	75	80
Have personally experienced discrimination by Anglos	23	20
Have personally experienced discrimination by older-established Cubans	52	37

Source: Alejandro Portes and Juan M. Clark, "Mariel Refugees: Six Years After," *Migration World* 15 (1987): 14–18.
Note: Sample size in 1983 was 520 drawn at random from a two-stage cluster design in the principal areas of Cuban concentration in Dade County. The sample decreased to 400 in 1986 because of respondent attrition, but it was statistically unbiased with respect to the original.

tion existed had increased: now close to one-third of the refugees felt discriminated against by Anglos. Still, this figure was but a fraction of the almost 80 percent who reported discrimination by other Cubans.

These numbers, impressive as they are, do not fully capture the depth of the frustration expressed by many of our Mariel respondents at being treated as second-class citizens by their compatriots. As late as 1987, a Mariel informant reported: "These older Cubans are very difficult. If you object to their very narrow and reactionary view of things, they make a scene and accuse you of being with Fidel. They are very dogmatic. I am an educated person and have a right to my own ideas."[16]

The accusations of the Castro government, echoed by the North American media, did succeed in stigmatizing the Mariel inflow and creating a deep rift within the exile community. But a second effect arose almost simultaneously. Faced with a rapidly spreading reputation as "undesirables," Cuban-Americans were forced to turn their attention inward and confront their condition as a domestic ethnic minority. Like other ethnic groups before them, the exiles responded to strong outside prejudice by undergoing a process of reactive formation: they worked to redefine the situation in terms more favorable to their own self-image and their role in the community.[17] The key factor separating Cubans from most other ethnic groups in this effort was the array of resources they were able to muster.

Meanwhile, as a direct outgrowth of Mariel, a grass-roots movement of native whites was organized in Miami. Its overall goals paralleled those promoted by the *Herald*, but the immediate objective was somewhat different: "My parents were immigrants and they had to learn English promptly; Cubans should do likewise," announced one of the leaders. The movement gathered enough strength to put the language issue before the voters in the election of November 1980. The Cuban community was still unorganized in local affairs, and the "antibilingual" referendum passed overwhelmingly. From then on, Dade County officials were prohibited from funding programs or activities "other than [those] in the English language."[18] The referendum victory marked the high point of the Anglo-centered effort to hang on to hegemony. David Rieff explains the feelings of Miami's native whites, many of them children of immigrants, thus: "Within living memory, they had given up languages and habits of being in order to feel themselves more American. Moreover, they were not given a choice. . . . But the Italians (and the Jews and the rest) had not expected America to adapt to them, so why were the Cubans so intransigent?"[19]

The 1980 election marked the beginnings of the process of reactive formation on the part of Cuban-Americans as well. The following statements are typical of exile community leaders' reactions in the years following Mariel and the passage of the "antibilingual" referendum:

Cuban-American executive of Knight-Ridder Corporation, parent company of the *Miami Herald* (1983):

There were three reactions to Mariel. The first reaction was positive: to help all those who came. The second reaction was negative, even by Cuban exile leaders. There were obvious differences of values, of appearance, of ambition between the old and the new refugees. There was great fear of the criminal element. The third reaction was that of the press. It was not "Freedom Flotilla," but boatlift; the newcomers were not "escapees from communism," but economic immigrants. . . .

At that time, we Cubans began to receive blows from everywhere. Negative press and stereotypes apply to all, not only to the Mariels. Then came *Scarface*, the reedition of a 1930 movie about Al Capone, but this time with a Marielito as a drug mafia boss. These were the events that led to the creation of FACE [Facts about Cuban Exiles]. The organization has two programs: one to counteract all the anti-Cuban articles and stereotypes; a second to promote the Cubans' image through articles and films. FACE started with thirteen people in Miami, but now has chapters throughout the country.

Cuban-American Dade County official (1981):

The Anglo power structure is scared to death about the Cuban rise in this community. It has tried cooptation through an "interethnic relations committee" of the Miami Chamber of Commerce, which is really a sham. There were four stages to Mariel and its aftermath:

In the first, there was great solidarity by Cuban-Americans with the Mariel refugees. One million dollars were contributed after a telemarathon, and fifteen hundred volunteers showed up daily to assist with the processing. Metro-Dade County government was in charge of operations. This lasted from April 21 to May 9.

In the second, the Feds took over. The campaign against Mariel in the press got tougher. Cuban-Americans began to believe it and abandoned the new arrivals. There were riots in the camps. In all, a disaster orchestrated by people at the highest level of government.

In the third stage, there was the antibilingual referendum, which was a slap in our face. People began to feel "more Cuban than anyone." There was anger at the insult, but no organization yet. In the fourth stage, there is embryonic organization promoted by the business leaders; the plan today is to try to elect a Cuban mayor of the city and perhaps one or two state legislators.

Following the events of 1980, Cuban-American businessmen who had believed themselves integrated into the mainstream began to withdraw from Anglo organizations or to combine participation in them with the creation of parallel ethnic associations. Facts about Cuban Exiles (FACE) and the Cuban-American National Foundation (CANF) were founded at this time. Plans were made to run candidates for local office. More important, a new perspective began to emerge, a response to that advanced by the antibilingual movement. In this alternative perspective, the exile community itself represented the solution to Miami's problems and the builder of its future. Luis Botifoll, a leading Cuban-American banker, became one of the principal exponents of this view:

Before the "Great Change," Miami was a typical southern city, with an important population of retirees and veterans, whose only activity consisted in the exploitation of tourism during the sunny winters. No one thought of transforming Miami into what it is today. It is no exaggeration to say that the motor of this Great Change was the Cuban men and women who elected freedom and came to these shores to rebuild their homes and face with courage an uncertain future. . . . These last decades of the twentieth century have witnessed the foundation of a dynamic and multifaceted Miami over the past of a Miami that was merely provincial and tourist-oriented. Today, the level of progress has reached unanticipated heights, beyond the limits of anyone's imagination.[20]

Even Mariel refugees became integrated into this optimistic framework, which rescued them from the gloomy purview of the mainstream press and redefined them as contributors to the city's future. The Cuban-American assistant county manager defended them as follows:

So far, from a population of 120,000, we have 2,750 potential "bad apples"—less than 2.5 percent. That leaves 117,250 immigrants who are good, hardworking people seeking political and economic freedom. . . . Let's talk about these people. Let's talk about the benefits we will derive from them. . . . Cubans have, for the past two decades, made a tremendous contribution to Dade County. We all know the success stories of Cuban lawyers and bankers. Indeed, commercial liaisons with Latin American clients and land development ventures have established Cubans as economic leaders. With the passing of time, upward mobility has created openings at the semiskilled levels. Now the labor force is suddenly here to fill the gap. Of course, the new arrivals will need time to retrain, to adjust to life in an environment of abundance and freedom. . . . So they, and therefore we in this community are now in a state of flux. History shows us that this too will pass and that we are on our way to greater prosperity.[21]

The Cuban-American "success story" is already evident in these statements. What is often neglected is its reactive character. The Anglo attempt to reassert hegemony was in essence an offensive against two central goals of the exile community: family reunification through the opening provided by Mariel, and the preservation of the Spanish language. The establishment campaign did not, however, yield the expected results; indeed, it led to novel consequences, mostly the opposite of those intended. Instead of subduing the Cubans, the hegemonic discourse of the *Herald* and its allies transformed the exile community into a self-conscious ethnic group that organized effectively for local political competition.

By mid-decade, the mayors of Miami, Hialeah, West Miami, and several smaller municipalities in Dade County were Cuban-born, and there were ten Cuban-Americans in the state legislature—quite a step up from the one or two envisioned in the "embryonic organization" plan outlined by the Cuban-American Dade County official in 1981. And significantly, these changes took place in the context of an aggressive alternative discourse, one that portrayed not old Miamians, but former refugees, as the primary builders of the city's future. Local Anglo elites were thereafter compelled to bargain in a transformed environment, where their view had ceased to be hegemonic and where de facto pluralism became the norm.

Chapter Three

A Year to Remember

The Riot and the Haitians

Blacks and Refugees

The third consequence of the anti-Mariel campaign spearheaded by the *Miami Herald* was an increase in the mood of tension in the city. Not only Mariel Cubans but also Haitians were coming (sometimes washing) ashore, and the sense of being under invasion by the Third World fused with the unresolved racial tensions of this southern city. Even as the local establishment battled the Cubans in its effort to fend off new waves of immigrants, it persisted in its old ways with regard to the native ethnic proletariat—the Blacks. These ways involved relegating Blacks to a permanently subservient status and then, when civil rights legislation made this impossible, simply ignoring them.

When the first Cuban exiles began arriving in the early sixties, they confronted the unfamiliar spectacle of Blacks queuing up to seek and be refused admittance into whites-only movie theaters. This was just the tip of the iceberg. Blacks could not eat at white restaurants, they paid their taxes at a separate window in the Dade County courthouse, and they did not even have access to Miami's famous beaches. Blacks had to travel by boat to Virginia Key or go all the way to Broward County "to swim in salt water."[1]

The early middle-class exiles may have deplored the scene of NAACP activists being turned away at the movie box office, but when it came to jobs they, too, brushed the Blacks aside, taking over positions that might have been the ticket to economic advancement for the native minority. As Cubans began to consolidate their hold in certain areas of Miami and Hialeah, they forgot about the Black community as well. Little Havana and Liberty City, the largest Black area of Miami, are scarcely two miles apart; socially they could be in different countries.[2]

For Black Miami, the 1960s and 1970s were tough years in which they had to contend not only with a Deep South legacy, but also with the Cuban-inspired transformation of their city. During the sixty-odd years prior to the arrival of the first Cubans, Blacks had been the traditional source of manual labor in Miami, simultaneously needed and rejected by the city that they were building. A succession of white sheriffs had made it their business to keep the "Negroes" in their place, both socially and physically. Their zeal was reinforced by the Ku Klux Klan, which tarred and feathered, beat and bombed, any uppity Negro who tried to leave his crowded ghetto. Although Blacks fought back as best they could, it was only in the 1960s with the upsurge of the civil rights movement that they began to make significant headway toward racial equality. The sixties were also the years in which the first Cuban exiles arrived.

In 1966, Martin Luther King, Jr., noted Miami's emerging racial triangle and warned against the pitting of refugees against Blacks in competition for jobs.[3] By the mid-seventies, the Cuban presence had become too large for anyone to ignore. If the Anglo establishment found it difficult to fathom what was happening to their city, for Blacks the Cuban presence and its consequences was a social cataclysm.

Thus far, the story of the effect the Cuban influx had on the native minority has been told with an emphasis on two themes: first, competition for jobs between the two groups, and second, the consequent deterioration of the living standards of the Black population. One Black leader bluntly asserted: "It is a fact that Cubans displaced Blacks."[4] Bruce Porter and Marvin Dunn, comparing figures for Black employment for the period 1968–78, observed that it was like economic progress suddenly thrown into reverse gear.[5]

Neither assertion is entirely accurate. Although middle-class Cubans in the 1960s took whatever jobs were available and in this sense "displaced Blacks," their stay in those jobs was relatively

brief. Subjectively, the exiles did not see themselves competing
with the native minority; they were simply making do until they
could return to Cuba. As those prospects became progressively
dimmer, many moved rapidly into self-employment in such areas
as garment subcontracting, landscaping, and residential construction. This evolution did not so much displace Blacks as transform
the local economy. Indeed, figures on ethnic employment by industry indicate that the rising representation of Latins (overwhelmingly Cuban) was primarily at the expense of native whites rather
than Blacks.

Table 3 illustrates this trend with Census figures for the garment, construction, hotel, and restaurant industries. Although
these figures must be interpreted with caution because of changing
Census definitions, they indicate that native whites were the primary losers, at least in these sectors. The garment industry, for
example, evolved from 94 percent native white in 1960 to only 10
percent in 1980, when Spanish-origin workers represented 83 percent of the garment labor force. Blacks did not reduce their representation in this sector, but held steady at 5–7 percent. More
telling is the evolution of the hotel industry, commonly cited as the
core locus of "displacement." The Cubans did more than double
their presence between 1970 and 1980—from 18 to 40 percent—
but again the gain was entirely at the expense of native white
workers. Blacks, in fact, increased their representation in this industry from 14 to 23 percent over the same period.

A variant of the same story is told in figure 4, which portrays
employment in professional, executive, and labor positions by ethnic category for 1970 and 1980. Of the new jobs generated during
the decade, Blacks garnered about 20 percent, a figure commensu-
rate with their proportion of the Miami population. As figure 4
shows, Blacks increased their representation across the board. The
proportion of Blacks in the professions alone almost doubled, from
7 to 13 percent. It is true that the Cuban presence grew faster, but
once again, this occurred at the expense of Anglo workers. Between 1970 and 1980, the Spanish-origin group secured 65 percent
of all new jobs, a figure well above their approximate 40 percent
representation in the area's population.

Black economic advancement during the decade is evident in
other areas as well. For example, the median income of the Black

TABLE 3. *Ethnic Groups' Employment by Sector, Dade County, 1960–80*

	1960		1970			1980		
	White	*Black*	*White*	*Black*	*Spanish origin*	*White*	*Black*	*Spanish origin*
Garment (Textiles)	94.4%	5.6%	17.8%	3.7%	78.5%	10.4%	7.0%	82.6%
Construction	80.1	19.9	60.1	19.4	20.5	43.8	16.6	39.6
Hotels	83.8	16.2	77.5	14.1	18.4	37.3	22.9	39.8
Restaurants	90.7	9.3	61.7	12.9	25.4	60.5	9.3	30.2

Source: U.S. Bureau of the Census, *Florida* (Washington, D.C.: U.S. Department of Commerce, 1960, 1970, and 1980).
Note: The 1960 Census did not have a category for persons of Spanish origin. In the 1970 and 1980 censuses, Spanish-origin overlaps with the other categories. However, in 1970 and 1980 Dade County had relatively few black Cubans or black Latin Americans, so the categories "Black" and "Spanish origin" may be taken as mutually exclusive. The figures for whites are then determined by subtraction.

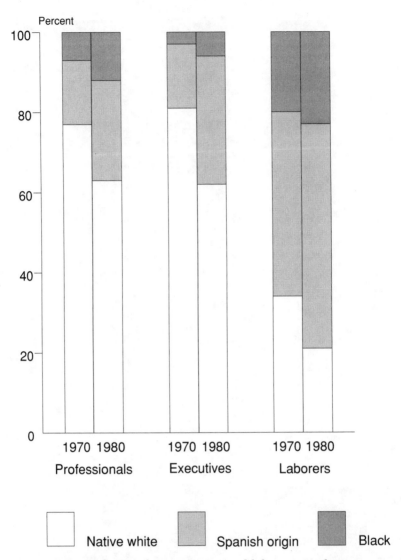

Figure 4. Professionals, executives, and laborers, Dade County, 1970 and 1980. *Profile of the Black Population* (Miami: Metro-Dade County Planning Department, 1984), tables 25 and 26.

population of Dade County rose 7 percent between 1970 and 1980; by the latter year, moreover, Black median income was 68 percent of the national average, compared to 60 percent for Blacks nationwide. Affluence among Black families also grew rapidly; by 1980, 7 percent of the area's Black families were earning $50,000 or more. Indeed, fully one-third of all Black families in this income category in the state resided in the Miami metropolitan area.[6]

There was no one-to-one substitution of Blacks by Cubans in the labor market, nor was there direct exploitation of one minority by the other. There was, however, a new urban economy in which the immigrants raced past other groups, leaving the native minority behind. Hence, after decades of striving for a measure of equality with whites, Miami Blacks found that the game had drastically changed. Anglos were leaving, and other whites who spoke a foreign language were occupying their positions. As a result, most Blacks were in a similar position as before. Nowhere is this part of the story clearer than in the evolution of income, poverty, and unemployment. Figure 5 compares relative incomes and poverty levels for the three major ethnic groups in Miami in 1980; figure 6 graphs unemployment between 1980 and 1990. In both data sets, there is a wide gap between Blacks and native whites in favor of the latter. There is also, however, a significant gap between Blacks and the intermediate Spanish-origin group.

These aggregate figures do not convey the full story because they pertain to everyone, employers and employees alike. It was, rather, in the development of small enterprises that the differences became most visible. Perhaps most devastating to the Black community was the apparent ease with which the Cubans ensconced themselves in the local economy, all the while claiming that their stay was temporary for they would soon return to their island. In 1977, only eighteen years after the Cuban Revolution, Cuban-owned firms in Dade County exceeded eight thousand in number, or four times as many as were owned by Blacks; average gross receipts of Cuban firms amounted to almost $84,000, or twice as much as the typical Black enterprise.[7] By 1980, approximately half of the largest banks and enterprises owned by Spanish-origin groups in the United States were in Miami, even though the area claimed a mere 5 percent of the country's Spanish-origin population. By contrast, only one Miami Black business made the list of the three hundred top Black enterprises in the nation.[8]

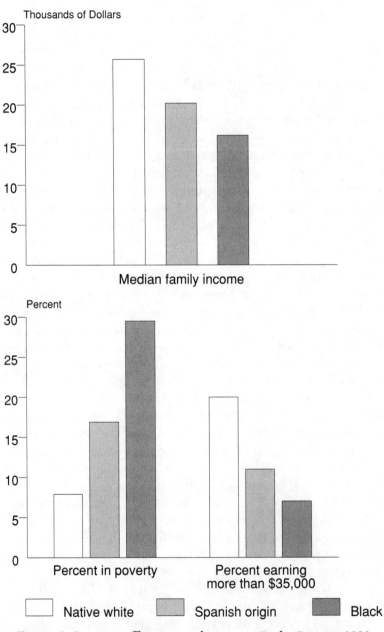

Figure 5. Income, affluence, and poverty, Dade County, 1980. *Profile of the Black Population* (Miami: Metro-Dade County Planning Department, 1984), tables 29, 32, and 33.

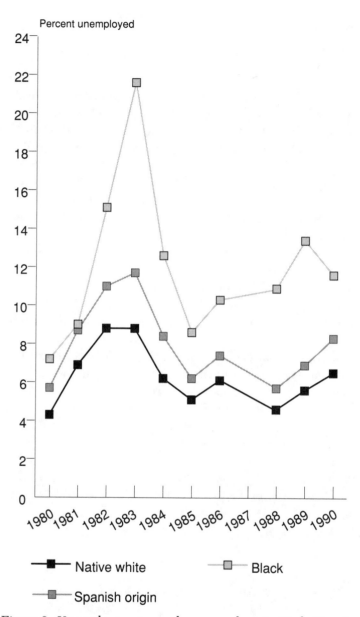

Percent unemployed

■ Native white   □ Black

□ Spanish origin

Figure 6. Unemployment rates by race and origin, Dade County, 1980–90. *Florida Statistical Abstracts* (Gainesville: University of Florida Press, 1973–90), tables on unemployment by county. (Data for 1987 not available.)

The rapid entrepreneurial advance of the Cubans was not due entirely to their business acumen or community solidarity. U.S. government agencies also looked with sympathy on the exiles' fledgling businesses and favored them disproportionately. In 1968, for example, the federal Small Business Administration (SBA) distributed $1,078,950 in loans to Cuban-owned small firms in Dade County and $82,600 to Black enterprises. Between 1968 and 1980, 46 percent ($47.7 million) of SBA Dade County loans went to Cuban and other Spanish-origin businesses, versus only 6 percent ($6.5 million) to Black firms. By the same token, the construction of Miami's rapid rail transit (Metrorail) during the late 1970s employed only 12 percent Black contractors, compared to over 50 percent Cuban.[9]

Such patent inequalities sharpened the sense of double subordination felt by Miami Blacks as the seventies progressed. After all, it was they who had fought the civil rights battles to gain access to public and private facilities. Affirmative Action and other programs had been designed to rectify the years of abuse that *they* had suffered, not to help a recently arrived group of white immigrants. As far as the Cubans were concerned, however, America's race problem was not theirs and they were certainly not about to make it so. Their history and concerns were different; hence, they took no responsibility for the racial inequalities that they encountered in Miami.

During the 1970s, the two minorities never clashed directly; each remained absorbed in its own situation and problems. Yet the immigrants' presence increasingly altered the character of the city, adding a new twist to the perennial subordination of Blacks and to their rising discontent.

The Riot

For outsiders, I think, it would be impossible to appreciate the shock that went through the Black community. I think it is safe to say that you'd almost *have* to be Black to understand. All their grievances, all their distrust of the system. . . . Suddenly, it all turned out to be true.

Major Clarence Dickson,
highest-ranking Black officer,
Miami Police Department[10]

By 1980, this situation of double marginalization had not yet been articulated into a coherent Black discourse, although the reality of powerlessness was there for all to see. At the street level, powerlessness was reflected in the traditional police practice of treating Blacks with relative impunity. Seen by respectable white citizens as the vice-ridden "bad" parts of town, Liberty City and other Black ghetto areas were places where the police were given a freer hand. People living in these areas had to fear not only violence from crime, but also violence from their would-be protectors. This adversarial culture between the Black citizenry and the local police departments then became exacerbated in the wake of the civil rights movement, just as an increasing number of officers came to bear Spanish names.

"McDuffie," as the case was known locally, represented the culmination of this hostile trend. In March 1980, a thirty-three-year-old Black insurance agent named Arthur McDuffie died in Miami's Jackson Memorial Hospital from injuries sustained after being chased by city and county police units. The cause of the chase was a rolling stop at a red light plus an obscene gesture toward a nearby officer. Police claimed that McDuffie had died as the result of accidental injuries during the chase. Black Miami knew better. On March 31, four white Dade County Public Safety Department officers were charged with playing some role in the beating of McDuffie and subsequent attempts to cover up the cause of his death. Sensing the mood of tension in the city, a local judge granted a change of venue to Tampa. As he put it, the case was "a time bomb."[11]

Mariel had not yet started at the time of the March indictment, but by mid-May, when the jury's verdict came in, some fifty thousand new refugees were camped in the Orange Bowl and in public land under I-95, the city's main north-south thoroughfare. Their visibility was compounded by dire forebodings in the press about their presence. Just a week before, the *Miami Herald* had published its survey of significant negative reactions to the new refugees and the "potentially dangerous disagreements" among native whites, Blacks, and Latins.[12] The anti-Mariel campaign only added to the rising tension in the city. Hence, as Cuban exiles and native whites focused their attention on the comings and goings in the Straits of Florida, Black Miami remained fixed on that Tampa courtroom. For Miami native whites, the city was under siege from the outside; as Blacks saw things, *their* city had long been under siege by the forces of the local establishment.

The verdict, reached in less than three hours of deliberation by an all-white jury, was broadcast by the Miami media on a clear Saturday afternoon. All four white officers were acquitted of all charges. It took the Black community about as much time to react to this verdict as it had taken the white jury to arrive at it. The news was known in Miami at 2:42 P.M.; less than three hours later the first rocks and bottles were flying in Liberty City.

The 1980 Miami riot was different from similar urban uprisings in three ways: first, it was isolated rather than part of a national trend; second, it was unusually violent; third, it took place with at least the tacit approval of many Black leaders, who under other circumstances could have been trusted to oppose it.

It had been twelve years since the other great Black Miami uprising. But unlike the 1968 riot, which was timed to coincide with the National Democratic Convention in Miami Beach, the 1980 civil disorders were not matched by similar events in other cities. Black Miami rose alone. Its action stood as yet another manifestation of the singularity of the city, and as a reflection of the uncommonly harsh conditions endured by its nonwhite citizenry.

The riot was also different in its viciousness. Porter and Dunn estimate that total property loss reached about $80 million. All kinds of businesses were hit, including manufacturing plants where no consumer goods were to be found. White-, Cuban-, and Black-owned businesses were torched indiscriminately. By the end of the disorders, commercial life in many parts of Liberty City had virtually ceased to exist.[13] Nevertheless, the pent-up anger reflected in the rioters' drive not just to steal but to destroy was nothing in comparison with the way they went after random whites, Anglo and Latin alike. There was an eye-for-an-eye mood which led hitherto powerless Blacks to attack any unfortunate representatives of their perceived oppressors who happened by. Driving down the wrong street during those days could lead to a nightmarish experience, if not death. Whites were doused with gasoline and set afire in their cars; others were dragged out and beaten repeatedly with chunks of concrete and bricks, run over by cars, stabbed with screwdrivers, and shot. One was left dying in the street, a red rose in his mouth. Eight whites died in such terrible ways, most on the first day of the riot.[14]

Similar uprisings in other cities have brought Black leaders into the streets to calm down the masses, and older Black citizens have generally tried to rein in ghetto youth. There were such attempts in Liberty City and other Black areas of Miami, but they were countermanded by the opposite trend. A peaceful rally called by the local branch of the NAACP the day the verdict was announced turned into a full-scale riot involving both ghetto teenagers and Black professionals. During the incident, the seat of Dade County's justice system, the courthouse itself, was broken into and torched. Adults on ghetto street corners were observed egging on youths as they stopped and attacked cars driven by whites.[15] "During the riot, we hit everybody, Anglo, Cuban, it didn't matter," a Black community leader told us in 1985—the pronoun "we" speaking volumes; "it was the only way left for this community to show its ire."[16] The local head of the Urban League refused to go into the streets and calm the crowds, noting that "anyone who had any understandings of the ramifications of dehumanization and social isolation could understand the riots. . . . Whites thought it was irresponsible . . . because they assumed that black leaders were there to protect them and not to lead black folks."[17]

The 1980 riot expressed in actions what words had not been able to. American Blacks have always defined their reality in reaction to the subordination and discrimination laid on them by whites; indeed, this is the core of a nationwide Black discourse. In their study of American race riots, for example, Stanley Lieberson and Arnold Silverman noted that cities where riots occurred as a rule had: (1) too few Black police officers relative to the Black population; (2) too few Black entrepreneurs and store owners; and (3) an electoral system that led to too few Black representatives in local government.[18] Miami fulfilled all three conditions amply, but in addition the native minority confronted the reality of a changed city, where a new immigrant group was elbowing them aside. "McDuffie" was, without doubt, the trigger for the riots, but the resentment of being always left out, of remaining invisible and forgotten as other groups marched forward, was the background against which the extremely violent actions of May took place.

Mariel and the Black riot had this in common: they galvanized the two ethnic communities and provided the basis for a vigorous effort at reinterpretion. The stigma of Mariel compelled the Cubans to invent a "new Miami" in which their own role was both central and positive. Similarly, the deaths and deliberate destruction during the May uprising forced Black leaders to rethink the city in terms not bounded by the standard urban-minority frame. The militant double-subordination perspective that took shape during the next decade was born out of these events.[19]

The Boat People

My name is Jean and I came to the United States in 1978. Well, what happened to me was that a Macoute[20] came to rent a bicycle from me for a dollar. When I asked for it back, he told me, "Don't you know that I bought this bicycle from you for a dollar?" I held the bicycle and took it away from him. Right away he hit me with a club. As I was trying to get away, four more came and started beating on me. I ran and hid in the woods.

A cousin came to tell me that they had taken one of my brothers. When he couldn't tell them where I was they took him to a park in front of everybody and killed him. I spent two or three months hiding, and then I went to the Northwest to find a boat. That wasn't hard, but I had to get the $1,500 for the passage. I sold one of my small plots. Anyway, I thought that, once in Miami, I could earn enough to buy it back and probably more. Other families in the town received as much as $200 a month from relatives in Miami. . . . That's more than most could earn in three years.[21]

Between Port-de-Paix and Cap-Haïtien on the north coast of the Republic of Haiti, there were at the start of the 1980s some sixty boats capable of carrying people on a long sea voyage. Charging two or three times the commercial air fare and packing dozens of people in every trip, the captains of those boats created one of the most lucrative businesses in the country. The destination was Miami.

People sold everything they had, including land that had been in their family since the Haitian Revolution in 1804, to buy passage aboard those boats. Their desperation was understandable. In May 1980, the military commander of Haiti's Northwest Province called together all the area's pastors to inform them that the government wanted to stop the exodus. He asked the religious community for its assistance. In fact, the flow did stop for about a week. But after the brief embargo, the first boat to leave departed from directly below the military commander's headquarters. All along, his intent had been not to control outmigration but to obtain a monopoly on kickbacks.[22]

To try to leave the poorest country with one of the most corrupt regimes in the hemisphere is a rational course of action. Indeed, for several decades Haitians of all classes had been streaming out. During the 1960s and 1970s their main destination was New York City. As with other immigrants, New York simply absorbed the newcomers. Middle-class professionals escaping the Duvaliers' oppression were followed by artisans and workers, who simply overstayed their temporary visas. No matter: New York took them in, adding them to its global mix.

Miami, however, was different. Between 1977 and 1981, approximately sixty thousand Haitians arrived by boat in South Florida. The number was only about one-fifth the size of New York's Haitian population, but the impact that these "boat people" had in the receiving city was immeasurably greater.[23]

More than numbers, it was the manner of their arrival that garnered attention, both locally and nationwide. Photographs of shirtless black refugees huddled aboard barely seaworthy craft evoked images buried deep in the American collective mind. Like the slave ships of yore, these boats also brought a cargo of black laborers, except that this time they came on their own initiative, and this time nobody wanted them. Still more pathetic were those black bodies washing ashore Florida's pristine beaches when their craft did not make it. For native whites, this new immigrant wave reinforced the state-of-siege mentality created by Mariel.

In 1980, the Third World laid claim to Miami. The Haitian boat flow peaked right at the time of the Cuban flotilla, the two becoming one in the public mind. Yet despite this conflation, the two refugee streams were very different.[24] Mariel had been, after all, sponsored from Miami, the creation of nostalgic Cuban-Americans. The majority of Mariel entrants had relatives awaiting them and a strong community that understood their language and culture. Cubans, moreover, had been a familiar presence in South Florida for two decades.

Haitians were not sponsored by Miami, nor did they have any

solid ethnic networks on which to rely. Few people in South Florida understood either Haitian Creole or the abysmal conditions that the would-be refugees were leaving behind. Not surprisingly, the reaction of native whites was to reject the new arrivals and to try to stop their entry. Unlike Mariel, this effort met with greater success.

In response to representations made by Miami leaders and local staff of the INS, federal officials in Washington initiated a "Haitian Program" in 1979. The core of the program involved accelerating deportation proceedings and making a concerted effort to discourage Haitian boat people from applying for political asylum. Those who did apply did not have much luck: "Five minute answers to such questions as 'What do you think would happen to you if you return to Haiti?' were reduced to a single sentence in translation. 'Why did you come to the United States?' was virtually always answered on the official form as 'I came here to find work,' as if each of the Haitians had used precisely the same words."[25] The INS would either fail to advise Haitians of their right to a lawyer or else tell them that a lawyer would only get them into trouble. A favorite tactic was to schedule multiple hearings simultaneously. Attorneys for the would-be refugees were expected to argue fifteen different cases in five different locations at the same time.

The culmination of this campaign came not in government offices, but on the high seas. Soon after the installation of the Reagan administration, Coast Guard cutters were ordered to patrol Haitian waters around the clock so that Miami-bound boats could be intercepted at sea before reaching U.S. jurisdiction.[26] Faced with such determined efforts to prevent their arrival, it is remarkable that so many Haitians managed to slip through and remain in South Florida.

Ironically, the reason the "Haitian Program" did not thoroughly succeed was its victims' own defenselessness. Their plight elicited public compassion and the concern of churches and philanthropic organizations. The National Council of Churches sponsored the Haitian Refugee Center (HRC), led by an activist Haitian priest named, most appropriately, Gerard Jean-Juste. The three or four young attorneys who worked pro bono at the center, with support from national law firms, probably did as much to sustain the fledgling Haitian community as the refugees themselves. These lawyers in effect interposed the American legal system between the power-less newcomers and the government's efforts to be rid of them. Their efforts culminated in a class action suit heard in Miami's Federal District Court the same week that the first boats from Mariel came streaming in.[27]

Cuban-Americans also provided unwitting support for the Haitian refugees through their efforts to bring their own kin from Mariel. The coincidence of the two flows only underscored the glaring disparities in the receptions accorded to each group. No government official ever attempted to summarily deport a Mariel refugee; U.S. Coast Guard cutters towed and escorted boats carrying Cubans to Key West, not back to Cuba. No matter how disparaged Mariel entrants were by the media, they were still Cuban and thus effectively insulated from the fate awaiting the boats from Cap-Haïtien and Port-de-Paix.

The U.S. government's justification for the differential treatment hinged on the distinction between "political" refugees and "economic" migrants. The argument did not wash. Clearly many Mariel refugees had left in search of better opportunities, while many Haitians had experienced genuine persecution. The Miami District Court repeatedly heard testimony like that of Mr. Solivece Romet:

Held by the Tonton Macoutes for four days during which he was forced to stand in a 2 by 3 foot cell. Beaten repeatedly as a consequence of which he showed deep scars in his skull and developed a speech impediment. After escaping to Florida in a sailboat, he was detained by the Immigration and Naturalization Service. INS was trying to deport him on the grounds that he was an economic immigrant.[28]

In fact, the difference between the Cubans and Haitians streaming into Miami had less to do with individual motivations than with the country they left behind, the community that received them, and their color. This last realization mobilized the Black political establishment in defense of the Haitians. "If we can take in the refugees of other countries, we can take in the refugees of Haiti," declared Andrew Young in a March visit to Miami.[29] On April 19, 1980, Jesse Jackson led a march of one thousand people to a hotel in Miami where the government was holding sixty Haitian women and children who had arrived by boat the preceding week. In

Washington, the Congressional Black Caucus led the political battle. U.S. representatives Shirley Chisholm, Walter Fauntroy, and Mickey Leland all argued on the Haitians' behalf in personal meetings with the attorney general, the secretary of state, and the president himself. Shortly thereafter, Senator Edward Kennedy attacked U.S. policy as racially biased and demanded to know if Haitians would be treated the same as Cubans.[30]

Faced with this combined offensive, the government relented. Processing of the two flows was assigned to a new administrative entity—the Cuban-Haitian Task Force, housed in the State Department. The creation of this task force and the appointment of a new "Cuban-Haitian refugee coordinator" by the Carter administration further stigmatized the Mariel arrivals, but proved invaluable to Haitians seeking stays from deportation. From then on, any government action toward the "entrants" (as both Mariel Cubans and Haitians were now officially labeled) would have to be on an equal basis.[31]

Haitians gradually won enough class action suits, and sufficient numbers gained permanent or temporary reprieve from deportation, to consolidate a small ethnic community. The Ford Foundation and other philanthropic organizations stepped in with support for the Haitian Refugee Center and the newly founded Haitian Task Force, created to stimulate small businesses in the model of nearby Little Havana. Middle-class Haitians came from New York to join the entrants released from INS custody and those who managed to slip in undetected. Together they forged a new neighborhood—Little Haiti—occupying about nine census tracts in Miami's northwest. A small strip of brightly painted shops emerged in this section, "gypsy" cabs began to make the rounds, and the slow cadences of Creole came to be heard over local radio. City and county governments eventually threw their support behind a new organization, the Haitian American Community Agency of Dade (HACAD), established to provide social services to the new immigrant neighborhood.[32]

Haitians and Miamians

If the creation of Little Haiti was a victory for the national Black political establishment and for the refugees themselves, it was seen in a very different light by the local population. Embattled Miami Anglos, seeking to preserve what remained of their life-style, viewed it as yet another harsh blow. It seemed that they could not win, no matter how hard they tried. Their effort to stop Mariel had fizzled in the face of the Cuban exiles' clout with conservative forces in Washington; attempts to stop the Haitian boats had been similarly short-circuited, this time by liberal activists. Miami's old resort way of life was being relentlessly undercut by the intrusion of national and international forces. Not surprisingly, the rhetoric of "Paradise lost" and the popular bumper sticker reading "Will the last American leaving Miami please take the flag" made their appearance about this time.[33]

The Black community also had reason to look upon the Haitians with ambivalence. True, prominent Black figures had defended the newcomers against government deportation, but they had done so in the interest of racial equality—because they were black, not because they were immigrants. Once settled, however, the newcomers proceeded to compete directly with Black Americans for manual labor jobs, accepting almost any wages and work conditions. For Liberty City, Overtown, and other Black ghetto areas reeling under the impact of double marginalization, the appearance on the labor scene of yet another competitor was not welcome. Black leaders never publicly attacked the Haitians, but confrontation between the two groups mounted nevertheless. The Creole-speaking newcomers were too docile, too subservient to white employers, and, above all, too foreign to the realities of Black America.

Discrimination on the part of native Blacks did not go unreciprocated; Haitians did not see the common circumstance of race as sufficient reason to join a subjugated minority. Instead they set their sights higher, seeking to become an entrepreneurial group. The self-conscious attempt to pattern Little Haiti after the business community of Little Havana was part of this effort. The Haitian quarter abuts Liberty City on the east, but contacts between the fledgling immigrant neighborhood and the Black ghetto were scarce and uneasy. A Haitian-American community leader described the situation in the early eighties thus: "Haitians rarely cross 7th Avenue or I-95 [the locally agreed-upon limits of Liberty City]. They call the area 'Black Power' and do not want to live close to it. Haitians will not melt into the larger Black community. There is just too much animosity between both groups—both in school and at work. The competition for jobs is tremendous."[34]

The difficult circumstances of arrival and the indifference, if not hostility, of the local population combined to make the initial years in the United States a trying experience for the boat people. In 1983, as part of our study of immigrants in South Florida, we interviewed five hundred Haitian entrants who had settled in Miami's Little Haiti and, in smaller numbers, in Fort Lauderdale and the nearby town of Belle Glade.[35] The results of this survey offer a profile of the background of these immigrants and their situation during the first several years of settlement (table 4). Predictably, most 1980–81 Haitian arrivals were young, a prerequisite if one was to withstand the grueling sea journey. About half came by boat directly to South Florida, but a third made a stop in either Cuba or the Bahamas. Most of these young immigrants traveled alone.

The story of their reception in the United States is told in the body of the table. The typical Haitian had few or no relatives awaiting her or him in this country, the average being 1.5. (By contrast, Mariel refugees interviewed in the same year had three times as many relatives already living here.) One-third of all Haitians—and 42 percent of the males—were interned in INS detention camps upon arrival. When finally released, they and others went to live in areas where their immediate neighbors were either American Blacks or other Haitians. The concentration of the newcomers in the poorest ghetto areas is not surprising, given the unwelcome official reception and their own modest backgrounds. Although Haitian entrants were somewhat better educated, more highly skilled, and more urban than their compatriots still in Haiti, they nevertheless compared poorly with American Blacks or Mariel Cubans. On average, none had advanced beyond the fifth or sixth grade, and about four-fifths spoke little or no English. In Haiti, about a third had been jobless (unemployed or not looking for work) before they decided to leave.

By 1983, the Haitians' tribulations had not yet begun to pay off. True, over half were enrolled in English and other courses in order to improve their labor market chances, but fully two-thirds (and 80 percent of the women) were jobless. By way of comparison, that

TABLE 4. *Characteristics of Haitian Entrants in South Florida, 1983*

	Males (N = 205)	Females (N = 294)	Whole Group (N = 499)
Median age	30	29	29
Percent single	53.6	48.5	49.8
Percent traveling alone to U.S.	81.3	70.7	74.9
Means of travel (percentage)			
Airplane	15.7	12.7	14.0
Boat, direct to U.S.	46.1	52.8	50.3
Boat, stop in Cuba	21.2	16.2	18.2
Boat, stop in Bahamas	17.0	18.3	17.6
Average number of relatives present at arrival	1.6	1.5	1.5
Percent jailed by INS upon arrival	41.8	33.1	34.6
Ethnicity of neighbors (percentage)			
Haitian	61.2	67.2	64.8
American Black	20.5	20.6	20.6
Anglo/Latin/other	18.3	12.2	14.6
Average years of education	5.9	3.7	4.6
Percent fluent in English	30.1	11.9	19.2
Percent pursuing English or other courses in the U.S.	54.6	56.6	55.8
Percent jobless			
In Haiti	28.2	33.0	31.0
In U.S.	35.7	81.4	63.0
Percent professionals/managers			
In Haiti	9.0	2.5	5.2
In U.S.	1.0	0.0	0.4
Source of help in securing first job (percentage)			
Kin and friends	75.2	66.4	70.7
Self	23.0	27.9	25.5
Government agencies/other	1.8	5.7	3.8
Current individual income (dollars per month)	600	440	563
Current household income (dollars per month)	712	508	600
Percent in poverty[a]	46	71	59
Percent receiving welfare aid[b]	12.7	40.3	29.2

Source: Alex Stepick and Alejandro Portes, "Flight into Despair: A Profile of Recent Haitian Refugees in South Florida," *International Migration Review* 20 (1985): 329–50.
[a] Percent of households below the federal poverty level for a household of three in 1982 ($7,963).
[b] Includes cash, food, and all other forms of aid, except medical, from private or public agencies.

figure is about twice the jobless rate among Mariel refugees and, for males, three times the jobless rate reported by the Census for all pre-1980 Haitian residents nationwide.[36] As a result, the average household income for Haitian entrants was less than half that reported for the pre-1980 U.S. Haitian population; indeed, close to 60 percent of the new households were below the poverty line. Despite their dire situation, only 29 percent of the immigrants received any form of public or private assistance during their initial years in the United States—a clear indicator of the social environment they confronted here. Of those lucky enough to have found jobs, the overwhelming majority had done so with the aid of kin and friends or by themselves; fewer than 4 percent had been helped by any public or private agency.

The pariah status of Haitian boat people was a consequence of both their race and the highly visible manner of their arrival, which contrasted with the low profile that their co-nationals had been keeping in New York for years. The two factors combined to insure a negative reception by both the federal government and the local population. For the latter, the pathetic image of the arriving Haitian boats suggested that not only Cuba, but the entire Caribbean, was about to empty itself in Miami. The association in the public mind of incoming Cubans and Haitians became one of the few lucky things going for the latter. Yet despite this coincidence and the help of churches and private charities, the situation three years after arrival was anything but enviable.

Haitians were not so much at the bottom of the labor market as outside it; they were neglected by public welfare agencies and looked down on by all other segments of the local community, including native Blacks. Reflecting this situation, 53 percent of our 1983 Haitian entrant respondents reported that they were discriminated against by Black Americans; 65 percent indicated that Anglo-Americans considered them inferior; and 86 percent had had few or no contacts with a single native white.

The City at Mid-Year

Now picture the situation by the late summer of 1980: Mariel had added some ninety thousand to Dade County's Cuban population. The exile community had gotten away with the boatlift, but Fidel

Castro had succeeded in stigmatizing the rescue effort. Although most Mariel refugees had integrated themselves quietly into the community, a visible minority was causing enough trouble to garner national attention. Seriously disturbed mental patients roamed the streets of Little Havana, overwhelming the local mental health system;[37] former convicts survived by preying on Jewish retirees in South Miami Beach; Mariel drug gangs peppered each other with gunfire in any neighborhood shopping center.

Meanwhile, much of the Black northwest section of Miami lay in shambles following the latest assault by its own citizens, a rebellion against the city that immigrant newcomers were overcoming all obstacles to reach. The May riot had made abundantly clear just how tall the barriers were separating native whites, Latins, and Blacks. Next to the wasted Black ghetto, immigrants of the same color but a different mind-set had started building a community of their own. For old-time Miamians, this activity was a harbinger of things to come. French Creole was now added to Spanish in what was quickly becoming a polyglot boardinghouse.

Monolingual Anglos, meanwhile, responded by voting solidly for the primacy of English. Cubans paid no attention. Haitians enrolled in English classes, but they learned Spanish on the job too. By now, *Miami Herald* columnists had run out of expressions to describe the new events, each one a blow to the city as they had known it. Their cries of anguish also went unheeded. Miami was a very different place eight months into the year because the remarkable happenings beforehand had fundamentally altered its ethnic makeup and, in the process, subverted an entire social order.

The city had never been a place conducive to self-reflection. For its once-dominant Anglo majority, it was essentially a vacation spot turned permanent residence. What was there to contemplate in a city barely eighty years of age? Transplanted whites paid more attention to the weather, especially in contrast to the frigid north that they had left behind than to political revolutions in the Caribbean. Miami Blacks were not much for introspective analysis either. The city's race relations were solidly cast in a Deep South mold, one that was both familiar and oppressive. The local Blacks' situation was not too different from that of their brethren in Georgia or Alabama, and its causes had already been written about at great length. As for the growing Latin population, Cubans reserved their capacity for self-reflection to ponder events in the island and their prospects for return. The city where they resided "temporarily" was taken largely for granted.

Nineteen eighty changed all that, forcing each group to look inward and devise a novel definition of themselves and their city. Attacked by Anglos and denounced by Blacks, Cubans reacted to the threat of a pariah status with a novel discourse that placed their role in and their contribution to Miami in a strongly positive light. This reactive frame did not stop at self-defense; it went all the way to laying claim to the city. And the considerable resources of the exile community made this aim a serious challenge.

Blacks did not go that route; rather, pressured from all sides, they expressed their sentiments in the desperate violence of May. These actions had to be explained, however, and in so doing Black leaders pieced together a novel discourse not heard anywhere else in the South. In confrontation with native whites, Cubans, and Haitians, Black Miamians found their voice. From that point on, it was to be heard energetically, staking out the claims of the native minority.

Even such a recent immigrant group as the Haitians found that life in Miami meant more than hard work and sending money home. The process of rapid change that they themselves had helped to create also compelled their fledgling community to reinvent itself, as they sought a legitimacy that others were only too quick to deny.

For Miami Anglos, this sudden ethnic conflagration was too much, and many just fled north. Those who remained also had to rethink their city, no longer as a tourist destination but as an international crossroads. It became a less relaxed, but more complex and interesting place. In jockeying with each other and bringing down the old order, Miami's ethnic groups produced a unique urban experiment.

Although the events of 1980 were the immediate determinants of the current profile of Miami, they themselves had more profound roots. These are to be found in the history of the area and in its long-neglected Caribbean nexus. Those groups that crossed the Straits of Florida in that year and those that resisted their arrival were unwittingly reenacting and bringing full circle a historical saga begun four and a half centuries earlier.

Chapter Four

The Early Years

*Civic spirit may be said to exist in a city where
there is widespread participation in civic affairs on
the part of those able to benefit the community by
voluntary management of its civic enterprises.*
C. Wright Mills and Melville J. Ulmer,
"Small Business and Civic Welfare"

Sipping a drink on a terrace down by the mouth of the Miami
River, the visitor may fancy that the Hyatt and Dupont Plaza hotels
there are the first civilized tenants of this area, it exudes such an
aura of newness. Yet the impression is deceiving. While the city of
Miami is less than a century old, the site where the river empties
into Biscayne Bay has hosted successive visitors for over four hundred years. A stranded Basque sailor gave the bay its name in the
early sixteenth century. It was here that Spanish missionaries,
complaining bitterly about the mosquitoes, settled in 1568. Almost
three hundred years later, in 1836, American soldiers erected Fort
Dallas on the same site as that first mission during the Seminole
War. And sixty years or so later, Henry Morrison Flagler built the
Royal Palm, the first grand hotel of Miami, where the Dupont
Plaza stands today.

Throughout these four hundred years, the successive occupants
of the place—Indians, Spanish friars, American soldiers, southern
colonists, and black slaves—left such tenuous imprints that by the
end of the nineteenth century the area was thought to be as wild
and empty as it had been in the sixteenth. The first white men did
not settle on the reef island eventually known as Miami Beach until
1870, when an adventurer named Henry B. Lum conceived the
idea of putting the sand to use as a coconut plantation. The enterprise failed, but Mr. Lum's coconut trees still grace the beach. On
the mainland, a few scattered plantations survived by shipping

61

their products to Key West, where they were transshipped to places north.[1] As late as 1890 there was no city at all, but only a small agricultural community in the area known as Cocoanut Grove.

Standing some three miles to the south of the first Spanish mission, an early Yankee pioneer recorded his impressions of the place: "Fancy yourself on a broad piazza facing southeast. The wind, almost constantly from that direction, brings with it the refreshing smell of salt water, which is as clear as that of the Mediterranean, bedded as it is with a pure white sand and coral rock."[2] Yet such impressions of unspoiled natural beauty concealed a turbulent past, for the area had been crisscrossed and fought over by Indians and Europeans for over three hundred years. Within view of our charmed observer, not three miles away, was the lighthouse of Cape Florida, sacked and burned by a desperate Seminole party some sixty years earlier. In retribution, Lieutenant Colonel Harvey of the U.S. Army hunted and hanged the Seminole chief and forced the others to scatter into the Everglades. The emptiness that was South Florida, ready for the white colonist's hand, was molded by a history of struggle.[3]

The city of Miami was founded not by a European empire, an army, or a group of planters, but by a handful of brash millionaires bent on turning the Mediterranean dreams of early Biscayne Bay settlers into reality. An enterprising Cleveland widow, Julia Tuttle, who owned land by the mouth of the river, made up her mind to turn the wilderness into an orderly metropolis. According to local lore, the high point of this venture came during the hard freeze of 1894–95 when, with citrus dying south of Orlando, Mrs. Tuttle dispatched a bouquet of orange blossoms to railroad magnate Henry M. Flagler, proving that South Florida remained frost free. Whether the story is true or apocryphal, the fact is that Mr. Flagler was in the area shortly thereafter, with a spur of his Florida East Coast Railway following from West Palm Beach. The first train arrived in 1896, and with it Miami came into being.[4] "Commodore" Ralph Munroe, a Cocoanut Grove planter and yachtsman thus said his nostalgic farewell to the past: "There are many advantages in the new life which has flowed so irresistibly since the railroad came to the Bay, but let no one think that this great change did not bring disadvantage as well. The charm of wide spaces and the simple life are gone and they are blessings not to be despised."[5]

Florida and Cuba

For almost five hundred years, the history of the Florida peninsula has been marked by a series of sudden jolts that tied its course now to men and places of the south, now to those of the north. Early-sixteenth-century navigational charts portrayed Florida and Cuba as a single land mass. Although the error was soon corrected, the Spanish Crown lost no time in claiming the new territory as its own. For the next three centuries, the destiny of the peninsula was to be intertwined with that of the island to the south, and especially to its capital, Havana, from which Florida was governed.

Juan Ponce de León had sailed with Columbus on his second voyage and was later sent to pacify the island of Puerto Rico. He succeeded in this task, but failed in his court battle against Diego Columbus, who claimed the governorship as his own. Ponce was fifty-three when, as *adelantado* of the unknown northern peninsula, he sailed three shallow-draft ships from Puerto Rico in early 1513. The expedition made landfall at latitude 29°32' north on Easter Sunday—or Pascua Florida, which gave the land its name. Contrary to local lore, the Fountain of Eternal Youth did not rank high in the old sailor's priorities, for he never wrote about it. Instead, Ponce and his men sought what Spaniards everywhere in the new continent thirsted for: gold and native empires to subdue. Nothing of that sort met them along the interminable low coast. The Fountain of Youth endured, however, as the first of Florida's many myths.[6]

Sailing south, the expedition rounded the island of Santa Marta, today Key Biscayne, and came into sight of the great emerald bay. The Indians by the mouth of the Miami River were friendly enough; Ponce named them Chequescha, as he thought they called themselves. The *adelantado* went on to explore the west coast of the peninsula, endured a hurricane, and eventually returned home.[7] Eight years passed before he ventured again into these domains. Spurred by the incredible achievements of Hernán Cortés in Mexico, Ponce finally boarded five hundred men in two ships and sailed again for the west coast of Florida. Again neither gold nor eternal youth met the Spaniards. Indeed, this time they were greeted by hostile Indians and a hail of fire-hardened arrows. Mortally wounded, Ponce was taken back to Cuba where he died. He left little behind, except an unshakable myth and the mystery of a forbidding land.[8]

The next Spanish attempt to claim the land was made in 1528 when Pánfilo de Narváez, humiliated by a misfired attempt to subdue Cortés in the name of Cuba's governor, tried to redress that failure with a conquest of his own. Banners flying, he again took possession of Florida in the name of the king. But the land was unyielding: it just swallowed Narváez and his expedition, all of whose four hundred men perished except four. One of these survivors, Cabeza de Vaca, returned to Spain to warn future would-be conquerors against the futility of the enterprise.[9]

But his effort was in vain. Hernando de Soto had been with Francisco Pizarro during the conquest of Peru, where he acquired great wealth and a reputation for bravery. Appointed governor of Cuba and *adelantado* of Florida by Emperor Charles I, De Soto organized and financed the expedition from Spain himself in hopes of replicating Pizarro's great feat. In 1538, a fleet of ten ships with a thousand men and 350 horses arrived in Cuba. After a year's preparation, De Soto appointed his wife temporary governor of the island and sailed to the Gulf Coast of Florida. That tearful farewell in the Havana harbor was the last seen of him. The expedition hoped to encounter an advanced civilization like the Aztecs or the Incas that would guide it to great wealth. Instead it encountered primitive villages and a forbidding swampland. After marching along the Gulf Coast, De Soto established his winter quarters in the north of the peninsula, near present-day Tallahassee. From there the Spaniards hacked their way into Georgia, venturing as far north as the mountains of Tennessee. Then they turned west, discovering the Mississippi River and reaching the Arkansas.[10]

De Soto alternatively made treaties with local chieftains and fought fierce battles with them. Exhausted by the struggles and the march, he died of fever at the mouth of the Arkansas River. The few survivors from the doomed expedition built brigantines and sailed down the Mississippi, arriving in Tampico, Mexico, three years after their original departure.[11] For the next quarter of a century Florida was left alone, the Spanish Crown now being convinced that nothing was to be gained from settling this barren and hostile land.

But although the peninsula itself had nothing to offer, it did sit on the route of the *Flota de la Plata*, a fleet of ships taking the silver and gold of the New World to the king's coffers. Pirates and hurricanes made innumerable victims of the slow and overloaded cargo ships. Particularly feared were the many French, English, and Dutch pirates who based themselves in the small islands of the Caribbean and the Bahamas; and now, to make matters worse for the Spanish, a French Huguenot expedition was dispatched to take possession of Florida in the name of their king. To combat these evils King Philip II turned to his best captain, Don Pedro Menéndez de Avilés, whom he appointed the third *adelantado* of Florida.[12] Don Pedro promptly mounted a five-galleon expedition to the peninsula's east coast in order to destroy the French settlement of Fort Caroline, at the mouth of the St. Johns River. On August 28, 1565, Saint Augustine's Day, he entered the deep, easily defended bay that was to harbor Spain's first settlement in Florida. The inlet at the southern tip of the bay became known as Matanzas (lit., Slaughters), a name well earned during the following days.[13]

After several indecisive encounters, the Spaniards succeeded in capturing Fort Caroline, and in defeating the Huguenot fleet that came to its rescue. "Are you Catholic or Lutheran?" each prisoner was asked. Upon declaring their Protestant faith, the captives were taken in groups of ten behind a sand dune and put to the knife. Seventy Frenchmen were thus executed at Matanzas, including their commander, Jean Ribault. With the Huguenot peril out of the way, Menéndez concentrated on consolidating his hold on this slippery land. He traveled up and down the coast establishing forts and signing peace treaties with local chieftains, such as the powerful Carlos, head of the Calusas. But wherever the *adelantado* was not present, things reverted to their original state. Soldiers mutinied and left their garrisons; tribes captured shipwrecked sailors and burned them in honor of their gods. The wild land resisted in every possible way the hold of the empire.[14]

And so it would continue for 250 years. Every attempt at colonizing the interior of the peninsula with forts and missions was eventually repelled, first by the Indians and the elements, and later on by marauders from the rival colonies to the north. Only in St.

Augustine did Spanish Florida maintain an enduring existence, and this thanks only to its enviable natural defenses and to a continuous stream of settlers and supplies from Cuba. Captured and burned on several occasions, the settlement was each time rebuilt. Francis Drake strode contemptuously into the puny little fort before putting it to the torch in 1586, but on his departure a stronger one was erected.

Finally, the discovery of the white shell rock "coquina" and the arrival of Spanish engineers from Cuba made possible the completion of the castle of San Marcos in the early eighteenth century.[15] Surrounded by a deep moat, the high walls of San Marcos proved unassailable. Several times during the next decades, the population of the town took refuge in San Marcos as pirates and English troops from Georgia and the Carolinas came calling, only to be beaten back. The castle and the town were finally surrendered in 1763, not because of military defeat, but as the outcome of the vagaries of European politics. On that occasion, Havana and Florida, both outposts of empire, were traded for each other. Lord Albemarle had taken Havana from Spain in 1762 during the Seven Years' War (the French and Indian War in North America). The next year, the Treaty of Paris sealed Britain's complete victory over both France and Spain.

For Spain, the loss of Havana, the key to her colonial empire, was irreparable. In exchange for the city, the Bourbon king agreed to surrender all of Florida. He was compensated in turn, by his cousin and ally the King of France, with the vast but unsettled territory of Louisiana. A Spanish governor took over in New Orleans at the same time that the dejected townspeople of St. Augustine embarked for Havana. The English were finally able to enter the unconquerable castle, which they renamed Fort St. Marks.[16]

Florida was now divided into two colonies, East and West Florida, with capitals in St. Augustine and Pensacola. The English moved quickly to consolidate their hold on the region, establishing plantations, adding incongruous chimneys to open Spanish courtyards, and otherwise anglicizing the landscape. This effort proved short-lived, however. The revolt of American colonists, eagerly supported by France and Spain, deprived England not only of its original thirteen colonies, but of its fourteenth and fifteenth as well. Marching from New Orleans, Governor Bernardo de Gálvez retook Pensacola for the Spanish Crown in 1781. In Havana, society ladies gave up their jewels in support of the American troops during that bitter winter.[17]

By the Treaty of Versailles in 1783, the American colonies gained their independence and Spain regained Florida. British royalists who had taken refuge from the rebellious Americans in St. Augustine learned that they would have to move yet again.[18] Although the returning exiles from Havana found their dwellings strangely changed by English additions, otherwise the town was the same. Florida once more found itself Spanish and dependent on the Captaincy General of Cuba. The destinies of the island and the peninsula were proving inextricably bound together.

The Empty Land

If the loyal subjects of George III had been forced into a second exile by the return of the Spaniards to St. Augustine, others found in Florida a refuge from oppression in the newly liberated colonies. Slaves running away from their masters in Georgia and Alabama could gain their freedom by simply disappearing into the peninsula's wilderness. There they joined a population of half-Hispanicized Indian tribes, half-breeds, and even a few descendants of white settlers. This odd mix that formed Florida's native population at the beginning of the nineteenth century was called the Seminoles. The word did not correspond to the name of any Indian tribe; rather, it apparently evolved from the Spanish word for runaway slaves, *cimarrones*, pronounced now as "seminolies."[19] Seminole "Indians" were thus far more familiar with the ways of white men and far more in contact with their cultures than the images of scalping savages diffused by books and films a century later.

Andrew Jackson saw an opportunity. American "property" was escaping by the droves into Florida, a repugnant state of affairs to the mind of the planter class, of which the Tennessean general was a prominent member. Life, liberty, and the pursuit of happiness were fine for white citizens, but they did not apply to others. The disorderly state south of the Georgia border where former slaves were beginning to enjoy just such freedoms aroused concern and alarm in the southern states—reason enough to annex the peninsula. Florida was "a pistol pointed at the head of Louisiana," remarked President Monroe, though this hardly seemed a significant threat.[20] Recovering from the Napoleonic invasion of her own territory, Spain was in no position to be belligerent, or to resist an American invasion of Florida.

Jackson entered Florida and roamed at will, despite repeated protests by the Spanish minister in Washington. On one occasion, he kidnapped the hapless Spanish governor and stole the royal archives; on another, he had 250 Blacks massacred with the justification that they were after all "American property." In the Suwannee River, he took prisoner an old British trader said to be friendly with the Indians and had him shot for "conspiring with the enemy."[21] Publicly, President Monroe disclaimed any responsibility for these deeds; his government, however, secretly encouraged them. The undeclared war in Florida put much pressure on the Spanish Crown to cede the peninsula, as the Americans repeatedly requested. Unable to resist by force of arms, the Spanish government stalled, hoping that diplomatic effort would save it Florida. International law was fully on Spain's side, but Jackson held the ground.

In February 1821, after three years of haggling, the king finally ratified the treaty of cession. Most histories report that Spain received $5 million in compensation. In fact, the U.S. government agreed only to settle claims of American citizens against Spain up to that amount. Spain never saw a penny. At a brilliant ceremony on July 15, 1821, Jackson and his men stood at attention in the main plaza of Pensacola as the Spanish flag came down, marking the end of three centuries of domination.[22] So much suffering, and only to end in this—ignominious surrender in a little Panhandle town. No longer would men, weapons, and ideas come up from the island of Cuba. Now they would come from the north, and quickly, in the wake of Jackson's victory.

Before the new conquerors could impose their own brand of colonialism, though, the land had to be rid of its old-time occupants. The remnants of centuries-long Iberian rule were rapidly cleared out as the few Spanish settlers returned to Cuba and as Black runaways were captured and sold back into slavery. Native Seminoles were informed, in no uncertain terms, that they had to vacate the land. In 1830, the U.S. Congress passed the Removal

Act, the purpose of which was nothing less than the forced displacement of Florida's entire native population into the barren lands west of the Mississippi. Today, as we visit the elegant beach resorts and the manicured theme parks of Disney World, it is difficult to imagine that for all this to come about, weeping Indian men, women, and children were marched at rifle point down the Trail of Tears. Many men, Black and Indian alike, committed suicide rather than be sold back into slavery or removed from their land.[23]

The Seminoles, being pushed ever deeper into the Everglades, resisted. Two army companies under Major Francis Dade were wiped out as they marched east from Tampa. Chiefs Alligator and Osceola met the remaining troops shortly after at the Withlacoochee River, inflicting many casualties. Like other Seminoles, Osceola was not a full native but the son of a white father and a Creek Indian mother. In Marjory Stoneman Douglas's words, "He fought savagely, yet he refused to make war on women and children or permit torture. He was unquestionably the greatest Floridian of his day."[24] Unable to defeat him in battle, General Thomas S. Jesup tricked the Seminole chief by sending him a flag of truce. As Osceola and his retinue entered St. Augustine for the parley, they were promptly enchained and remitted to Charleston, where, in 1838, the chief died of illness and grief. His head was then cut off and exhibited for a while in circus shows.[25]

Thus the whites moved relentlessly forward with their occupation of the long territory. The attack on the lighthouse at Cape Florida by the last of the "Spanish Indians" in the Miami River was a final desperate act of resistance. By 1843, however, it was all over. The "Red Peril" had been put to an end and the land made safe for white settlement and cotton planting. To achieve this end, the U.S. Army had conducted a scorched-earth policy that led to Florida's demographic collapse. By the end of the Seminole War, the total population had fallen to an estimated thirty-five thousand, and the peninsula acquired that empty look that was to endure well into the twentieth century.[26]

In the middle years of the nineteenth century, Florida was largely vacant, having been made so by the logic of America's imperialist expansion. Before there were beach resorts, Fort Myers, Fort Pierce, and Fort Lauderdale were military outposts of that empire; Miami at the time was known as Fort Dallas.[27] Visiting the present-day Miccosukee reservation twenty-five miles west of Miami, one wonders whether these impoverished descendants of the fighting tribes are aware of their historical link with the descendants of Spanish colonists who now inhabit the city. For it was under the tenuous rule of Spain that the Seminoles emerged as a people and prospered, having little to fear from the indifferent colonialism of their neighbors to the south. The sudden end of that rule marked the natives' near extinction under a far more lethal form of empire-making.

Shallow Dixie

Now Florida came under the influence of its northern neighbors as it was discovered that cotton could be grown in the newly cleared lands. Demand for the fiber, and exhausted soils on older plantations, led to a wave of migration and investment from Georgia, Virginia, and the Carolinas. A new planter class emerged, securing a firm grip on the territorial government in Pensacola and later in Tallahassee. The northern counties—Leon, Jackson, Gadsden, Jefferson—acquired that peculiar Old South coloration as graceful mansions with classical Greek porticoes rose in the countryside and as society came to rely on slaves for all manual labor. Ownership of slaves and land was the key to wealth in the territory, and those who had them were determined that things stay that way. In 1845, Florida entered the Union as a slave state; in 1861 it seceded, briefly becoming an independent republic. American domination, which killed off so many native Floridians, had lasted just fifty years.[28]

The newly independent republic then joined and fought along with the rest of the Old South, and was defeated with it. But unlike in Georgia or Alabama, plantation society did not return to the peninsula. For Florida, the end of the Civil War also spelled the end of that peculiar order. Because it had been merely an outpost of the Spanish empire, Florida had escaped the destiny of a Caribbean sugar colony. And because it had remained in Spanish hands well into the nineteenth century, it also managed to escape the "curse of cotton."[29] Despite dominance in state government of the young planter class, that coterie never succeeded in consolidating its hold on the territory as a whole. The sparsely settled lands left in the wake of the Seminole Wars encouraged a more democratic frontier style of life. South and east of the cotton-growing counties, where slaves were few, sentiment for the Union remained strong throughout the war.[30]

Unlike its Dixie neighbors, then, Florida escaped the unenviable fate of a one-crop economy, tenancy and sharecropping, and demagogic rural bosses. Instead, a vast social vacuum emerged. Lacking a dominant planter class, state politics became fundamentally atomized. Neither Spanish nor southern, not yet firmly under Yankee rule, the state developed an amorphous political system. This system persisted well into the twentieth century, when the political scientist V. O. Key described the situation thus: "Florida is not only unbossed, it is also unled. . . . Factional lines in the Tennessee fashion simply do not exist. Nor does there seem to be any clear-cut fundamental cleavage within the state that reveals itself starkly in times of political tension as in Alabama."[31]

Centuries of marginal colonization followed by a war of extermination and another of secession had failed to produce a social order worthy of the name. The two conflicts successively lopped off the bottom and top of Florida society so that, by the last quarter of the nineteenth century, the state had reverted to a vacant land awaiting resettlement. South of Lake Okeechobee, in particular, the landscape was much as it had been at the time of Ponce's visit—a tangle of swamp and mangrove where the saltwater crocodiles and alligators vastly outnumbered the few human residents.

Like Juan Ponce de León, Henry M. Flagler was fifty-three when he landed in St. Augustine in 1883. Close to where the Spaniard had planted his flag 370 years earlier, claiming the territory for Emperor Charles I, Flagler erected a $1.25 million resort hotel. With a fine historical sense, he named it after Ponce. Flagler had no doubt who the new conquerors would be.[32]

An American Riviera

By the time Julia Tuttle sent her bouquet of orange blossoms twelve years later, the future of Florida's northern Atlantic coast was certain. Flagler's elaborate chain of hotels now extended all the way down to Lake Worth—from the Ponce de Leon and the

Alcazar in St. Augustine to the Breakers in newly fashionable Palm Beach. They were impressive structures, capable of attracting the New England and New York gentry who arrived aboard their private railroad cars on Flagler's Jacksonville, St. Augustine, and Indian River Railway. The late nineteenth century was not the time of the common man, nor was Mr. Flagler about to make it so. His establishments were strictly for the rich; after the ball season ended around mid-March and the magnates returned home, they closed for the year.[33]

Yet there was some doubt about the land west of Biscayne Bay. Its fame was due, after all, to the fact that oranges did not freeze there in winter. The weather plus the few groves around Cocoanut Grove augured for the area a tranquil rural future as a citrus shipper. But the railroad that was supposed to transport the fruit north brought instead a mixed bag of hucksters and visionaries who, in no time, changed for good the fortunes of the place. Miami was literally built up from swamp and mangrove to become an assortment of theme parks featuring "sun and sand, bathing beauties, glamorous hotels, palatial homes, night clubs, race tracks, and a certain dash of sin."[34]

First off the train was Mr. Flagler himself, whose Royal Palm Hotel, built over a Tequesta burial ground by the Miami River, continued the tradition of extending a winter welcome to the well-born and powerful. Flagler's baronial style is perhaps best captured in the very founding of the city in July 1896. Miami was incorporated at a meeting attended by 368 persons, 162 of them Black laborers from Flagler's railroad. This "black artillery," brought to the assembly by John Sewell on Flagler's orders, voted as it was told to, thus insuring that the interests of the Florida East Coast Railway had priority. After the election, the Blacks were promptly sent back over the tracks and forgotten. Even Mrs. Tuttle and her dreams of a liquor-free, genteel city were pushed aside as more daring adventurers poured from Flagler's train cars. They gave the city, from its beginnings, a more extravagant, unruly, and democratic flavor than the second Palm Beach contemplated by the lady pioneer and the baron.[35]

Of these early entrepreneurs, none was more important to the new city's future than a Quaker horticulturist from New Jersey named John S. Collins. He came to Miami when the idea of tropical fruit production there still had currency, and immediately bought the barrier island between the Atlantic Ocean and Biscayne Bay with the notion of turning it into an avocado plantation. The land resisted this crop, as it had resisted Lum's coconuts two decades earlier. As the avocado farm went bust, old Collins yielded to his children's entreaties to sell the place in lots to tourists. But in order to get the fruit out and the people in, communication to the mainland was necessary. Collins strained his credit in New Jersey and Miami to build a wooden bridge across Biscayne Bay—only to see construction stop, for lack of money, half a mile short.[36]

Sinking one hundred thousand 1912 dollars into a bridge leading nowhere was heartbreaking, especially since demand for ocean-front lots was on the rise. Relief came in the form of an Indiana huckster and self-made millionaire by the name of Carl J. Fisher, builder of the Indianapolis Speedway, inventor of Prest-o-lite, and promoter of the first cross-country highway. With the same irrepressible energy, Fisher set out to finish what Flagler and Collins had started. He completed the bridge and cleared the land, actually making more of it by the simple expedient of dredging sand from the shallow bay. On top of this new land he put golf courses, baroque-style hotels, and grand mansions.[37]

As his vision of Miami Beach took shape, one of Fisher's few concerns—shared by most of his fellow developers—was to prevent the place from being turned into another Atlantic City, by then virtually a Jewish colony. Signs specifying "Gentiles Only" blossomed as Fisher and Collins moved to keep moneyed Jewish shopkeepers out of their new resort. Lots in their developments were deeded with provisos that read: "Said property shall not be sold, leased or rented in any form or manner, by any title either legal or equitable, to any person or persons other than of the Caucasian race."[38] At the southern tip of Miami Beach, meanwhile, the Lummus brothers—developers with less capital and fewer prejudices—were not about to let good money pass them by. It was on their land that the original Miami Jewish community gained a foothold.

Back on the mainland, Salomon Merrick's citrus plantation had also gone bust, leaving the former New York pastor with a lot of idle land. Like the sons of farmer Collins, those of Merrick quickly saw the light and, with some outside backing, began to improve the area. The exclusive residential city of Coral Gables netted its developers a profit estimated at more than $20 million during its first five years alone.[39]

The tycoons, hucksters, and visionaries who were mining gold out of the sands of Miami had something in common more peculiar than a simple love of money. Northerners all, it might have seemed reasonable for them to conceive of a seaside resort on the model of Newport or Cape May. Yet this did not happen because, almost to a man, these Yankee developers were obsessed with the Mediterranean, and in particular with Spain. Henry Flagler set the tone with hotels that reproduced, in minute detail, the hues and arabesques of Andalusian architecture. St. Augustine to our day is a counterpoint between the majestic fake-baroque structures of the Ponce de Leon and the Alcazar and the unpretentious remnants of the original settlement. The "nation's oldest city" became far more Spanish under the Yankee tycoon than it had ever been during three centuries of Spanish domination.[40]

Not to be outdone, Henry M. Plant spent three million 1890 dollars on his Tampa Bay Hotel, whose thirteen Moorish towers and minarets, its shining crescents and piazzas, made it, in the mind of its owner, "the greatest hotel in the world." Plant even built a railroad from central Florida to transport visitors to his hotel.[41] Down south, Biscayne Bay drew a swarm of visitors who saw in its magnificent vistas the beginnings of an American Riviera. One of these was James Deering, of International Harvester fortune, who decided to build himself a winter villa south of the Miami River. Completed in 1916, this magnificent structure features a coral rock pier in the shape of a Venetian gondola, a broad piazza overlooking the bay, and a vast collection of *objets d'art* imported from Europe. Despite its Venetian style, the villa was named Vizcaya—confirming David Rieff's observation that in South Florida, Spain and Italy were always getting confused.[42]

Hispanophilia was taken to an extreme by the younger Merricks, who conceived Coral Gables on a scale and at an expense that boggles the mind. It was to be not merely a pleasant residential area, but the best resort in the world; it would boast, among other things, the grandest hotel and the most prestigious university in the country—today's Biltmore Hotel and the University of Miami.

Metropolitan Miami, indeed, is probably the only city in the world with two copies of Seville's Giralda Tower. One is the Biltmore; the other, built at the bayfront, was home of the *Miami News* until it came to house the Cuban Refugee Center and was rebaptized Freedom Tower.[43]

The leitmotiv of the Merricks' grandiose project was, as the Biltmore architecture symbolizes, Andalusian. Even today, one enters Coral Gables through fake Spanish fort gates to face shaded streets named Granada, Giralda, Galiano, Oviedo, and Ponce de Leon. Unlike the place and street names of southern California, often in comically anglicized Spanish, those in southern Florida are always correct. The Merricks kept their dictionary close by. Their Andalusian theme park came complete with Moorish minarets, a baroque frontispiece for the Congregational church, "Spanish" moss everywhere, and a coral rock swimming place named (perhaps in answer to "Villa Vizcaya") the "Venetian" pool.[44]

The lead of these pioneers was followed by myriad others during the boom of the twenties. Everyone wanted a Spanish villa by the water. Places called Mar-a-Lago, Miramar, and Buen Retiro housed the lucky entourages of the Fishers and the Firestones. A self-appointed architect named Addison Mizner dotted the Florida coast with a style that mixed, in astonishing proportions, everything Mediterranean that money could buy.[45] South Florida's demand for Spanish grillwork, Italian terraces, and Moorish tile became so great that artisans from all over Europe came to Miami to help turn this mix of fad and obsession into reality: "By 1930 . . . Miami Beach's oceanfront was covered with Casas de Playa whose red-tiled roofs and stuccoed walls looked as if Ponce de Leon had really colonized Florida after all."[46]

For the first three hundred years of its history Florida was settled from the south; for the last hundred, the process shifted direction to come from the north. Even so, the peninsula could not shake off Spain. Her distant influence came first in the galleons of visionary conquerors and soldiers from Cuba and then in the brief-cases and dreams of Yankee entrepreneurs. The notion that history repeats itself, the second time being a parody of the first, could find no better evidence than in the ornate minarets, baroque hotels, and Spanish-style villas built by the Merricks and Mizners.[47] Although few residents of Coral Gables could pronounce the names of their streets correctly, it did not matter: the place stood as a peculiar link to Florida's past and a premonition of things to come.

The Blacks

Beneath the dreamlands built by northern developers, a real city was taking shape, and it was substantially Black. By 1910, fully 42 percent of Miami's five thousand–odd inhabitants were Black. Yet few tourists or moneyed residents had contact with this population, except in the latter's capacity as servants and manual workers; the city fathers took good care to keep them isolated in remote quarters. The land within city boundaries, originally owned by Julia Tuttle and Mary Brickell, another early settler, was deeded in such a fashion that whites received all the bayfront property and that on both sides of the Miami River. Blacks were confined to a northwest quarter across the railroad tracks, which became known as "Colored Town," later Overtown.[48]

The Miami Black population was unique in that it contained, in addition to migrants from Georgia and the Carolinas, a sizable number of Bahamians, who had been brought to work on agricultural plantations and subsequently in railroad and hotel construction. Many settled in Cocoanut Grove, giving the area a distinct "island" atmosphere that lasts to our day. Unlike Blacks from the Deep South accustomed to servile status and heavy discrimination, the Bahamians arrived without a strong sense of stigma. In 1908, Judge John Grambling of the Miami Municipal Court noted that, until they were taught a lesson in manners by the Miami police, "The great number of Nassau Negroes . . . upon their arrival here considered themselves the social equal of white people."[49]

Putting Bahamians in their place was important, but by no means was it the white establishment's only worry vis-à-vis the Blacks. As the tourist boom took off, large numbers of reliable manual laborers were needed, and those workers were overwhelmingly Black. They built the railroad, the villas, and the hotels and later staffed them with porters, maids, waiters, and gardeners. Yet even as Black workers built Miami, their growing numbers posed a problem to hoteliers and developers who had to make sure that their presence did not sully the image of an unspoiled Mediterranean paradise. The solution was to confine Blacks to restricted residential quarters and to control them with various forms of intimidation, mostly entrusted to the police.

In 1898, soldiers of Camp Miami, built by the U.S. Army during the Spanish-American War, amused themselves by harassing the hapless residents of Colored Town. On one occasion, they killed a Black and injured several others for no apparent reason. On another, they invaded in force when a rumor spread that a Black had killed a soldier, forcing the residents to flee in terror. Not a single soldier was ever arrested for these deeds. Regular "necktie parties" were visited upon Blacks accused of attacking whites, especially if the alleged deed involved rape. The first city newspaper— optimistically named the *Metropolis*—made a specialty of arousing anti-Black feelings on such occasions, suggesting measures for the wholesale disposal of the "black fiends." Epithets such as "darky" and "coon" appeared regularly in the pages of both the *Metropolis* and its rising competitor, the *Miami Herald*.[50]

The campaign of intimidation against the Black minority was not aimless; indeed, it had two very clear goals. The first was to prevent Black expansion into adjacent neighborhoods. The second was to prevent the minority's enfranchisement through the electoral system. Until the 1930s, every attempt by Black families to move out of the crowded and unhealthy living conditions in Colored Town was met with violence. A 1911 *Miami Herald* article declared that "the advance of the Negro population is like a plague and carries devastation with it to all surrounding property."[51] The few Blacks who had managed to leave Colored Town by 1915 had to abandon their homes in a hurry after being visited by masked men who threatened their lives. This pattern of intimidation persisted for more than fifty years. As late as 1951, Black families attempting to move into an apartment building outside Overtown were greeted by a series of dynamite explosions. In that second year of renewed American involvement in Asia, these blasts were large and frequent enough to earn for the area the nickname "Little Korea."[52]

Forceful attempts to exclude Blacks from the polls were less frequent, though no less violent. They dated back to the days of work on Flagler's railroad, but began in earnest with the arrival of the Ku Klux Klan in Miami in 1921. The Klan, founded in Georgia in 1915 on the model of its Reconstruction era predecessor, made a specialty of running out of town ministers and leaders of the Black community who advocated racial equality or greater Black participation in the political process. In 1939, the Klan attempted to prevent Black voting in a primary election by holding a parade through Colored Town with hooded men aboard dozens of cars. Klansmen burned crosses at one-block intervals. A dummy hanging by a noose from a power pole bore a red-lettered sign: "This nigger voted."[53]

Up to 1960, Black Miami closely resembled similar areas in other Southern cities, despite the city's projected image of a cosmopolitan world-class playground. As late as 1982, the *Economist* observed that "Miami is not a good city in which to be Black."[54] From the start, a vast rift developed between the white fantasyland mingling Italian and Andalusian dreams and the stark reality of the Black proletariat. For Blacks were Miami's true working class, even though their economic subordination was both concealed and compounded by racial lines and officially sponsored discrimination. They were, more than white workers would have been, cut off from the benefits of the city they were building—to such an extent that, to "swim in salt water," they had to leave Dade County.[55]

Despite poverty and meager resources, the Black population fought back. Churches, business organizations, and publishing concerns emerged, providing leadership for the community's development and for the struggle against oppression. By 1905, a business district had developed on a half-mile strip along Avenue G in Colored Town. Black-owned businesses in the district included grocery stores, an ice cream parlor, a pharmacy, a funeral home, and a newspaper. Later, and farther north, a series of jazz and blues nightclubs emerged in the same street (now renamed Northwest Second Avenue), earning it the sobriquet "Little Broadway." Marian Anderson, Nat King Cole, and many other Black stars of the thirties and forties performed there.[56]

As in colored sections of other American cities, the confinement of the entire Black population into tight quarters led to social differentiation and the emergence of a small but active middle class. David A. Dorsey, Colored Town's first and only millionaire in the 1910s, built the area's first park, library, and school. Henry

Reeves published the *Miami Times*, the largest Black newspaper, which provided a minority alternative to the views aired in the *Metropolis*. These leaders and other prominent citizens founded the Civic League of Colored Town, the Negro Uplift Association of Dade County, and the Colored Board of Trade, organizations that took the lead in fighting discrimination and the Klan.[57]

Although failures were common in the face of what amounted to official support for racism, there were some scattered successes. Liberty City, for example, today Miami's main Black neighborhood, was born out of one such effort spearheaded by a Black Episcopal minister and the Greater Miami Negro Civic League in the early 1930s. They persuaded the *Miami Herald*'s editor to run a series of exposés on the deplorable living conditions in Overtown and the consequent proliferation of contagious diseases. At that time, the infant mortality rate in the area was twice that of white Miami, and there were sporadic outbreaks of influenza, yellow fever, and smallpox. The news reached Washington and contributed to the decision of Roosevelt's Public Works Administration (PWA) to build the first housing project in the southeastern states. Located between N.W. 62d and 67th streets, the project consisted initially of thirty-four apartment units and was baptized "Liberty Square."[58]

There is evidence, however, that the Black leaders' petitions to the New Dealers were successful only because they coincided with the interests of the Miami establishment. The formal application for Liberty Square to the PWA's housing division was submitted by the Southern Housing Corporation, organized by leading members of the white business elite. Their point man was John Grambling, the same former judge who had praised the Miami police for putting Bahamian immigrants in their place. His efforts in 1933 to get the PWA to eradicate Colored Town's "slum" stemmed less from a change of heart than from the desire to push Blacks even farther away from an expanding central business district.[59] Nor was the choice of the project's location entirely casual. Grambling was at the time the personal attorney of Floyd W. Davis, a developer who owned much of the empty land around Liberty Square and who stood to profit enormously from the exploding Black demand for housing. In short, as historian R. Mohl, puts it, "The availability of federal housing funds mobilized the civic elite, who saw in slum clearance a golden opportunity to push the Blacks out of the downtown area."[60]

Hence, even the small victories of Black leaders did not occur without the support of the downtown establishment. Better housing and political representation were the long-term goals of the Black community that organizations like the KKK attempted to thwart. However, the main confrontations, those in which the minority population poured out into the streets, had less to do with long-term improvement efforts than with proximate incidents of violence. Soldiers, Klansmen, and police felt free to attack individual Blacks with complete impunity. The absence of legal redress in such cases was the principal motive for most spontaneous mobilizations and near riots in Overtown and then in Liberty City. Not until 1928, after a seemingly endless series of violent attacks on Colored Town's citizens, were the first white police officers indicted for beating a Black man to death. But then, after deliberating for three hours, the all-white jury acquitted the officers.[61]

Similar events took place with almost monotonous regularity during the next forty years. More than housing or political representation, what drove Blacks into the streets was the need to defend the most basic right of all, life itself. This pattern of confrontation, firmly implanted in the Black collective consciousness after decades of oppression, created the backdrop against which the "McDuffie" riot and other violent uprisings during the 1980s must be understood.

The Cities

Before 1949, the laws of the state of Florida allowed twenty-five or more persons of any hamlet, village, or town who were freeholders and registered voters to establish a municipal corporation. If, after legal public notice, two-thirds of the inhabitants, but no fewer than twenty-five persons, met and agreed to form a municipality, they could do so, earning for themselves all the powers of taxation and regulation granted by the state to municipal corporations.

The developers who invented Miami found it convenient to give their creations legal standing so as to gain for themselves all the powers granted by the state. Under the easy incorporation laws, they quickly moved to turn their orange groves and failed plantations into full-fledged cities. Miami made its debut in 1896, followed in Dade County by Homestead, incorporated in 1913, and Florida City in 1914. All three places were stations along the new branch of Henry Flagler's Florida East Coast Railway. Subsequently, Collins and his followers incorporated Miami Beach (1915), and the Merricks did the same with Coral Gables (1925). Opa-Locka—developer Glen Curtiss's dream of the "Baghdad of America," with streets named Sheherazade and Ali Baba—became a city in 1926. Miami Springs, South Miami, and North Miami followed during the next two years.[62]

The proliferation of local government units slowed somewhat in the aftermath of the Great Depression, though five more cities were created during the 1930s: Miami Shores (1931), Biscayne Park (1931), and El Portal (1937) on the mainland, and two tiny barrier islands across Biscayne Bay, Surfside (1935) and Indian Creek Village (1939). The pace accelerated in the 1940s with the incorporation of Sweetwater (1941), Bal Harbour (1946), Bay Harbor Islands (1947), Virginia Gardens (1947), Hialeah Gardens (1948), Medley (1949), and Pennsuco (1949). In 1949, the state legislature finally passed a measure that prevented further municipal incorporations. The law was reinforced by an informal legislative agreement in 1953 prohibiting the creation of new cities by special acts.[63]

But the damage was done. Lax regulation had led to a hodgepodge of twenty-six "cities" that, in 1990, ranged in size from 358,548 (Miami) to 13 (Islandia). Areas that in other cities would be small or midsize neighborhoods, in Dade are full-fledged municipalities. The proliferation of local authorities, petty rivalries, and overlapping jurisdictions resulted in inefficient provision of basic services to the true "city" that encompassed almost the entire county. In addition, after 1949 many residents moved to the "unincorporated" area of Dade County, serviced by county agencies but untaxed by any municipal authority. The obvious need to provide countywide services and the equally obvious inequity of service costs for city versus county residents was to shape the local political agenda for years to come. The struggle to create a badly needed metropolitan form of government in the face of determined municipal resistance and the paradox of an "unincorporated" area two and a half times larger than the largest city (1,036,925 vs. 358,548, in 1990) was the legacy of the developers' chaotic dreams.[64]

Florida Politics

Politics in pre-1960 Miami was not so much a struggle between well-defined party forces as a beauty contest among members of a single party. The Democrats reigned supreme. The Republican party, turned by the Reconstruction era into a permanent minority force, was riddled with factionalism. To understand the character of Miami politics in the first half of the twentieth century, one must first look at the singular state context in which it was embedded.

Florida, that long-vacant land, was being resettled. The Old South, too weak to dominate the new territory, became a passageway for those coming from farther north. Farmers victimized by boll weevil and drought in their home states settled by the Indian River; hordes of retirees discovered St. Petersburg and Tampa; and well-heeled eastern families were seduced by the manicured playgrounds that Flagler planted along his railroad. By the mid–twentieth century, 48 percent of Florida's population had been born elsewhere, compared to 11 percent in Georgia and 10 percent in the Carolinas.[65]

The settlement profile of the peninsula also contrasted in multiple ways with the neighboring states. By 1940, only 16 percent of Florida's population lived in rural areas, compared to 48 percent in South Carolina, 57 percent in Arkansas, and 64 percent in Mississippi. Florida agriculture became increasingly diversified and technology-driven. Its weight in the state's economy was balanced, however, by lumbering and fishing interests, construction, and, above all, tourism. This diversification gave the state the highest income per capita in the South, with the exception of oil-rich Texas, and a paradoxical political system dominated by a single party yet free of the hegemony of any interest block.[66]

In Florida, candidates for Congress and for the state legislature often ran as individuals, rather than as part of a "ticket" as in the rest of the South; local officials frequently refused to endorse candidates for state office, lest they antagonize local opponents of those candidates; and former governors seldom had enough clout to get themselves elected to the U.S. Senate or even to other state offices.

The outcome of elections depended on shifting coalitions in which the farmers, the developers, the insurance industry, and other special-interest groups participated but which no one dominated. This gave to Florida politics that atomized, amorphous quality unique in the South.[67]

The system is best reflected by the peculiar character of the Florida executive branch, established by the constitution of 1885. This document provided for a collegial executive in which not only the governor, but also the secretary of state, attorney general, comptroller, superintendent of public instruction, state treasurer, and agriculture commissioner were elected statewide. The governor could not serve in a second four-year term, but cabinet officials could be reelected indefinitely. Many actually died in office. During their tenure, they served ex officio and with the right to vote in all key state boards and commissions. This anachronistic "cabinet system," which severely restricted the power of the chief executive and diluted responsibility for government decisions, was actually defended by many as providing the only measure of stability in a shifting political order. In V. O. Key's opinion, "It may not be mere coincidence that such an institution developed in the southern state with the most disintegrated structure of political organization."[68]

It takes time to put down roots in a place, to cultivate stable loyalties, and to identify reliable enemies. Factions consolidated elsewhere over the course of generations had but a feeble base in a population of sun-seeking retirees, part-time tourists, and newly arrived farmers. The radical individualism displayed in Florida elections was but the political reflection of a still-unsettled social order. By the mid–twentieth century, Florida, though no longer a vacant frontierland, was still in search of an identity and far more permeable to outside influences than the older societies of its erstwhile Confederate partners.

The Fight for Metropolis

What was true of the state as a whole was more so at its southern tip. Dade County's population was even newer and more unsettled than that of the rest of the state. Crisp Bostonian accents mixed with the nasal twang of midwesterners, the slow cadences of Georgians, and the harsh New York intonations. This population had little connection with the area's past and little in common among themselves, except perhaps the love of sun and sand and of the money that could be made from them. With the exception of Blacks, whose condition did not differ much from that of their brethren in other southern cities, Dade's populace could have been found anywhere in the country. Developers took full advantage of this fragmentation to quickly and easily transform newly drained swamps into political jurisdictions.

The loyalties that eventually emerged in Dade County did not encompass the entire metropolitan area, but went only as far as the municipal borders. Residents of Coral Gables, the best-laid-out resort in the area, developed an image as a privileged enclave, jealous of its municipal prerogatives and weary of any close inter-course with the less fortunate citizens of other subdivisions. In contrast, Hialeah deteriorated from the stylish neighborhood-by-the-racetrack advertised by Glen Curtiss into a jumble of cheap bungalows and trailer parks, becoming progressively poor and falling under the influence of a series of notorious political bosses. To the north, Curtiss's Arabian-style Opa-Locka city hall peeled and faded as fast as the inhabitants' social standing; the city became increasingly Black and poor, housing refugees from Liberty City and Overtown.[69]

In that avocado plantation cum tropical resort called Miami Beach, the most interesting development occurred as the one ethnic group explicitly barred by Fisher and Collins settled en masse, displacing the original gentile proprietors. New York Jewish tourists had started coming for short vacations, settling in the modest hotels and houses of the Lummus brothers' subdivision south of Fifth Street. As the boom of the 1920s came to an end and wealthy vacationers started bypassing Miami Beach for more exotic destinations, local realtors quickly became less squeamish about the ethnic background of their customers. When it came right down to it, a Jewish millionaire was better than no millionaire at all.[70]

The depression years were hard on Miami Beach, but wealthy Jews arrived to pick up the slack both as customers and as buyers of property. With them came Yiddish and synagogues, delicatessens, and even Hebrew private academies and universities, transforming the resort into an extension of their Jewish New York enclave. Where Carl Fisher had dreamed of an exclusive playground for wealthy Anglo-Saxons, the hitherto discriminated-against minority erected a city in its own image that obliterated the resort's early social ambiance. Jews were city people, and they conceived of *their* playground in urban terms—a Warsaw by the sea. Their influence was most marked south of Lincoln Road, where the quaint little hotels and numerous small shops exuded an unmistakable ethnic flavor. The human dimensions of the place, in fact, were to save Miami Beach from ruin half a century later, when this "Art Deco" district was rediscovered.[71]

No stable political coalition gained hegemony over Miami itself, however. During the 1930s, Daniel J. Mahoney, publisher of the *Miami News*, and Florida senator Ernest G. Graham forged a political coalition that took control of political patronage, functioning for a while as a "Little Tammany." After its dissolution and until the 1950s, the familiar political vacuum reemerged, filled only in part by the growing influence of the *Miami Herald* and its associate editor John Pennekamp. In the absence of a well-articulated power elite, the newspaper assumed this role by default, becoming a power broker in its own right.[72]

Lack of a true bipartisan system and of a consolidated elite was nowhere more evident than in the fight to establish a metropolitan system of government. The complexities of managing a growing city squeezed into a narrow strip between ocean and swampland had become painfully obvious. A patchwork of ad hoc solutions had emerged, such as the arrangements by which the city of Miami sold water to Hialeah, Miami Springs, and Miami Beach and provided the use of the Miami police communications system to smaller municipalities. Areawide agencies had been created by the state legislature to attend to the most urgent needs. In 1945, for example, an act of the legislature did away with the Greater Miami Port Authority and replaced it with the Dade County Port Authority under control of the County Commission and with jurisdiction over "all harbors and airports, tunnels, causeways, and bridges."[73]

But these short-term solutions were not enough. The true city, growing in all directions, required unified governance. The myriad incorporated "cities," led by Coral Gables, however, orchestrated a fierce opposition to all proposals for metropolitan government. The fight pitted downtown business and civic leaders, who saw a pressing need for coordinated authority, against local residents bent on protecting their own particular life-styles. The independent "cities" were backed by their own employee unions and their suppliers; opposing them was a loose coalition led by the *Miami Herald* and including the Dade County legislative delegation, the Dade County Research Foundation, and the Miami-Dade Chamber of Commerce.[74]

Despite their impressive roster, the pro-Metro forces suffered a series of defeats at the hands of the municipalities. Miami Beach complained tirelessly that it contributed far more in sales taxes from tourism than it received from the county in services. Other localities had gripes of their own. Beneath these protests and the effective resistance they articulated was the fact that social structure and community solidarity barely transcended local boundaries. Residents identified with their immediate surroundings, be they in Coral Gables, Miami Beach, or Hialeah. In this context, the voices calling for a citywide discourse faced an uphill battle, despite the pressing needs on which they grounded their position.

Metropolitan government ultimately came to Miami in a two-stage process that required approval of a Home Rule Amendment for Dade County by the Florida electorate and then passage of a metropolitan charter by county voters. Home rule garnered a full 70 percent of the state vote in the elections of November 1956. Passage of the metropolitan charter would seem an easy last step. The municipalities, however, had other ideas and bitterly contested the reform. The Metro Charter passed in the special election of May 1957 by a mere 1,784 votes—44,404 for versus 42,620 against. Not a single precinct in Miami Beach and Hialeah voted in favor, and most smaller cities also turned the reform down. Only a massive vote in the central city enabled Metro to become law.[75]

The clash between the city of Miami and the surrounding municipalities was not the classical confrontation between a low-income central city and its affluent suburbs, for, with the exception of Liberty City and Overtown, most of the metropolitan area was in fact "a giant suburb."[76] The conflict had to do instead with the petty loyalties built over the short span of the area's existence as a city and with the vested interests created during the early fever of incorporation. For a large part of this population of New York retirees, transplanted New Englanders, and Chicago businessmen, the idea of "metropolitan Miami" was still an abstraction. Downtown leaders who had begun to think in these terms scored their first tangible victory with the passage of the Metro Charter. It paved the way for acceptance of the city as a real place and for the expansion of a civic spirit confined thus far to narrow local boundaries. This victory, however, occurred in 1957, just two years before the triumph of the revolutionaries led by Fidel Castro in Cuba.

On the Threshold of the Sixties

The most prominent political figure in Florida in the early years of the twentieth century was Napoleon Bonaparte Broward. A committed populist, Broward was the antithesis of Henry Flagler, whose baronial style he opposed. As governor, he began the draining of the Everglades, a project he believed to be in the public interest, while simultaneously fighting the "wild capitalism" he saw growing everywhere around him. His rough brand of populism came as close to dividing Florida politics into entrenched factions as anything before or after.[77] Broward had made a name for himself smuggling arms to the Cuban insurrectionary army fighting Spain in the 1890s. His interest in the island a hundred miles to the south was, like his politics, exceptional for the time. Most Florida politicians directed their sights exclusively northward, to the places from which people and money were flowing in a seemingly endless stream. In this mental landscape, Havana, and for that matter the entire Caribbean, were, at best, a remote presence.

This view of things was widely shared in the fast-growing city by the bay. Miami's "Spanishness" did not come from Cuba, but from New York. During its first half-century of existence, Miami had evolved into a tourist resort, a playground, even a Jewish enclave—anything but the "Capital of the Caribbean." That designation—which today is one of the city's claims to fame—would have been incomprehensible to a population arrived recently from the north who had but the faintest idea of Florida's Spanish past. On the threshold of the sixties, Miami reveled in its newly gained metropolitan status and took the first hesitant steps toward an urban identity that would transcend its puny subdivisions. The political concerns of its citizenry continued to focus, however, on the endless bickering between Metro and the "cities," and on the threat posed by the continuous inflow of northern migrants seeking the same life-style that the locals already enjoyed.[78]

Those who inveighed at the time about the dire consequences of this influx of northerners could not have dreamed that the bulk of the city's population in the next decades would come from the opposite direction. Once again, the destinies of the island and the peninsula were to be intertwined, this time in a most unexpected way. The rising flow of exiles from Cuba's socialist revolution did not go to Tampa and Key West, places of Cuban settlement at the time of the island's earlier war of independence. Rather, and overwhelmingly, they chose the glittering Biscayne Bay metropolis, then groping for some sense of urban identity. The first exiles encountered a social and political order that, if not entirely amorphous, was a far cry from the consolidated power structures in place farther north, and therefore far more permeable. As the *Miami Herald* and its allies struggled to build a serious city out of an assemblage of theme parks, the entire Cuban bourgeoisie arrived on the doorstep. The Andalusian settings so presciently built by George Merrick half a century earlier now became populated by people who knew their origins and could pronounce the street names correctly. After four hundred years, history had come full circle.

Chapter Five

Enter the Cubans

Tucked among the royal palms and frangipani of South Street in Key West, the southernmost urban way in the United States, is the John Dewey House. The bungalow was the winter home of the famous American philosopher, who found in this community and its weather a balmy respite from the rigors of the north. It is a white wooden structure built in a style familiar throughout the Caribbean; it looks south toward Cuba.

Less than two blocks away, as one turns north onto Duval Street, El Balcón de Martí, the second-story balcony from which the Cuban revolutionary José Martí addressed throngs of exiled cigar workers commands the sidewalk. The humble monetary contributions of those workers, plus similar collections in Tampa and Jacksonville, armed a series of expeditions against the Spanish colonial regime in the island during the 1890s. Today the building graced by El Balcón houses an inn and a fancy restaurant.

One block north along Duval is the San Carlos Club, a structure reminiscent of the architecture of old Havana but actually built in the 1920s to replace a nineteenth-century gathering place of Cuban revolutionaries. The new San Carlos was dedicated on October 10, 1924, the anniversary of the beginning of the first Cuban war of independence. The building's founding stone was brought from *La Demajagua*, the sugar mill where that rebellion started.[1]

Before there was a Miami, the city of Key West was a well-established and thriving center of Caribbean commerce. The supplies and men who carved Henry Lum's coconut plantation out of the jungle that was then Miami Beach came from there. Mail also

89

came from the Key aboard the schooner *Flora*, which sailed regularly to the Brickell trading post by the Miami River and to the tiny settlement of Cocoanut Grove.[2] In Key West, the two oddly mixed currents that were to shape Miami's history in the twentieth century were already present in the final decades of the nineteenth.

The Dewey House is today a lingering symbol of what northerners of all stripes came south for: the sea breezes, the sunlight, the ocean in multiple hues of emerald. The San Carlos and El Balcón de Martí stand for the other, earlier South Florida, inhabited by people to whom sand and sea meant little, since they were born with them. This last group dedicated its energies to other pursuits, usually of a political nature. In Key West at the end of the 1800s, pale Yankee tourists intermingled with olive-skinned exiled workers and veterans of past insurrectionary wars. Heavily armed expeditions set sail right next to beach resorts packed with northern vacationers.

The Two Floridas

This counterpoint was not just a colorful historical oddity; it prepared the way for the forces that were to transform South Florida and Miami after the Cuban Revolution. The common history of the island and the peninsula under Spanish rule constituted the backdrop against which the events of the 1970s and 1980s were to unfold. The more immediate social explanation for those events, however, lay in that peculiar juxtaposition of tourist-oriented development and revolutionary expeditions, the construction of beach resorts and the arming of men, that marked the late nineteenth century. Florida meant very different things to people coming from the north and those coming from the south, and the combination took a number of dramatic turns.

In late 1894 the Cuban Revolutionary party, founded by Martí, readied to rekindle the insurrection in the island, organizing a well-armed expedition of three ships to set sail from Fernandina Beach near St. Augustine. Owing to the carelessness or treachery of its commander, however, the expedition was discovered and the vessels seized by U.S. authorities on January 14, 1895. It was a major blow. The monies accumulated after endless rallies and speeches in Tampa and the Key were lost with the ships.[3]

Meanwhile, the heartbreak of the arrested revolutionaries was echoed across Central Florida, but for very different reasons. A record frost that winter had ruined countless citrus growers and compromised the finances of Flagler's East Florida Railroad. The year was chilling all around. Insurrectionists, growers, and railroad workers struggled mightily that winter in close physical proximity, even if their worries were not at all the same.

On February 24, 1895, Martí finally succeeded in taking the war to Cuba, where he himself landed at the head of a new expedition. The confiscations of January had in fact energized the Cuban cause by proving the revolutionaries' seriousness of purpose.[4] That same month, the frost peaked in Florida, triggering a similarly energetic response. Flagler's railroad organized the distribution of free bags of fertilizer and cheap loans for the growers, whereas in Miami, Julia Tuttle saw her golden opportunity.[5]

The following years were marked by feverish activity both in South Florida and across the Florida Straits, as one group of newcomers sunk their energies into building new resorts and another into achieving national independence. Yet a curious mutual indifference was apparent throughout this entire period. It seemed as if there were two Floridas—one being built out of the swamp with the dreams and ambitions of Yankee entrepreneurs; the other looking ever to Cuba and to Spain thanks to centuries of trade and political tradition. In 1896, Miami became a city and construction of Flagler's luxurious Royal Palm Hotel was proceeding at full steam. In the same year, expeditionary boats played cat-and-mouse with U.S. revenue cutters up and down the Florida coast, taking vital supplies to the rebels in Cuba.[6]

Of these expeditions, none were more colorful than those organized by Napoleon Bonaparte Broward and the Cuban Revolutionary Council of Jacksonville. Broward's powerful, fast tugboat the *Three Friends* was ideal for outrunning the U.S. cutters and the Spanish gunboats that blockaded the island. After some vacillation, Broward signed a secret agreement with the council and himself captained the first expedition. On March 15, 1896, the *Three Friends* delivered to the north coast of Matanzas Province some sixty Cuban soldiers and a cargo consisting of two field cannons, five hundred Remington rifles, three hundred Winchester rifles, five hundred machetes, five hundred pounds of dynamite, and three hundred thousand rounds of ammunition.[7]

Although the trip was successful, the tugboat was discovered by the Spaniards, who nearly captured it. Only its superior speed allowed it to escape. But the Spanish minister in Washington protested, and, after the adventure became known, the *Three Friends* came under close scrutiny by U.S. Treasury officials and Spanish government spies. Broward and his men were quite adroit at eluding this vigilance. More than once he explained his boat's activities by saying that he was towing Flagler's barges or doing other work for the resort developers in South Florida. To the Spanish consul in Jacksonville, Señor de Mariátegui, he retorted on one occasion, "I've got one hundred twenty tons of coal and a whole boatload of arms and ammunition for Key West."[8] He then invited the Spaniard to be a guest on his next trip.

The Cuban Revolutionary Council in Jacksonville could never have gotten away with this trafficking of men and arms were it not for the open sympathy of many Americans to the rebel cause. Freight cars loaded with guns and ammunition for the Cuban army arrived in Jacksonville's yards from the north, while recruits came from Tampa by the dozens—and neither Mariátegui nor the U.S. authorities could do anything about it. The *Three Friends* took three more expeditions to Cuba, the third, which delivered seventy-five men and a thousand rifles, landing only a few hundred yards from General Maceo's rebel army in Pinar del Río Province.[9] During its fourth incursion, the *Three Friends* was discovered and chased by a Spanish gunboat south of Pinar del Río Province. Answering its fire, the tug's rapid-fire cannon scored a direct hit that crippled the Spaniard. Another, larger gunboat gave chase, but the tug managed to escape in the fog. The episode became known as "Cuba's first naval battle."[10] It took place in December 1896, at about the same time that the Royal Palm Hotel was being readied for its New Year gala opening and the steamer *City of Key West* delivered its first boatload of winter tourists to Cocoanut Grove.[11]

In 1897, a Supreme Court decision reaffirmed U.S. neutrality in the Cuban war and ordered all filibustering boats to be impounded. Fortunately for Broward and other pro-Cuban owners, the U.S. battleship *Maine* was sent to Havana harbor, where it mysteriously exploded, leading President McKinley to declare war on Spain. The Supreme Court ruling on Florida's Cuban supporters was never implemented.[12]

Florida as a Stage

Miami in the late 1890s was as yet too insignificant to serve as a base for conspiracies and was thus spared the revolutionary fever. Miami's confrontation was not between Cuban rebels, their American sympathizers, and a cornered Spanish government, but between Flagler's railroad and those old-timers who, like the Munroes and the Brickells, were trying to preserve what they could of the bay's old charm. Just a hundred miles to the south, meanwhile, Captain General Valeriano Weyler of Spain was starving the Cuban peasantry by relocating people away from the land; at night, the skies were lit by the brightly burning cane fields.[13]

The Spanish-American War was the first major event to unite the destinies of the young Florida city and the island colony. Shortly after the hostilities began, the U.S. Army moved troops to Camp Miami in preparation for invading the island. As it turned out, no invasion took place because the Spanish resistance crumbled quickly; instead the idle troops amused themselves by harassing the inhabitants of Colored Town.[14] It would not be the last time that affairs in Cuba would end up with the victimization of Blacks in Miami.

The defeat of Spain was a bittersweet victory for the Cubans. As the exile colonies of Tampa and Key West began to empty out, the returning revolutionaries carried to the island ambivalent feelings toward the country that had given them refuge. True, the American intervention had brought a bloody war to a swift end, but the favor had come at a cost: Cuba was now a political protectorate. American generals governed the island from 1898 to 1902, and when they finally left, the new republic found that it was anything but fully independent. Senator Orville H. Platt proposed, and the U.S. Congress approved, an amendment to the Cuban constitution giving Washington the right to intervene in the country's internal affairs.[15] Under the Platt Amendment, the American ambassador became in point of fact the colonial overseer of Cuba.

With such political assurances in place, U.S. capital started pouring into the island. The pattern of investment was not too different from that taking place in Florida at the same time: money went into agriculture, primarily sugar cane, and tourist ventures. In 1902, the most plausible future for the nascent republic was as a

southern extension of Florida, formally independent but subject to
the economic and cultural hegemony of the north. Had this occurred, the remarkable counterpoint of Yankee developers and Cuban
revolutionaries that was so apparent in South Florida during the
1890s would not have repeated itself. Instead the homogenizing
logic of capital, bent on extracting profit from warmer weather and
fertile land on both sides of the Straits of Florida, would have
prevailed.

That things did not turn out that way is a consequence primarily
of the kind of country Cuba was. Weak economically, it nevertheless possessed a strong national identity. The anthropologist Sidney
W. Mintz, in attempting to explain Cuban national character, contrasted the colonial history of the island with that of her Caribbean
neighbors. The plantation system, so inimical to nationhood as it
filled one colony after another with masses of slave laborers ruled
by a few overseers, made its appearance late in the history of
Cuba. For the first two centuries of Spanish rule, the island had
been left alone to develop an independent society of Creole commercial farmers and small subsistence cultivators. There were few
slaves; even after the large-scale introduction of sugar cane in the
second half of the eighteenth century, the proportion of slaves to
the total population remained much lower than in the other Antilles:

By the time the plantation system began to expand in Cuba, that society
had a people and a culture of its own. . . . Cuban society gradually took
a special quality: rural in emphasis, anti-Spanish but pro-Hispanic, folk-
Catholic, Creole. . . . It was Cuba's subsequent struggle for political and
cultural autonomy from Spain that gave her the focus she needed to
become a cohesive nation. Cuba as a Spanish colony had more nationhood
than the colonies of other European powers in the Antilles might have had
as sovereign states.[16]

This peculiarity of the subordinate new republic now came into
play as a counterweight to American economic and political influence. The successors of Flagler and Fisher could not simply push
south into more "open space," as they had at Biscayne Bay. Although weaker economically, Cuba was a very different place from
the semivacant peninsula. Instead of becoming its appendage,
Cuba gradually converted Florida into her own political backstage,

where the dramas, and sometimes comedies, of exile were regularly enacted. The counterpoint of the late 1890s was hence repeated, but each time with a different cast of characters and a
slight alteration of place. Now, as Miami continued to develop
along the lines envisioned by its founders, the upheavals of Cuban
politics regularly deposited a new wave of exiles on its shores.

For many years, the resort-bound vacationers and political con-
spirators coexisted in the city with the same mutual indifference
they had exhibited in Key West during the Spanish-American War.
Polly Redford's history of Miami, which ends before the Cuban
Revolution, contains only two references to Cubans, both as hired
help in Miami Beach hotels.[17] In turn, Hugh Thomas's voluminous
history of Cuba does not have a single index entry for Miami, even
though much political maneuvering went on there in the twentieth
century.[18] For Miami hotel owners and developers, Cubans represented little more than an occasional source of low-wage labor. For
the exiles, the city was but a rear base for organizing offensives
against the government in Havana.

Several factors contributed to this casual attitude of Cubans
toward a city that was, after all, in a different country. Weather
and geography played a part, no doubt, but so did the built environment. Old Key West had been built by Cubans, and its architecture naturally reflected styles familiar in the island. Miami was
built by Yankee developers, but their blueprints were also dominated by Andalusian and Mediterranean themes. Up and down the
beach, wrought iron, red tile, and villas with Spanish names
abounded. An architecture designed to attract tourists came to
provide, unwittingly, a receptive setting for former Spanish coloni-
als.

When General Gerardo Machado, democratically elected president of Cuba, decided to change the constitution in the late 1920s
so that he could stay indefinitely in power, he triggered a new flow
of exiles going to both Miami and New York.[19] The Platt Amendment, still in force, enabled the U.S. ambassadors to Cuba to play
a key role in the ensuing struggle. American economic interests in
the island, moreover, supported the dictator, just as they had supported the colonial regime during the war of independence.[20] "Indeed," Thomas observes, "it was all too easy for both government
and opposition to slip into the roles of Spaniards and Nationalists—

with the U.S. playing a similar if more ambiguous role than in the 1890s: its home territory acting as a base for rebels, its citizens in Cuba being a support for the Cuban government, both helping to provide specific financial assistance."[21]

The American ambassador, Sumner Welles, was at first friendly toward Machado, but soon the increasing violence and political instability in Cuba persuaded him that the general had to go. Thus, through Welles's efforts, the first Cuban dictatorship came to an end: on August 12, 1933, Machado flew to Nassau with a few friends—some still in their pajamas—and seven bags of gold.[22] Many of his closest supporters ended up in Miami, where Machado was eventually buried. His tomb is in the Woodlawn Cemetery, today in the heart of Little Havana.

The intense participation of the American ambassador in the events of 1933, as well as the comings and goings between Washington and Havana under the Platt Amendment, gave Cubans an object lesson in the politics of empire. The unfortunate status of being a semicolony had the unintended effect of giving the islanders a thorough apprenticeship in the political ways of the north. The Cuban upper class learned henceforth to monitor the government in Washington as carefully as they did their own in Havana.

In Miami, those August days of 1933 had witnessed the departure of exultant revolutionaries, their places taken by crestfallen incoming *machadistas*. The city, however, was in no mood to pay much attention to this change of the guard: it was in big trouble. The land boom of the nineteen twenties had turned into a complete bust, and the population had declined by more than half in less than ten years. The Royal Palm Hotel was boarded up, and many other businesses had closed. With no paying jobs anywhere, locals rediscovered the natural bounty of the tropics, nearly forgotten since the arrival of Flagler's railroad. Avocadoes, mangoes, and guavas were still plentiful in Miami backyards, and fish still swam in great numbers in the bay; the subsistence that they provided came to substitute for store-bought provisions.[23] As the despondent Machado exiles made their appearance, they found a city where a good part of the economy had reverted to what it had been half a century earlier, replacing that run on tourist dollars and rampant land speculation.

The Leader Cometh

On a sunny day twenty-three years later, the authorities of Daytona Beach gathered to honor a famous local resident. The man in question, General Fulgencio Batista y Zaldívar, had left Daytona a few years earlier to organize opposition to the democratically elected president of Cuba, Carlos Prío y Socarrás. On March 10, 1952, Batista engineered a military coup that sent Prío packing to Mexico and eventually to Miami. The new regime was very favorably disposed to Americans, be they legitimate businessmen or gambling racketeers, and the sugar-led prosperity of the island insured happy returns to all. Accordingly, the Daytona city fathers saw nothing wrong in proclaiming March 24, 1956, "Batista Day" in honor of the new Cuban dictator, in a ceremony held only a few hundred miles away from Miami, where the deposed legitimate president sulked in impotence.[24]

Prío was down but not out. He now dedicated all his energies and his considerable personal fortune to the overthrow of Batista. And although Prío was not up to leading an expedition himself, he supported almost anyone who did. First the Luzerne Hotel in Miami Beach and then Prío's own Casa Reposada in South Miami became hubs of conspiracy where politicians and adventurers of all stripes came to avail themselves of the former president's largesse. Miami once again became the center of opposition to the regime in Havana.[25]

It was thus to Miami that, in late 1955, a young exile came who could boast of having led the only major armed attack on Batista's dictatorship. The attack failed, and many of the participants were killed, but Fidel Castro survived and was amnestied two years later. Although Castro had been an active political opponent of former President Prío, all was forgotten now in the two men's common struggle against the Batista dictatorship. From Miami, therefore, Fidel was able to take back to his headquarters in Mexico a hefty financial contribution and the promise of more to come.[26] One year later, Fidel and his band of revolutionaries embarked on the fifty-eight-foot yacht *Granma*, bought with $15,000 of Prío's money, and landed in Oriente Province, Cuba, on December 2, 1956.[27]

From that day until the overthrow of Batista in 1959, the center of revolutionary action shifted to the Sierra Maestra Mountains, where the rebels had established their headquarters. Miami became a support base. Thenceforth a tacit struggle broke out between Castro supporters, whose mission was to send arms and supplies to the rebels, and the rest of the anti-Batista factions, who felt increasingly upstaged. Prío's plan had succeeded only too well in creating an armed challenge to the dictatorship, but in the process the deposed president had lost control of the situation.

An attempt to bring the revolution back into the hands of those who were paying for it was made in Miami in the early winter of 1957. At a meeting attended by representatives of Castro's Twenty-sixth of July Movement, Prío's Autentico party, and other exile factions, a Council of National Liberation was established, with Prío's former prime minister, Manuel Antonio de Varona, named head. The council immediately issued a manifesto designed to reassure both Washington and the Cuban elite about the revolution's procapitalist leanings. Prío, who helped organize the meeting and who financed most of the groups present, emerged as the clear winner.[28]

There was one hitch, however, and that was that Fidel Castro had never been consulted. He learned about the "Miami Pact" in the *New York Times* and immediately denounced it. His protest letter to the council exemplifies the language he would use to silence all opposition after his arrival in power: "For those who are fighting against an army incomparably greater in number and arms, with no support for a whole year apart from the dignity with which we are fighting . . . bitterly forgotten by fellow countrymen who, in spite of being well provided for, have systematically . . . denied us their help, the Miami Pact was an outrage."[29]

With the withdrawal of Castro's Twenty-sixth of July Movement and later of other forces, the council disintegrated. The exile community in Miami was thereafter torn in a double struggle: against Batista and between the increasingly dominant *fidelistas* and other revolutionary groups. Prío helped organize and finance several subsequent expeditions, aimed at balancing the increasing hegemony of the Sierra Maestra rebels.[30] But it was too late. Fidel Castro had captured both the imagination of Cubans and the fancy of the U.S. press, and when Batista finally fled on December 31, 1958, power fell right into the hands of the Sierra Maestra leader. Other revolutionary groups were compelled to fall into line or were eliminated.

In the wake of Fidel's triumph, many Miami Cubans returned to their homeland. Like the returning exiles of 1895, they harbored decidedly mixed feelings about the country left behind. True, the United States had given them refuge, and influential American voices had supported their cause, but the U.S. government had also waited until the last minute to reverse its active support of Batista. Like the Daytona Beach city council, State Department officials put North American economic concerns first and human rights and democracy in Cuba a definitive second. A famous remark by the Cuban desk officer at the State Department, William Wieland, was kept well in mind by the returning exiles: "I know Batista is considered by many as a son of a bitch . . . but American interests come first. . . . At least he is our son of a bitch, he is not playing ball with the Communists. . . . On the other hand, Fidel Castro is surrounded by commies."[31]

As for ex-president Prío, the early patron of Castro's rebel movement, he was courted at first by the new regime, which sent him on a series of diplomatic sorties abroad. Deprived of any real power and confronted with a radicalizing revolution, though, he sought asylum during one such trip to Brazil. A few days later, he was back in Miami. Years later, his fortune and influence gone, he committed suicide at his home in Coral Gables. Like Gerardo Machado, he is buried in the Woodlawn Cemetery, in the middle of Little Havana.

Off-Season Tourists

Another facet of the relationship between Cuba and Florida became apparent during the Prío/Batista decade (1948–58). Miami in the 1950s was not just a place where political manifestos were issued and revolutionary pacts signed; for the growing Cuban middle class, it was also a popular vacation spot. The island sold sugar, nickel, and tobacco and imported almost everything else, mostly from the United States. It made sense, then, to go shopping for the latest fashions and consumer goods on the mainland and, in the process, partake of the glitter of Miami Beach's "Gold Coast" along Lincoln Road and Collins Avenue. Pan American Airlines was born when it began service to Cuba, and the Miami-based hydroplanes that took thrill-seeking tourists to Havana also brought back loads of Cuban shoppers. Cubana Airlines, originally a Pan Am subsidiary, added several daily flights, turning the Miami run into a routine event.

For many middle-class Cubans, a South Florida vacation was a yearly ritual; for the wealthy, it could be a daily excursion. Businessmen and well-heeled government officials could fly to Miami in the morning, shop on Lincoln Road and have lunch at the Fontainebleau Hotel, and be back in Havana by evening. For those with access to government or private planes, it was a popular trip indeed.[32] Miami hoteliers, who had ignored the revolutionaries except perhaps as a source of casual labor, welcomed the Cuban tourists, for now they could keep their establishments open year-round. Northerners came fleeing the cold and snow in winter, a time when no self-respecting Cuban, or South Floridian for that matter, would dream of going near the water. Cubans, however, came in the summer, the "off-season"; after all, it was not weather that attracted them to Miami. They simply enjoyed partaking of American culture in a familiar environment. The temperature, the fauna and flora, even the architecture were common; the thrill consisted mainly in seeing them labeled in a different language and arranged somewhat differently in the flat Florida landscape.

By the mid-1950s, the Miami tourist industry and the semipermanent colony of Cuban visitors had settled into a comfortable relationship. Expelled politicians came to Miami to live in leisure, if they had the economic means, or to work for low hotel wages if they did not. Tourist accommodations were discounted in the summer months, and the Cuban middle class took advantage of the cheap rates for its pilgrimages north. None of these tourists imagined that they would walk the same streets as penniless refugees only a few months later.

Cuban political militants remained nearly invisible in Miami at least until the early 1960s; at that point, though, the erstwhile summer vacationers began to join their ranks in increasingly large numbers. When the Cuban middle class did start to exit the island, it went to a social environment made utterly familiar by years of prior travel. No culture shock here. Unlike later refugees from other communist regimes—Vietnamese, Cambodians, Ethiopians—Cuba's exiles did not really move to a foreign land.[33] Southern Florida was known territory. This perceptual frame allowed early escapees from the revolution—members of the old elite who came to await the "inevitable" downfall of Castro—to define their sojourn to South Florida simply as an extended vacation.

The Exodus

In July 1960, a young student leader recently escaped from Cuba was collected at his Miami hotel and taken to a secret meeting of the Cuban Movement for Revolutionary Recuperation (MRR). The purpose of the meeting was to expel three of the four founders of the movement so as to put it under the sole control of the fourth, a CIA-backed former lieutenant in Castro's rebel army, Manuel Artime. Those at the meeting were made to sign a formal document of "expulsion"; subsequently the young exile was escorted to a house where he would reside with other members of the movement until his departure for the clandestine training camps set up by the CIA. The hotel where the youth was living was in Miami Beach, the house where the secret meeting took place was in Coral Gables, and the would-be freedom fighters' dormitory was in South Miami.[34]

Even at this early date in the exodus, there were Cubans all over the city. Meetings like this one in Coral Gables proliferated as self-proclaimed leaders of post-Castro Cuba jockeyed for power; at the airports, traffic was heavy as planeloads of new refugees arrived from the island and secret CIA flights departed for training camps in Central America. All the while, Miami's white establishment ignored all the activity, confident that, as in times past, it would eventually go away.

On January 1, 1959, the forces that had been building for so long on either side of the Straits of Florida had begun to converge. This first day of the year marked the beginning of the revolutionary regime in Cuba, as well as the birth of a new social order in Miami. As so often happens in history, the old order looked on the event that marked its demise with indifference. The struggle in Cuba did not even make the front page of the *Miami Herald* on that fateful New Year's Day. Instead the newspaper informed its readers about the King Orange parade and the end of the Eastern Airlines strike. While Cuban exiles in Miami took to the streets to celebrate, native Miamians paid scant attention to the news that General Fulgencio Batista had fled the island.[35]

The first wave of the post-Castro exodus consisted of officials from the deposed Batista regime. The familiar changing of the guard took place, with exultant *fidelistas* leaving, to be replaced by defeated *batistianos*. Scuffles broke out in the Miami airport between passengers arriving from and departing for Havana, causing local police reinforcements to be sent in. Otherwise, things were normal. As expected, the new exiles created their own organizations and newspapers and set about the improbable task of wrestling power away from the revolutionaries they had been unable to defeat while they still controlled the government in Havana.

This first batch of exiles was numerically insignificant, and given the mass return to the island following Batista's downfall, the Cuban population of Miami probably diminished for a while. Had the revolutionary regime carried out the promised return to elected government, the situation might have stabilized at that point. Instead, Castro opted to "deepen" the revolution, moving it steadily leftward. In reaction, a slow but growing trickle of business people and former landowners, who had at first tried to negotiate with the new authorities only to see their properties and land confiscated, began to leave the island as well. In Miami, the Batista followers awaited them with an "I told you so" smirk. The first two years of the Cuban Revolution thus saw the gradual return to Miami—in the guise of political exiles—of the very groups who had known the city as a playground: first, the privileged for whom Miami was a day trip, and then those who could afford to come every summer. Approximately 135,000 Cubans arrived during this early period— between January 1959 and April 1961.[36]

Implausible as it may seem, regular Havana-Miami flights continued after the Bay of Pigs invasion of 1961, ferrying a growing number of escapees. The newcomers came increasingly from the lower middle class and were much less likely than their predecessors to hold the illusion of exile as an "extended vacation." Commercial flights to Miami ceased during the Missile Crisis of November 1962. From that time on, escape from Cuba became possible only by securing a visa to a third country, a difficult process at best, or by crossing the Florida Strait on a clandestine boat or raft. By 1965, annual Cuban refugee migration to the United States had dwindled to only 16,447; the cumulative total since the revolution stood at 210,000.[37]

The superpower confrontation over the Russian missiles in Cuba in 1962 was resolved at the eleventh hour when the Soviet Union agreed to remove its weapons; in turn, the Kennedy administration agreed that there would be no new armed actions against Castro's government—including any initiated by Cubans in Miami. With the Soviet Union backing Fidel and Washington preventing raids on the island, the Miami Cuban community was effectively reduced to impotence. This state of affairs was not lost on the city's civic leaders, who did not relish the prospect of a permanent population of two hundred thousand impoverished refugees. By 1965, the presence of the Cubans was no longer a matter of public indifference in Miami. Elected South Florida officials now petitioned Washington for federal help in solving the "refugee crisis."

In response, the U.S. government organized a large-scale initiative to resettle anti-Castro exiles away from Miami. The new Cuban Refugee Program, created by the Kennedy administration to aid the exiles during their "temporary" stay, focused almost immediately on resettling them across the country. Cuban professionals were retrained as high school teachers and dispatched to remote northern locations; government aid to individuals and families, in fact, was made contingent on acceptance of resettlement. By 1967, the program's head, John Thomas, could proudly proclaim that the resettlement of Cuban refugees in the United States had been a complete success.[38] With immigration from the island reduced to a trickle and a vigorous resettlement program in place, Miami officials breathed freely again. Miami would continue to be what it had always been—a purveyor of sun and sand to northern tourists, its politics dominated by the perennial struggle between Metro and the municipalities.

Alas, it was not to be. In September 1965, the Cuban government opened the fishing port of Camarioca to all exiles wanting to take their relatives from the island. In a rehearsal of Mariel fifteen years later, five thousand Cubans were ferried across to Miami. response to this incident, the Johnson administration si "Memorandum of Understanding" with Havana allow daily flights of refugees from Varadero Beach to Miami. Between December 1965 and April 1973, when they were unilaterally terminated by Castro, these "freedom flights" brought approximately 340,000 new refugees.[39]

It is unclear why Washington agreed to such a massive airlift—perhaps to avoid another Camarioca, but then again, the daily spectacle of these refugees had political value: what better indictment of Caribbean-style communism? Cuba's escapees may also have been regarded as an asset because of their educational and occupational credentials, particularly during this period of sustained economic growth in the United States. In reality, however, the refugees' educational qualifications were continuously falling as the elite exodus gave way to a more representative cross-section of the Cuban population. Before 1970, the proportion of professionals among the exiles hovered around 15 percent; but in a representative sample of 1973 arrivals, professionals represented only 4.8 percent. Even so, average educational attainment of the new refugees was still above the average of the population on the island. The exiles were also disproportionately urban in origin, and the proportion of blacks and mulattoes remained much lower than in Cuba.[40]

All the time that the freedom flights were coming into Miami, resettlement flights were leaving it in an attempt to distribute more evenly the burden of refugee resettlement. By 1978, 469,435 Cubans had been settled away from Miami. To federal and local bureaucrats, this was ample evidence that the "problem" of refugee concentration in South Florida had been resolved.[41] In the late 1960s, however, a discreet countertrend started that saw resettled Cuban families trek back to Miami on their own. In 1973, a survey estimated that 27 percent of the Cubans residing in the Miami metropolitan area had returned there from other U.S. locations. A survey conducted by the *Miami Herald* in 1978 raised that valuation to about 40 percent.[42] As a consequence of this accelerating return migration, by 1979, on the eve of Mariel, close to 80 percent of Cubans in the United States were living in Miami, making it, in effect, Cuba's second-largest city and the refugees the most concentrated foreign-born minority in the country.[43]

Evidence that returning Cuban exile families regarded life in the north much as immigrants often view their stays abroad, namely as an opportunity to accumulate savings with which to start a business at home.[44] Once they had accumulated a substantial sum, they headed back to Florida. But not to just any place. Jacksonville and Tallahassee were as alien to the refugees as the frigid cities they had left behind. Miami, on the other hand, was warm and familiar. It was relatively easy to learn the ropes of business there; Cubans knew the city, and most had kin there who had remained despite the entreaties of the Cuban Refugee Center. The ties built over half a century now worked to promote a mass return migration to this single city. As a substitute for lost Havana, only Miami would do.

By the time the chartered boats began to cross the Straits of Florida for Mariel, a large and diversified exile community had emerged in South Florida, acting as a magnet for all Cubans elsewhere. An estimated 80 percent of the 125,000-odd Mariel entrants settled there,[45] at once expanding the community in size and prompting its transformation from a political exile group into a self-conscious ethnic minority.

Uneasy Neighbors

The flight from Varadero Beach had already arrived. Most passengers had been greeted with the usual tears and embraces and whisked away to the homes of their kin. Sitting alone in the reception area was a middle-aged man reflectively puffing on his cigar. The interviewer approached him and a conversation in Spanish began:

"Why are you still here?"

"I'm awaiting a flight to New Jersey."

"Do you have relatives there?"

"Yes, a few."

"And they will surely help you."

"I don't expect so."

"Do you speak English?"

"Not a word."

"But look, New Jersey is not Miami. If you're going there without knowing English and with no one to help you, how do you expect to survive?"

A condescending smile. "That's what 'they' always told me. The *fidelistas* where I worked were always saying that I could never get as good a job, could probably get no job at all here. And I replied: *Chico*, in North America, how do the deaf-mutes survive? Because that's what I'm going to be there—deaf and mute. And if they can survive, so will I."[46]

It was March 1973. Even at this late date, with the freedom flights about to end and a large exile community resident in Miami, new arrivals were still willing to try their luck in northern cities. It was difficult, however, to remain deaf and mute and at a cultural disadvantage when a better option existed. Six years after the above exchange took place, our confident respondent came back to Miami. Many others had preceded him.

After the 1962 Missile Crisis, the Cuban exile community resigned itself to a long period of waiting before a return to Cuba would be possible. By the end of the decade, many had become convinced that their "temporary" move had turned permanent. For those arriving aboard the freedom flights, coming from progressively lower strata of Cuban society, there was no doubting that fact. They had left to escape communism, not to engineer its demise. As they joined older Cubans in South Florida, they were confronted with a novel problem: how to coexist with their Anglo neighbors.

Just as it had influenced the selection of Miami as the choice place of exile settlement, the history of Cuba-U.S. relations also affected the refugees' approach to community. Resistance to Yankee hegemony, so prevalent among the revolutionary leaders in Havana, was not entirely absent in Miami. As a group, the refugees regarded the nation that had received them with a mix of gratitude and suspicion. Had not North Americans, after all, always put their own interests first? Had they not, after helping to liberate Cuba from Spain, then imposed the Platt Amendment? Had they not supported various dictators, even while they hosted successive groups of exiles working to overthrow those same dictators? Had they not, ten years earlier, armed the expeditionary force against Castro and then abandoned the men in the Bay of Pigs? Finally, had not Washington traded away the exiles' ability to confront Castro directly in exchange for its own security? All in all, a very spotty record.

Hence, when Miami native whites abandoned their traditional

indifference toward the refugees to speak in increasingly urgent terms about the need for assimilation, the Cubans balked. The Anglo elite discourse, which urged the newcomers to give up their culture, learn English, and take their turn in the ethnic queue, inspired little enthusiasm. Instead, despite its own myriad social and political cleavages, the exile community set about pursuing an alternative project. Tacitly, almost unconsciously, it attempted to recreate as far as possible the country left behind. This was to be no mere immigrant neighborhood, but a "moral community" standing for the values of old Cuban society and against the new order imposed by Castroism.[47] Throughout the seventies, this tacit project continued at a rapid pace. The rhetoric was that of return, but the reality was one of consolidation. The loud protests of the native elites went unheeded as, gradually, Miami, took on the hues of a "second Havana"[48]—giving to the Andalusian playgrounds and the Spanish-named boulevards a new meaning.

1. The Miami skyline, 1992. Photo by Sue Chaffee.

2. Sign at S.W. 8th Street and 27th Avenue, Miami. Photo by Sue Chaffee.

3. Chapel of Our Lady of Charity, patron saint of Cuba, built on Biscayne Bay. It faces south toward Cuba. Photo by Sue Chaffee.

4. Bay of Pigs Memorial, Woodlawn Cemetery, Miami. The inscription under the map of Cuba reads: "In memoriam, may God grant eternal rest to those who, for their love of God, Cuba, and family, preceded us in sacrifice and deny it to us until we win victory for Cuba." Photo by Peggy Nolan.

5. Cuban and U.S. flags in Woodlawn Cemetery. Two Cuban and one Nicaraguan president are buried there. Photo by Peggy Nolan.

6. Domino players in Little Havana. Photo by Sue Chaffee.

7. Funeral home in Miami. The city did not exist in 1857; the sign refers to the home's founding in Havana. Photo by Peggy Nolan.

8. Street scene, Little Havana. Photo by Sue Chaffee.

9. Billboard paid for by the Cuban-American National Foundation as part of its controversy with the local newspaper in early 1992. The sign reads, "I do not believe in the *Herald*." Photo by Sue Chaffee.

10. Downtown Little Haiti, Miami. Photo by Sue Chaffee.

11. Haitian street vendors, Little Haiti. Photo by Sue Chaffee.

12. Street scene, Little Haiti. Photo by Sue Chaffee.

13. Haitian boat and captain in the Miami River. The boat's name, in Creole, means "God Is Not Like Us." Photo by Sue Chaffee.

14. Haitian dock worker, Miami River. Photo by Sue Chaffee.

15. Haitian women at work in agriculture, southwest of Miami. Photo by Peggy Nolan.

16. Haitian bean picker, southwest Dade County. Photo by Peggy Nolan.

17. Haitian women shopping in a Cuban-owned market. Photo by Sue Chaffee.

18. Religious college in Miami Beach. Photo by Sue Chaffee.

19. Students at Talmudic University, Miami Beach. Photo by Sue Chaffee.

20. Hasidic Jews under the palm trees, Miami Beach. Photo by Peggy Nolan.

21. Monument to Carl Fisher, founder of Miami Beach. Its small size may be due to his anti-Semitic views in what became a predominantly Jewish city. Photo by Sue Chaffee.

22. Mural in northwest Miami. It marks the dividing line
between Little Haiti and Liberty City. Photo by Sue Chaffee.

23. Cubans protesting Nelson Mandela's visit to Miami, 1990.
Photo by Dezso Szusi, *Miami Herald*. Reproduced by
permission.

24. Anti-Mandela protester, 1990. Photo by Jon Kral, *Miami
Herald*. Reproduced by permission.

25. Cuban protester arguing with Mandela supporter, 1990. Photo by Dezso Szusi, *Miami Herald*. Reproduced by permission.

26. Tent city providing temporary shelter for people made homeless by Hurricane Andrew. Photo by Sue Chaffee.

27. Store destroyed by Hurricane Andrew. Photo by Sue Chaffee.

28. Home destroyed by Hurricane Andrew. Photo by Sue Chaffee.

Chapter Six

How the Enclave Was Built

The Recarey Case

The man in the sober dark suit appeared quite confident. "Let them complain," he said. "Our profits are legitimate and they come from bulk buying of generic drugs and from preventive medicine." The man had reason to be self-assured. In less than five years he had parlayed a tiny hospital in Miami into a chain of health mainte-nance organization (HMO) clinics grossing $30 million a month. The chain, International Medical Centers (IMC), had risen from nowhere to become the second largest Hispanic business in the country, right after Bacardi. The owner, Miguel Recarey, was catapulted into prominence as a leader of the Latin business com-munity and as the ultimate example of the self-made man. He adopted a life-style in accord with his success: a $1.2 million ocean-front house in Coral Gables Estates, a Maserati at the door, trips to a private island in the Bahamas aboard his forty-seven-foot yacht. Billboards in Little Havana proclaimed IMC as the largest Cuban firm in the nation and encouraged elderly Cubans to enroll.[1]

The splendid success of IMC was the product, however, not of competitive services and customer satisfaction, but of behind-the-scenes lobbying. The $30 million did not come from individual payments, but from the federal government, mailed to Recarey every month in a single check. Through political contacts in Miami, ranging from Congressman Claude Pepper to the then vice presi-dent's son Jeb Bush, Recarey had secured for IMC an exclusive contract for a pilot program under the sponsorship of the Department of Health and Human Services (HHS). The program was designed to reduce Medicare costs by paying HMOs 95 percent of average Medicare payments for elderly patients, regardless of the patient's health. If the HMO could maintain the patient's health for less than this figure, it would pocket the difference; if not, it would absorb the loss.

Recarey started by enrolling en masse the elderly Cubans of Miami, but soon moved beyond this core group to eye the large populations of American retirees in Broward County, Palm Beach, and Tampa Bay. There was a catch, however. To insure quality health care, HHS had stipulated that at least half of IMC's patients be from outside of the pilot program, the theory being that market competition would make the organization more efficient and guarantee its ability to deliver the best possible services. For the first three years of the program Recarey had been exempted from this requirement, but as 1984 rolled around he began to worry. The problem was that the IMC's rolls were heavily tilted toward program participants and it was difficult to attract outside patients. But instead of going after new clients, Recarey went after the politicians. A loyal aide to Pepper promised the congressman's support. On the Republican side, Recarey hired two former Reagan aides—Lyn Nofziger and John Sears—as lobbyists for astronomical fees (reportedly $400,000 and $300,000, respectively).

The effort paid off. Jeb Bush telephoned key HHS officials with assurances that Recarey was "solid" and would not prove an embarrassment. HHS secretary Margaret Heckler found these representations "persuasive." A letter denying the continuation of the exemption to IMC was replaced by one extending it for another three years. Recarey was in the money. Within a year, two hundred thousand new patients were enrolled in his clinics, almost 80 percent of them elderly Medicare patients. HHS officials who had played a role in extending the exemption quit the department to come work for IMC at much higher salaries. Juan del Real, the government's attorney during the negotiations, traded his $70,000-a-year government job for a $325,000 annual salary at IMC. C. McClain Haddow, the HHS official who actually signed the exemption, was paid $38,000 in 1986 as a "consultant" to IMC.

Soon, however, complaints and lawsuits started pouring in. While Recarey paid himself, his family, and his business associates fabulous salaries, he was squeezing the actual health providers. The aim was nothing less than to reduce costs per patient well below the 95 percent of average costs budgeted by the government. Early attempts to investigate Recarey led nowhere. A 1984–85 investigation by the State of Florida's Insurance Commission concluded that IMC was financially healthy and found no evidence of wrongdoing. A federal district attorney in Miami who opened an inquiry was advised to abandon it: Recarey was just too powerful.

But the avalanche of complaints and lawsuits continued. The scandal of elderly care in IMC clinics was just too big to cover up. In April 1987, Recarey and three associates were indicted by the federal government for bribery, and the IMC contract was revoked. In October Recarey, after quietly securing passports for his young children, left the country. He is still a fugitive. The remnants of IMC were acquired by the Humana Corporation of Kentucky, and with the merger, the "largest Cuban firm" in the United States ceased to exist.

Although not representative of the bulk of exile firms in Miami, the Recarey story illustrates well several aspects of the Cuban enclave. First, IMC was not the typical small ethnic business portrayed in the sociological or economic literature. This was no corner grocery store or loft garment shop, but a multimillion-dollar business with connections at the highest levels of government. Although IMC was the largest and fastest-growing exile enterprise, other Cuban firms reached, with less alacrity but better practices, a comparable size. Second, Recarey was the prototypical ambitious immigrant entrepreneur who goes too far too fast, paying little attention to the rules. He carried brashness to an extreme; nevertheless, the same orientation is found among other first-generation businessmen and politicians who believe that to succeed, one must not be too bound by legal niceties and formal procedures. As these people's deeds are regularly uncovered and they are hauled before the courts, they provide effective ammunition for those in the Anglo establishment who charge that these Latin newcomers cannot be trusted with the management of American institutions. Not surprisingly, Recarey's story was extensively reported on the front page of the *Miami Herald*.[2]

Third, the scandal rocked but in no way compromised the economic strength or the rapid growth of the Cuban business enclave. Other unscrupulous entrepreneurs like Recarey just shrugged their shoulders: he was caught, perhaps they would escape. The majority of Cuban firms and businessmen, those who played by the rules, lamented the incident as another episode giving the community a bad name. They made every effort to put the incident behind them, although the *Herald* would not easily let them forget. In the end, however, the number of entrepreneurial ventures and the sheer density of business networks were such that the Recareys could come and go without making a dent in the local economy. By the time IMC entered the scene, the Cuban business enclave had left the confines of Little Havana behind; it now encompassed the entire Miami metropolitan area. How this phenomenon developed as if out of the blue, lifting penniless refugees to national prominence, is the story of this chapter. This progression set the stage for the process of reactive formation that was to follow Mariel and the 1980 antibilingual referendum.

The Beginnings

Back in 1962, there were few if any Cuban businesses in Miami. The scattered restaurants were mostly from the previous, anti-Batista exile. By force of habit, they had made of nostalgia a specialty. Everyone expected to be back in Havana soon. Despite the Bay of Pigs fiasco the preceding year, the CIA continued to be very active in Miami. Its local station, located at the University of Miami and known as JM-Wave, was the agency's second largest next to headquarters in Langley, Virginia. Exiles who had been unable to bring enough funds to be self-supporting in Florida militated in anti-Castro organizations supported by the CIA. The agency, indeed, had become one of Miami's largest employers. The offices of the Cuban Revolutionary Council, the exile umbrella organization in Biscayne Boulevard, were known as "the Ministry" because of the many applicants both for current positions and for future ones in Cuba.[3]

The U.S.-Soviet deal that resolved the Cuban Missile Crisis in 1962 put an end to the militant period of exile politics, but the CIA did not abandon South Florida immediately. Only gradually did it dawn on the Cuban activists that the agency's goal had changed:

from overthrowing Castro to easing the exiles out of Miami. "Don't forget that we have a disposal problem," Allen Dulles was said to have told Kennedy on the eve of the Bay of Pigs by way of warning about the consequences of aborting the invasion.[4] The problem became urgent after the Missile Crisis concluded. To solve the "disposal problem," word was passed down from JM-Wave that the next step in the anti-Castro struggle consisted in joining the U.S. Army, which, in due course, would invade Cuba. Scores of young exiles enrolled and were promptly taken away from Miami. On the civilian side, the new federal Cuban Refugee Center strengthened the dispersal effort by making resettlement away from South Florida a common requisite for assistance.

The development of an ethnic economy of any substantial scale has three prerequisites: first, a stable market that small firms can control by offering to the immigrant community culturally defined goods and services not available on the outside; second, privileged access to a pool of cheap labor through networks within the community; and third, access to capital. The availability of a protected market and of cheap labor gives incipient ethnic enterprises an "edge" over firms in the mainstream economy. Access to capital, however, is the biggest stumbling block, since native bankers seldom lend to unknown newcomers.[5] In Miami in the early 1960s, prospects for the rise of a Cuban ethnic economy looked dim as the protected market and labor pool were constantly eroded by the resettlement flights out of the city and as major local banks proved unwilling to advance money for exile business start-ups.

Nonetheless, several countertrends were in evidence as well. Jewish garment manufacturers in New York soon discovered that the middle-class Cuban women of Miami made excellent workers. Desperate to maintain the living standard of their families during the "temporary" exile, these women would accept low wages and hard working conditions without protest. Thus, confronted with union trouble in New York, manufacturers moved their operations down to Miami and Hialeah in droves. The local garment industry thrived. A former president of the Florida Needletrade Association described the move this way:

You have to understand that Cuban workers were willing to do anything to survive. . . . At the same time, New York was experiencing a resurgence of union fervor. Manufacturers from New York who had homes in Miami Beach saw the advantages of opening new businesses and having the large number of fresh immigrants coming from Cuba. As a result the South Florida needletrade industry went from about seven thousand workers in 1964 to twenty-four thousand in 1973.[6]

A typical mid-sixties Cuban household in Miami featured a husband who had been a member of an anti-Castro organization and now strained to find employment and a wife who had never worked outside the home before but now sewed full time in a Hialeah factory. The large-scale employment of Cuban women in the needletrade had two important consequences. First, it allowed families to stay in Miami and bought time for husbands to learn English and find some local business niche. And second, it itself created some of these niches through independent subcontracting. Many Cubans, seeing what the Jewish jobbers were doing, decided to imitate them. The same Needletrade Association official reports: "In the beginning, all the factories were Jewish-owned, but by the mid-seventies there was a division of labor. The manufacturers were still Jewish, but most contractors were Cuban. Cuban garment 'factories' usually started in the owner's garage, with the wife, the mother, and other women in the family as the operators."[7]

Other market forces were also at play. The large number of former Cuban professionals and white-collar workers, who of course spoke fluent Spanish, began to attract the attention of companies operating in Latin America. Executives of North American companies that had had branches in Cuba pointed out to their employers the advantages of establishing their Latin headquarters in Miami. One enterprising employee of Coral Gables went so far as printing brochures highlighting the opportunities offered by the city, distributing them to all companies with Latin American operations. The result, in the words of a Cuban-American banker, was that "Coral Gables took on an unexpected dimension and soon consolidated into a world center of activity for the largest firms. . . . Cubans were then employed by these same multinational companies to travel and do business for them overseas."[8]

Capitalists throughout South America also became aware of the new labor market created in Miami by the Cuban Revolution.

Along with the drug trade that was to give rise to the "Miami Vice" image, many legitimate Venezuelan, Ecuadorean, and other Latin companies sought in the city a refuge from the economic vagaries and political instability of their own countries. South American flight capital plus Cuban management thus became a formula for the creation and growth of many banks and construction companies.[9] Their presence was to have a decisive impact on the subsequent development of the Cuban business enclave, as we will see below.

As the CIA abandoned Miami, its mission unfulfilled, it left behind a large number of former militants reluctant to resettle in the north and ready to avail themselves of the emerging business opportunities. Contrary to some scholarly accounts, there was apparently no direct connection between CIA involvement with the exile community and the rise of Cuban entrepreneurship.[10] Few of the agency's "front" operations prospered as legitimate enterprises, and there is little evidence that CIA salaries and secret accounts functioned as a major source of capital for exile firms. Instead, the main accomplishment of the agency's massive intervention in Miami was to support a substantial number of middle-class Cubans at a reasonable standard of living, allowing them time to monitor opportunities offered by the local economy and to find a suitable business niche. Painful as it was from a political point of view, the transition from militant exodus to entrepreneurial community was remarkably smooth. Few immigrant groups have commenced their economic adaptation to American life from a position of such relative advantage.

Three Stories

In 1966, Santiago Alvarez had had enough of the clandestine war and decided to settle down. He was twenty-five and, for the last few years, had worked as a boat captain for the CIA infiltrating men and arms into Cuba. Aside from an intimate knowledge of the Cuban coast, he had few skills. "I didn't have much of an education . . . I had to fight since a very young age," he said. In Miami, Santiago worked as a waiter, truck driver, and concrete salesman. Finally, in 1971, he opened his own construction firm, beginning with just himself, his pickup, and his connections. Such "back-of-the-truck" enterprises proliferated during the early seventies, but did not yet challenge the dominance of established Anglo-owned companies. Alvarez's operation, however, never ceased growing. By 1985 he was one of South Florida's most active real estate developers, having taken over from older companies the building of shopping centers and department complexes in Hialeah.[11]

After spending eleven days in jail for antigovernment activities, Remedios Diaz-Oliver and her husband, Fausto, left Cuba in 1961. A graduate of two Havana business schools, she went to work as a bookkeeper for Richford Industries, a container distributor. Fausto found work at Bertram Yacht, located nearby; that meant the couple could manage with a single old car. Within a year, Remedios had been moved to Richford's international division. Fausto took his two weeks' vacation, and the couple traveled to Central America with a bag of Richford's samples. They returned with $300,000 in orders from pharmaceutical companies in Honduras and Costa Rica. By 1965, Diaz-Oliver had been appointed Richford's vice president of domestic sales, in addition to her duties as president of the Latin American division.

These were the years in which former militant exiles were looking for permanent employment. From her Havana days, Remedios knew many people with the skills to make a business succeed. In 1966, she persuaded Richford to advance $30,000 in credit to one such person, with the promise that if he defaulted she would cover the debt with her own salary. The man paid, the account grew, and so did her commission. Following this experience and at her prodding, Richford agreed to advance credit to numerous exile clients. As these firms developed, the company's own business grew rapidly.

In 1976, however, Richford was sold to a division of Alco Standard Corp. of Omaha, Nebraska. The new employer required Remedios to sign a contract guaranteeing that she would not compete with Alco Standard if she left the company. Instead of signing, Diaz-Oliver decided to quit and form her own company. The construction trailer in which American International Container opened did not look like much, except that its owner had far more solid connections in the local market than the buttondown midwestern company did. By 1978, American International had taken over the inventory of Alco Standard after driving it out of Miami. Diaz-Oliver became exclusive Florida distributor for some of the biggest names in packaging, including Owens-Illinois and Standard Container. Her company had warehouses in Miami, Orlando, and Tampa and annual sales of over $60 million.

Remedios has been president of Dade County's American Cancer Society, the Hispanic division of the Red Cross, and the social committee of the Big Five—the private club created in Miami in nostalgic remembrance of the Havana Yacht Club and its four extinct peers in Cuba.[12]

All that Diego R. Suarez has done in his life is design and manufacture agricultural equipment, especially for the sugarcane industry. A graduate of the Vocational School of Havana and of the Civic-Military Institute of Ceiba del Agua, Suarez founded and operated a company called Vanguard National Equipment prior to the revolution. After Fidel Castro came to power, Suarez started moving his capital out of Cuba, and he himself left in 1961. With the monies smuggled out and a loan from a small Puerto Rican bank, he established in Miami the Inter-American Transport Equipment Company, a manufacturer and supplier of harvest, transport, and field machinery for the sugar industry. The company began by exporting light equipment to Puerto Rico, then expanded to all Latin American countries except Brazil. At present, over 90 percent of the equipment manufactured is exported to more than forty countries worldwide. In Suarez's estimate, the large majority of field equipment used today in Florida's sugar industry comes from his factories.

The company's headquarters and main factory are located in the vicinity of Hialeah, where it employs between three hundred and four hundred workers. Trade names include Vanguard and Thomson (tractors, transport equipment, and other machinery) and Claas (harvesters). By 1986, most of this equipment was designed and manufactured at these facilities, except the harvesters, which were made in West Germany. Inter-American's engineers are Cuban, Mexican, American, and British. Throughout the years, Suarez has maintained good relations with his workers and is satisfied with the strong bonds that exist with his close collaborators.

In 1980, Suarez initiated the Inter-American Sugar Cane Seminars, which bring engineers, technologists, and sugar mill owners from all over the world to Miami to discuss scientific and technical issues ranging from sugarcane diseases to computer automation of sugar mills. The seminars are financed by Inter-American Transport in cooperation with the city of Miami. Six U.S. universities, the universities of Puerto Rico and the West Indies, and the U.S. Department of Agriculture are the cosponsoring institutions. Suarez also presides over companies affiliated with Inter-American Transport and is one of the founders and directors of the Cuban-American National Foundation.[13]

Character Loans

Diego Suarez was fortunate to have brought money and contacts from Cuba. In general, the largest and best-capitalized firms of the emerging enclave were created by exiles experienced in business and having access to these resources. Many would-be entrepreneurs seeking a niche in Miami's economy during the early sixties were not so fortunate, however. Unlike Asian immigrant communities that make extensive use of the rotating credit association as an instrument for pooling savings, Cubans did not have this cultural practice.[14] In its absence, it seemed that business starts would have to rely on paltry family loans or small savings from wage labor.

There was another way. What Remedios Diaz-Oliver was doing at Richford—extending credit on the basis of personal reputation—became institutionalized as Cuban managers gradually took over the loan portfolios of local banks. To be sure, these were not the dominant Anglo-owned banks for whom the exiles were just another downtrodden minority, but small banks created with Latin American capital. South American owners had deemed it wise to put the management of their firms in the hands of experienced, but then unemployed, Cuban bankers. Once their own positions became secure, these officers initiated a program of lending $10,000 to $30,000 to other Cubans for business start-ups.

Access to this credit was not based on the applicant's balance sheet or collateral, but on his or her business reputation in Cuba. This unique practice became known as "character" lending and allowed numerous exiles who spoke little English and had no standing in the American banking world to get a foothold in the local economy. A leading Cuban-American banker who took part in this operation described it as follows:

At the start, most Cuban enterprises were gas stations; then came grocery shops and restaurants. No American bank would lend to them. By the mid-sixties, we started a policy at our bank of making small loans to Cubans who wanted to start their own businesses but did not have any capital. These loans of ten or fifteen thousand dollars were made because the person was known to us by his reputation and integrity. All of them paid back; there were zero losses. With some exceptions, they have continued being clients of the bank. People who used to borrow fifteen thousand dollars on a one-time basis now take out fifty thousand in a week. In 1973, the policy was discontinued. The reason was that the new exiles coming at that time were unknown to us.[15]

An early client, now a large factory owner, describes his impressions of differing banking styles:

The American banker looks only at the statement, the balance sheet of the company. If he doesn't like it, he doesn't give you the loan. The Cuban banker has a different technique: he looks for signs of your character. If he knows you, knows that you meet your obligations, he lends you without looking at the balance sheet. He knows you are not going to fail him. American banks have the habit of changing credit managers very often. They hire fresh college graduates who come here to Miami, know no one, and have to begin analyzing statements. There the Cuban banks have the advantage. Their loan officers know their clientele, they often even knew their families in Cuba—twenty, thirty years. It's a small technical detail, but important.[16]

Meanwhile, in the construction industry, Cubans with experience and who sought jobs as carpenters, plumbers, and bricklayers were being blackballed by local unions dominated by native whites. Undeterred, the Cubans created their own home repair businesses by buying a truck and going door-to-door seeking work. Eventually, some of them gained access to character loans, Small Business Administration loans, or pooled family savings to establish more substantial firms. By 1979, about 50 percent of major construction companies in Dade were Cuban-owned, and they accounted for over 90 percent of residential and commercial construction in the southwest zone of the county.

Developers like Santiago Alvarez gradually displaced older unionized companies. By 1985, six of the ten largest home builders in Dade were Cuban-owned, including West Miller Heights (P. Adrian), Atrium Homes (A. Sotolongo), H. G. Enterprises (H. Garcia), and Interam Builders (E. Pereira). These companies are uniformly nonunion. As they gradually expanded, unionized new construction in Miami plummeted from over 90 percent in 1960 to less than 10 percent in 1980. A Carpenter's Union organizer gloomily summarized the situation in 1984: "We paid dearly for not letting the Cubans in. They came to see us as the enemy, and workers in their companies would not touch us. Now even Anglo firms are 'double-breasting': they keep their unionized divisions as a façade, but all the work goes to new nonunion divisions."[17]

Grouped in the Latin Builders Association, the Cuban companies came to exert growing influence not only in the construction industry, but in local politics as well. Predictably, one of the goals of the association is to insure that the influence of the construction trades in Dade remains at a minimum.

There were other means of capitalizing new firms, both orthodox and unconventional. Established Cuban Jewish companies in Havana simply moved to Miami and continued their long-standing relationship with suppliers and creditors. This is the case of the Suave Shoe Company, a footwear manufacturer and one of the largest firms of the Miami enclave. Suave and similar manufacturers were able to secure credit from "factors"—bankers who specialize in advancing capital on the basis of work orders, bypassing the usual 90-to-120-days repayment period. Factor banking is not available to just any business newcomer, however; it is based on established networks and a solid commercial reputation. Thanks to this decided advantage, Suave became so successful that it went public and qualified to be listed on the New York Stock Exchange.[18]

Very small businesses without access to business networks or character loans had to fall back on family savings. A surprisingly common way of capitalizing such firms was to collect the cash value of insurance policies bought from an American company in Cuba by the entrepreneur or his or her parents. Many small businesses, from gas stations to book stores, were established in Little Havana by cashing in these old and nearly forgotten policies.[19]

But it was capital advanced by Cuban officials at the small South American–owned banks that played the decisive role during the sixties, fueling the development of a thick midlevel layer of enterprises between transplanted large firms and the small family businesses. By 1977, the Census of Minority-Owned Enterprises counted 30,366 Cuban-owned firms in the United States, most of them in Miami. The area was home to half of the forty largest Hispanic firms in the nation and to the largest bank. There was one firm for every twenty-seven Cuban-born persons.[20]

Networks and Social Capital

Clearly, social networks were essential in effecting the rapid transformation of political militants into ethnic entrepreneurs. Yet it is important to delve deeper into the social context in which these events took place. Language and a common culture provided Cubans with a basis for solidarity but by themselves were not enough to create a level of mutual support stronger than that typical of many other immigrant communities. Rather, the common circumstance of exile and the common experience of successive political defeats had cemented a strong sense of "we-ness" among these refugees. Expelled and despised by the government of their country, abandoned at the Bay of Pigs by a supposedly friendly government, traded off during the Missile Crisis, ridiculed by Latin American intellectuals who confined them to the dustbin of history, the exiles had little to fall back on but themselves. Bounded solidarity was the outcome, a mechanism that led the Cubans—despite diverse class origins and views—to patronize other Cuban-owned businesses and to prefer co-nationals as business associates.

Sharing a common political fate, and an unenviable one at that, had the unexpected consequence of promoting economic progress by cementing ties built originally on a common culture. The "discrimination" that Cubans suffered was not the usual type involving labor market opportunities or social acceptance. Instead, it concerned the failure of their overall political project and their inability to persuade others of its merit. Latin as well as North American intellectuals derided Cuban exiles as just a bunch of political losers stranded between two nations. This isolation defined the community and strengthened its internal solidarity in a way that even language or a well-defined national culture could not.

The physical boundaries of the Miami enclave are not clearly demarcated because Cuban businesses may be found throughout the metropolitan area. The social boundaries are, however, extremely clear; they define the operation and the limits of bounded solidarity, as well as of a second mechanism that contributed decisively to business development. Underlying the ease with which Cuban bank officials made character loans was the certainty that their clients would pay. Anyone defaulting or otherwise violating the implicit trust built into such deals could kiss good-bye his or her chances for business success; the entire Cuban community would know, and there was precious little opportunity outside of it. Hence, bankers were not simply being loyal to their friends, but displaying good business acumen. More than by a written promise, their loans were backed by a kind of enforceable trust inherent in the social networks of the enclave. The "zero losses" reported by our Cuban bank sources were entirely predictable.[21]

Norms of solidarity within an ethnic community raise the reverse problem of social support expectations that are incompatible with the logic of capital accumulation. In his study of commercial enterprises in Bali, Clifford Geertz observed how successful entrepreneurs were assaulted by job- and loan-seeking kinsmen. The petitioners' claims were buttressed by strong norms enjoining mutual assistance within the extended family and among all community members. The result was to turn promising businesses into relief organizations languishing at the margins of solvency.[22]

Family and ethnic obligations surely existed among Miami Cubans, but they did not go so far as to compromise the viability of most business ventures. On the contrary, such ties worked in the entrepreneurs' favor, as sources of low-cost family labor and start-up capital. There are several reasons for this situation. First is the fact that prerevolutionary Cuban society never enjoined the wealthy to support their less fortunate compatriots. Bounded solidarity emerged in exile out of the contingent circumstances described above, but it had clear limits in terms of mutual assistance.

Second, the precarious beginnings of many Cuban enterprises and the obvious fact that, to survive, they needed to maximize efficiency restricted their role as sources of employment. Early exile entrepreneurs, engaged in what amounted to economic guerrilla warfare against much larger firms, were in no position to honor other Cubans' welfare claims. Only kin and workers willing to work long hours for minimal remuneration could be employed by these fledgling businesses.

Third, larger enclave enterprises frequently shifted to more modern management practices that precluded particularistic obligations. As the ethnic economy grew and firms became better capitalized, they adopted more conventional forms of labor management. To be sure, Cubans were still preferred as workers and supervisors, and Cuban-owned companies did much of their business with each other, but the transactions acquired a more universalistic character that precluded exclusively ethnic criteria for hiring and contracting decisions.[23]

Most enclave firms could thus prosper without being turned into welfare hotels. The social mechanisms of bounded solidarity and enforceable trust produced entrepreneurial success that was celebrated by the entire community and presented as a model to follow. In political defeat, success in business gradually emerged as a source of collective self-esteem and as proof of the correctness of the refugees' ideological stance: while Cuba went down economically and regimes friendly to Castro also foundered, the Miami enclave flourished on the energies of exile entrepreneurs and the social capital created by their solidarity.

The Moral Community

"Miami: The World in Black and White," read the title of an editorial by a famous Cuban poet after spending a few months in the city. He summarized his impressions in a few poignant words: "You have to live in Miami, sleep in it each day, to really know how it is and how it has forged [the] profile [it has]. It isn't easy without a long historical recounting to understand the roots of so much incomprehension."[24]

His last word referred to the peculiar political intolerance that accompanied the rapid economic growth of the Cuban enclave. In Miami, an appearance by Jane Fonda had led to a boycott and a series of threatening calls to Burdines, the sponsor of her visit and the region's largest department store. Latin American artists who had visited Cuba at some point or another were barred from performing at the annual Calle Ocho Carnival. And the Miami City Commission permitted the Haitian community to celebrate the investiture of Haitian president Father Jean-Bertrand Aristide only provided Fidel Castro was not invited to the home-country ceremony in Port-au-Prince.

As the Cuban community gained political power it imposed a monolithic outlook on the city, often with little regard for the concerns and interests of other segments of the population.[25] A play by a New York–based Cuban writer suspected of being sympathetic to the regime in the island had to be removed from the program of the Miami Theater Festival after the organizers received numerous local threats. A Cuban businessman defended the protesters' point of view:

When so many persons have been affected by communism, when so many had to abandon the land in which they were born, when people could not visit the cemeteries where their loved ones rest, we do have to protest this kind of thing. Why not? Why do they have to impose on us such a painful thing? A person who has not suffered, who has not had relatives killed, can say coolly that there must be freedom of expression. We know better. It is too hard that they come here, to our center, to tell us these things.[26]

The play in question did not have much to do with conditions in Cuba, nor did it defend the regime. The exiles' objections were exclusively to the assumed political sympathies of the author. The expression "our center" in the above testimony encapsulated the belief that Miami was, above all, the capital of the Other Cuba. But other segments of the city resented the exiles' political intolerance. The *Miami Herald*, in particular, waged a relentless campaign against what it saw as the rising power of the Cubans and the threat that they posed to civic freedoms. Even before the Mariel confrontation, the paper castigated on numerous occasions the exile community's extremism.

During the 1970s, such attacks could be made with impunity, but after the exile community became organized for domestic political action in the aftermath of Mariel the story changed. This is what the Cuban-American National Foundation had to say about the *Herald*'s campaign in a full-page paid advertisement, published in the *Herald* in 1987:

All our achievements have been accomplished with a national press coverage that has often portrayed us as extremists. This has been the most unfair and prejudiced perception we have experienced in America. . . .

The Miami Herald bears tremendous responsibility for this injustice. . . . *The Miami Herald* is aggressive in its ignorance of our people. It refuses to understand that Cuban Americans see the struggle between totalitarianism and democracy as a personal, ever-present struggle. We live the struggle daily because our friends and families enslaved in Communist Cuba live it daily.[27]

As the enclave economy grew, so did the reach of this distinct political perspective, one that set the refugees sharply apart from the fairly liberal views of American journalism. The Cubans saw themselves as more militant in their defense of American values, more aware of the perils surrounding them, than the laid-back natives. The popular radio station WQBA, *La Cubanisima* (The "Cubanest"), for example, greets its listeners every day with this refrain: "It's noontime. Let us give thanks to God for living in a country of full liberty and democracy."[28]

Anglo Miamians who cared to listen reacted to such fervor with alarm, if not scorn. The effect was to sharpen the contours of the refugee community and increase its internal solidarity. Little Havana is no mere immigrant neighborhood, not even a lively business hub, but a moral community with its own distinct outlook on the world. If from the outside the exiles' political discourse appeared as raving intolerance, from the inside it helped define who was and was not a true member of the community. To be a Miami Cuban, it does not suffice to have escaped from the island; one must also espouse points of view repeated ceaselessly by editorialists in Miami's Spanish radio and press—the same voices that take care of denouncing any member of the community who strays too far from the fold.[29]

The political fallout of this ferocious right-wing frame has been generally negative with regard to the exiles' outside image, but its economic consequences are enviable. The consolidation of a moral community permeated imperceptibly the relationships between buyer and seller, lender and borrower, employer and worker in the ethnic enclave. A heightened sense of "we-ness" clarified the limits to which bounded solidarity would apply, while intensifying its hold. Cuban refugees bought from each other and sponsored each other's businesses to an extent seldom seen among Latin immigrant groups. Membership in this community defined, to a large extent, who was eligible for business loans and who was not. "Cuban-ness" by itself did not suffice.[30]

Union organizers similarly reported that whereas Cuban workers in mainstream firms would join unions, the same workers in Cuban-owned firms would be next to impossible to organize. The adversarial union-management relationship appeared inimical to the bond between workers and owners created by a common past and common political outlook. For this reason, firms like Diego Suarez's Inter-American Transport could remain indefinitely union-free.

If the exiles' political discourse had been more tolerant and less militant, it probably would not have been as effective in reinforcing the social capital on which their collective business advancement was cemented. The sense of having the truth but few allies with whom to share it strengthened considerably the moral bonds and self-reliance of this community: Cubans were *in* America, but not really *of* it, even after becoming U.S. citizens. Many feared that their situation and current well-being would be jeopardized by the moral laxity with which the nation's leaders were conducting the fight against communism. The following excerpt from a query by a Hialeah resident was published in *El Nuevo Herald*, the *Miami Herald*'s Spanish-language edition, in 1988:

Hundreds of Cubans live in fear after the changes in the Immigration Law following the Pact between Mikhail Gorbachev and the government of the United States with regard to Fidel Castro.

I have been in the U.S. for 25 years. I am married and have children. My wife and I have been American citizens for 15 years. My question is this: If we were deported to Cuba as a consequence of this Pact, would we still have a right to our social security pensions? Our children were born in this country, could we still have some rights as retirees with their consent?[31]

It had never occurred to this old Cuban that U.S. citizenship would protect him from deportation, even if the U.S. government came to an understanding with Castro and the Soviets.

Origins of the Moral Community

There is a Black-Cuban element in this dispute and there has been since June 26. That's the day that Mayors Gilda Oliveros of Hialeah Gardens,

José Rivero of Sweetwater, Pedro Reboredo of West Miami, Julio Martinez of Hialeah, and Xavier Suárez of Miami signed a letter unwelcoming Nelson Mandela. "We, Cuban-Americans . . . " it said. With these words, the five mayors made this in part a Cuban issue.[32]

The episode in question occurred in the summer of 1990, a few days before Nelson Mandela's arrival in Miami. The hero's welcome planned for the South African leader quickly turned into indifference and then opposition following acknowledgment of his friendship with Fidel Castro during an ABC television interview. Over the strenuous objections of Black community leaders, the Cuban-American mayors "uninvited" Mandela. Although the South African came to Miami only for a brief speech at a union convention and never accepted any local invitation, the mayors' action profoundly hurt the sensitivities of Miami's Black community. Black leaders responded by declaring a boycott of their own city, asking outside conventioneers not to come to Miami until the mayors formally apologized to Mandela.[33]

None of them did. To have done so would have been tantamount to losing the next election. Political power in these cities rested with Cuban, not Black voters, and the exile community was monolithic in its repudiation of anyone having anything to do with Fidel Castro. Although the Black boycott could easily have been prevented with a minor gesture of conciliation, elected Cuban-American politicians were unable to take that step. Any sign of an apology would have been immediately denounced by the Spanish radio stations as un-Cuban and a sign of weakness in the face of the enemy.

Where did this fierce rightism come from? It was not a foregone conclusion that escapees from Castro's leftist regime would move to the opposite end of the political spectrum. Indeed, the dominant political viewpoint among exiles during the days of active military struggle in the early sixties was very different: the revolution, embodying the legitimate aspirations of the Cuban people, had been betrayed by Castro and his henchmen; the fight, therefore, was to get them out in order to restore the country's constitution, organize free elections, and promote economic growth with social equality—in all, a social democratic or at least mildly centrist stance.[34]

Three successive events undermined this position and opened the way for the hegemony of extreme right-wing politics. First, the exiles' Assault Brigade 2506 was trained and financed by the CIA only to be abandoned to its fate at the Bay of Pigs. The decision to leave the men stranded, which directly contradicted earlier guarantees made by the U.S. government, was taken by the liberal Kennedy administration. The exiled leaders duped by these promises were also, by and large, members of the old liberal and centrist wing of Cuban politics.

Even after the Bay of Pigs, these leaders still heeded the promises of the White House; one year later, however, the Kennedy-Khrushchev accord during the Missile Crisis put an end to all hopes. The military deactivation of the Cuban community was a liberal Democratic feat, and the exile leaders who had tolerated it were of a similar political persuasion. Shortly after the Missile Crisis, the head of the Cuban Revolutionary Council, José Miró Cardona, resigned in protest, and the council, the exiles' umbrella organization, was disbanded.[35]

There was one more chance for Cuban progressives to prevail as the moral watchdogs of the exile community. It took the form of an organization built by former revolutionary leaders and militants and led by an ex-minister of one of Castro's first cabinets, Manuel Ray Rivero. They called themselves the People's Revolutionary Movement (Movimiento Revolucionario del Pueblo, or MRP) and for a long time maintained their distance from the CIA-supported Cuban Revolutionary Council, which they saw as excessively centrist and pro-American. The MRP reaffirmed the theme of the "revolution betrayed" and sought the overthrow of the regime through internal mobilization and the support of friendly Latin American governments. In the end, however, financial need forced Ray and his followers to accept covert U.S. support for their plans to launch a new invasion of the island. As with the Bay of Pigs three years before, political expediency again prevailed and the civil wing of Lyndon Johnson's Democratic administration betrayed its new clients. British authorities were notified as to the location of the would-be invaders in a Bahamian key, and Ray and his group were easily apprehended.[36]

The ignominious end of the MRP and the repeated betrayals of exile aspirations by Democratic party leaders in Washington paved the way for extreme-right elements to occupy center stage in Miami. Formerly discredited Batista supporters reemerged from the shadows with a claim to political foresight. "We told you so," they proclaimed; "Fidel has always been a communist, and his comrades of yesterday like Ray are not much better." Along with other conservatives, they forged a coherent interpretation of the exiles' plight. For them, the revolutionary triumph in the island had not been the result of social inequality or political oppression, because Cuba before Castro was already a quasi-developed country with enviable standards of living and economic opportunities for all. Rather, Castro's triumph was the result of an international communist conspiracy. The Cuban people had been deceived by Castro and his clique and then betrayed again by fellow travelers who had infiltrated the liberal Democratic establishment in the United States.[37]

Liberalism, according to this view, was nothing more than a convenient disguise, a front for communist objectives. Accordingly, leftists of all stripes had to be resolutely opposed; intransigent anticommunism was the only valid position for the exile community. This discourse had two significant advantages. First, it absolved earlier Cuban governments, including Batista's, of all responsibility for the ascent of Fidel Castro to power. Second, it provided a coherent interpretation for the immensely depressing fact that the U.S. government had repeatedly abandoned its fervent Caribbean allies at key moments in their struggle. Communist influence was everywhere, even at the highest levels of the American government. Cubans, who had suffered in their own flesh the consequences of such deceit, had the mission of opposing it everywhere and alerting others as to its terrible consequences.

The Cuban liberal discourse, labeled by the conservatives "Fidelism without Fidel," simply disappeared from view.[38] It had always had a difficult time reconciling its progressive claims with militant opposition to the Cuban Revolution. For left-leaning intellectuals and politicians in Latin America and for liberal academics in the United States, Fidel Castro symbolized the anti-imperialist struggle. His defiance in the face of Yankee hostility gained him much sympathy, which exiled liberals were hard put to counteract. In contrast, the conservative discourse was exceedingly coherent: since all these liberal academics and politicians were communist sympathizers anyway, there was no point in trying to persuade them on the appalling facts of the matter. Instead, Cubans should line up with militant anticommunist forces and seek their support to liberate the island.

The hegemony of extreme conservatism did not emerge all of a sudden but evolved gradually, growing in tandem with the business enclave. The two developments thus became intertwined, with militant rightism coming to define the vocabulary in which exile entrepreneurs expressed their views and with which they signaled membership in the bounded Cuban community. Even those who took exception to the extremist views aired ceaselessly on local radio had to keep their doubts to themselves for fear of the consequences. The moral community had taken firm hold, and its ideological trappings were unmistakably those of the far right, a direct outgrowth of the failed liberal promises of the early sixties.

Building on a Feeble Base

Monsignor Bryan D. Walsh, a longtime Miami civic leader who had witnessed the arrival of the first Cuban refugees, described the economic situation of Miami in the 1960s as follows:

Two things happened in the next years that caused all money for development of tourism in South Florida to dry up. One, Disney World started operating, and everybody with big money in New York knew it, they knew that 80 percent of the tourists who came to Florida came by car and Disney World would be like a Chinese Wall—nobody would drive further south. The state of Florida put a low priority on building major highways into South Florida. The second factor was the jet plane. It became just as cheap to fly to Jamaica or Puerto Rico, where you can get two weeks of sunshine guaranteed, than to fly to Miami, where you may get two weeks of rain if you're unlucky.

Had it not been for the Cubans, Miami would have been a dead duck. We had an economic depression in 1959; 1960 was a total disaster. The United Way failed, it did not raise one-third of its goal. . . . The Cubans moved into a vacuum; the place was full of empty stores. Southwest Eighth Street was boarded up from one end to the other. Very soon they went into the export-import business, they went into banks and everything else; they became the liaison between the United States and Latin America.[39]

From minimal character loans to becoming "the liaison between the U.S. and Latin America" was a long road. It took two decades for enclave firms to move from being a mere means of personal survival to achieving a position of influence in the local economy. Aside from the cohesiveness generated by a common political destiny and a monolithic ideology, the consolidation of the enclave benefited from the way the exodus from Cuba was paced. As we have seen, the arrival of Cubans in Miami did not occur all at once, nor was it a steady trickle; rather, Cubans came in a series of waves created by successive political crises. Each wave brought a mass of refugees with an average education and occupational status below those of the preceding wave.

For early enclave enterprises, access to capital was a crucial but by no means sufficient condition for survival. To maintain themselves and expand, they needed growing markets and a ready supply of cheap, hard-working labor. The successive refugee waves along a declining social gradient fulfilled both needs admirably. As consumers, new refugees created a growing demand for culturally defined goods and Spanish-language services that only enclave firms could provide. As workers, they readily accepted the modest jobs provided by Cuban-owned firms as a mode of entry into the American economy.

The moral community that developed among the refugees introduced a new element into what otherwise would have been pure market relations. Early enclave owners were expected to hire fellow exiles in preference to others, while workers were expected to labor diligently at the available jobs without making excessive demands. Low wages were accepted in exchange for preferential access to employment even in the absence of English or formal certification. Modest enclave jobs also provided an informal apprenticeship in how to establish and run an independent business later on.

Evidence regarding these developments comes from successive surveys of Cuban refugees in South Florida that we conducted during the 1970s. In 1979, for example, 63 percent of a sample of 450 refugees who had arrived six years earlier reported buying everyday goods from Cuban stores. Even purchases of major items such as cars and appliances were often made in the same way (32 percent of the sample), despite the scarcity of Cuban retailers of major appliances at the time. By contrast, in the same year a comparable sample of Mexican immigrants that had also arrived in the United States in 1973 reported proportions of coethnic purchases that were approximately half those detected among Cubans—32 percent for everyday items and 19 percent for durables.[40]

In 1976, 39 percent of the refugees in our sample were employed in Cuban-owned firms (including the self-employed). By 1979, the figure had increased to 49 percent, almost half of the total, whereas the figure among the Mexican immigrants was only 15 percent. Indirect evidence of how employment in the ethnic economy encouraged small entrepreneurship comes from figures on self-employment. Six years after arrival and despite low average levels of education and knowledge of English, 21.2 percent of the Cuban sample in Miami had become self-employed, as contrasted with 5.5 percent of the Mexican group. Self-employed Cubans earned much more than the rest of respondents in both samples. This was especially true of those whose firms had grown enough to hire salaried workers. Average monthly earnings for these entrepreneurs were $1,924 in 1979 dollars, compared to $974 for Cubans who remained as employees and $914 for all Mexicans.[41]

Further evidence of the role of enclave apprenticeship in business creation among new arrivals comes from an analysis of the determinants of self-employment in our Miami Cuban sample. It was found that the single most significant predictor of self-employment in 1979 was employment in a Cuban-owned firm three years earlier.[42] As an outgrowth of all these processes, Cuban exile enterprises expanded from an estimated 919 in 1967, to about 36,000 nationwide in 1982, and to 61,500 in 1987. Firms in the Miami enclave grew not only in number, but also in size. Aggregate receipts of Hispanic firms in Miami were $3.8 billion in 1987, a figure that exceeded by over $400 million that of second-ranking Los Angeles and was three times that of New York, despite these cities having much larger Hispanic populations. Cuban-owned firms averaged annual sales of $89,181, a figure that, though modest by national standards, exceeded by over $30,000 the average for all minority-owned firms nationwide.[43]

On the eve of Mariel, then, the exile community featured a monolithic political outlook, sustained both by conviction and the silencing of dissidents and by a rapidly improving economic situation. The staggered pattern of refugee migration had contributed to the latter state by furnishing Cuban firms with growing markets and reliable labor pools at opportune moments. Unwittingly, the successive waves of refugee migration reproduced in Miami the social pecking order of prerevolutionary Cuba: early-arriving, higher-status refugees created the first enterprises and took over command positions in the ethnic economy; subsequent arrivals came from more modest class origins and were employed by these firms in various subordinate roles. The growth of the enclave offered to these later arrivals the chance both to remain within their own community and to learn the ropes of a trade for later sallies into self-employment.

Conclusion

In May 1981, a few months after Mariel, a leading exile educator in Miami complained in these terms about the recent events:

The most important thing was the anti-Spanish referendum. This showed to Cubans how their Anglo neighbors in Dade really felt. It made Cubans see themselves for the first time, as a discriminated minority. The local power structure took an ambiguous stance: they didn't promote the referendum, but didn't oppose it either. Deep down, they shared the fundamental hostility of the Anglo citizenry toward the refugees. The reaction of the Cuban community was pitiful. There was barely opposition or mobilization. Everyone was too busy with his own affairs. Cubans came to realize what was happening the day of the vote.[44]

The overwhelming vote in favor of the antibilingual ordinance in late 1980 conveyed the impression that the refugees would be easily put back in their place, with control of the city thus reverting to its old-time elite. Cubans were made to feel at this time the full weight of Anglo discrimination. Not surprisingly, several local organizations, such as the Spanish-American League Against Discrimination (SALAD), started rehearsing the vocabulary common to all downtrodden minorities: complaints about discrimination, demands to be included and not marginalized from local decision-making, support of affirmative action programs.[45]

Appearances were deceiving, for behind the apparent vulnerability of the refugees was an ethnic economy that had not ceased growing for twenty years. Obsessed with the dream of return, Cubans so far had had little time for local politics. When the unexpected and fierce hostility of Miami native whites burst forth, the exiles were initially disoriented. It took time to fashion a response congruent with their past ideological stance. That response, when it finally came, stunned opponents both by its novelty and by its revolutionary implications.

The *Miami Herald* and its supporters had only wanted to restore normalcy to the city when they informed Cubans about how the political game was played in America and of their true position in the ethnic queue. The exiles responded by laying claim to the city. They put old elites in *their* place by portraying them as representatives of a provincial past. One of the most respected exile leaders articulated his community's response thus:

The Cubans' presence in Miami has an extraordinary importance. The rapid development achieved by the city is a feat that has no precedent in the history of the country and has been called, in multiple occasions, "the Great Cuban Miracle." For this reason, the exiles who came from the island after 1959 and others who arrived later with the same faith and hope must be proud of what they have achieved for themselves and for the community in general.

In order to appreciate the Cubans' contribution to Miami's development, it is convenient to go back to what the city was in 1959. Miami could be defined as a typical Southern town with a population of veterans and retirees. The sole activity was the exploitation of tourism in the sunny winters. Commercial activities were limited and industrial development incipient. . . . It was an underdeveloped area within the American economy, without any great perspective.[46]

The moral and material resources of the exile community, long prevented from confronting Fidel Castro directly, were now redeployed to check the looming local challenge within the framework of American politics. The term *Cuban-American*—seldom used before 1980—became the standard self-designation. The Cuban-American National Foundation (CANF) was founded, each of its many directors contributing free time for political lobbying plus $10,000 per year. Unlike other minority organizations, CANF did not ask politicians for money, but actually gave it to them through its political action branch, the Free Cuba Committee.[47] The exiles naturalized en masse and lined up at the polls to vote for their own candidates. If there was a measure of exaggeration in the refugees' claim to having engineered Miami's economic "miracle," there was precious little hyperbole in the political consequences of this claim. As one mayoralty and legislative seat after another came into the hands of the former exiles, their message about what Miami was and could become gained increasing credibility.

The extreme-right ideology of the exile community had great difficulty reconciling itself with the vocabulary in which downtrodden minorities customarily express their grievances. For this reason, the "minority" perspective never prospered in Cuban Miami after the early eighties. Instead the "success story" discourse gained precedence. Given the issues confronting the community, it had two significant advantages. First, it offered concrete proof of the superiority of the system advocated by the exiles over Caribbean-style communism. The implicit promise was that, after Castro's regime ended, the entrepreneurial successes achieved in Miami would be reproduced in Cuba. Second, the "success story" discourse conveyed a more optimistic message about the present and future of the city than that put forth by the natives. Whereas local whites deplored what Miami had become, the Cubans extolled it and promised a still better tomorrow. This positive frame of mind displaced both assimilationist and "minority" discourses among Miami's Latin population. The old hegemonic order was ruptured and the way paved for a novel set of definitions about what the city was and should become.

Chapter Seven

A Repeat Performance?

The Nicaraguan Exodus

For those residents of South Florida who still thought of the area as a resort, 1989 began badly, very badly. The worst seemed to be happening all over again. Immigrants, more Spanish-speaking ones, were rolling into the area. At the end of 1988, the U.S.-supported Contra war was winding down, and thousands of Nicaraguans began flowing up through Guatemala and Mexico to Texas and on to Miami. The stream of new immigrants swelled through the last months of 1988 until, at the beginning of 1989, it became a flood. U.S. Immigration and Naturalization Service (INS) officials estimated that as many as three hundred refugees a week had been settling in Dade County since the summer of 1988.[1] At the beginning of 1989, Greyhound assigned special buses to run continuously between the Texas-Mexico border and South Florida. In the second week of January 1989, ten buses arrived in Miami on one day alone.[2]

While the busloads may not have been as dramatic or as numerous as the boatloads arriving in Key West during the 1980 Mariel influx, the Nicaraguan refugees became a concrete part of the public consciousness after INS attempted to intercept and detain them at the Texas-Mexico border. The newly incarcerated Nicaraguans, who had been drifting almost invisibly into Miami for ten years, now appeared on national television, standing behind fences and looking much like the detained Mariel refugees of 1980. They were also saying, again like the Mariel entrants, that they would

150

head for South Florida as soon as they could. Then a federal judge
ruled INS's detention policy unconstitutional; the refugees were
released, and nearly everyone in Miami braced for "another
Mariel."[3]

The Nicaraguan flow did indeed appear similar to that from
Cuba. Nicaraguans, like Cubans, were fleeing a radical, left-wing
regime. The Nicaraguan exodus, like the Cuban, converged in
successive stages on Miami, beginning with the elites, then incor-
porating the professional and middle classes, and lastly the working
class.

But there were also important differences from the earlier
Cuban exodus. Most notably, Washington did not welcome the
Nicaraguans as it had the Cubans. Cubans had their passage from
Cuba paid for, were automatically granted permanent residence in
the United States, and received numerous other benefits. The federal government classified most Nicaraguans instead as illegal
aliens and actively tried to keep them out. The new refugees did
have the benefit, however, of coming after the Cuban enclave had
been consolidated, and so had in it a powerful ally. "Latin-ness"
alone was not the reason for the Cubans' support of the Nicaraguans. Rather, political ideology cemented the alliance—the common circumstances of militant opposition to an extreme-left regime.

Phases of Nicaraguan Migration

The growth and consolidation of Miami's Nicaraguan community
roughly followed the pattern established by the Cubans. Both
began in response to a major revolutionary upheaval. Both came in
successive waves, each distinct in terms of time of arrival, social
composition, and geographical concentration in Miami. In both
cases, the first to arrive were the ones most immediately and
directly affected by the revolutionary government—large land-
holders, industrialists, and managers of North American enterprises. Many of the Nicaraguan upper-class exiles also had economic roots in the United States and Miami before the upheaval.
In both migrations, a second wave of professionals and white-collar
workers followed the departure of the upper class. For Nicaraguans, this second wave commenced during the early 1980s. The

final wave, consisting primarily of urban blue-collar workers, peaked for Nicaraguans in the dramatic exodus of early 1989, the equivalent of the Cubans' Mariel.

The Wealthy

In 1978, Nicaraguan dictator Anastasio Somoza Debayle secretly bought a bayside estate in Miami Beach, paying $575,000 through a Virgin Islands corporation to the owner, Miami's Roman Catholic archdiocese. In 1979, two days before Managua fell, Somoza stepped off a plane at Homestead Air Force Base just south of Miami and was whisked to his sprawling new seven-bedroom house.[4] Even after his 1980 death, his relatives continued their opulent life-style. Hope Somoza, wife of the ousted dictator, and Matilda Debayle, Somoza's aunt by marriage, were among the richest people in Florida. But they maintained a low profile, not attending political rallies and making private visits to the grave of Anastasio Somoza—who, like Cuban presidents Carlos Prío and Gerardo Machado, is buried in Woodlawn Cemetery.[5]

The Somoza family is the most famous Nicaraguan clan living in Miami, but approximately fifteen thousand other rich exiles transferred their assets to Miami banks in the late 1970s, moved their furniture into fashionable residences in Key Biscayne and Brickell Avenue, and invested on condominiums in the suburban western edge of the city.[6]

The Middle Class

The early-arriving elite was soon able to rent and sell those condominiums to other Nicaraguans—the professionals and business people who made up the second wave of the exodus. These refugees established for the first time a visible Nicaraguan presence in Miami, clustering in the western suburb of Sweetwater, right next to the Everglades. Many of these middle-class Nicaraguans arrived on tourist visas, and sometimes they moved back and forth between Managua and Miami, eventually settling in the latter. Like other educated refugees, they initially experienced downward mobility as they retooled for their new environment. A survey conducted in the early eighties estimated that 70 percent of skilled

Nicaraguans were working below their training level.[7] Another study found that, of one thousand refugees surveyed, 34 percent were professionals in Nicaragua, but in their adoptive country "many are working outside their fields as laborers because they are so uncertain of their future."[8]

Those professionals who ended up staying did not usually remain laborers for long. Before the revolution, Jorge Savany held a cabinet-level post as the executive secretary of the National Cotton Commission. He fled Managua for Miami in July 1979, just as the Sandinistas ousted Somoza. With a younger brother he started selling hot dogs from a cart and eventually purchased eight such stands. A few years later, however, he was working as a salesman and assistant manager for a Cuban-owned furniture store on Little Havana's Calle Ocho, while his brother went on to become a real estate broker.[9]

Some of these refugees already had some work experience in North America, which they now put to use. The first president of the Nicaraguan-American Bankers Association of Miami, Roberto Arguello, was a Notre Dame graduate who became vice president of a Miami bank within a few years of his arrival in Miami.[10] The first Nicaraguan car dealership in Miami was similarly started by an individual who had attended the University of Miami in the 1970s. To obtain financing, he mobilized the friendships developed in school, especially with Cuban-American students.[11] Still others benefited from the heavy North American presence in Nicaragua before the Sandinista revolution. Another president of the Nicaraguan-American Bankers Association, Roberto Zamora, was a former trainee at the Citibank office in Managua who quickly made a fortune brokering Latin American loans in debt-equity swaps. And Leo Solorzano had attended the Harvard-affiliated Central American Institute for Business Management; in 1989, he headed the lending division of Miami's Capital Bank.[12]

The Workers

The third wave, comprising Nicaragua's workers and peasants, began in the mid-1980s, when the U.S.-sponsored Contra war disrupted the country's economy.[13] As early as 1984, nearly 20 percent of Nicaraguan migrants came from these modest backgrounds;[14] by the late 1980s, an estimated 50 percent of all Nicaraguans in Miami worked as laborers.[15] Much like Mariel Cubans in 1980, the newly arrived refugees could not afford to live in middle-class suburbs. Instead they occupied the poorest sections of Little Havana—where many Mariel Cubans had previously settled—creating a second Nicaraguan neighborhood.[16] Unlike Sweetwater, East Little Havana is poor and deteriorated. Despite its name, it is now mostly an area where Nicaraguans and other Central Americans live.[17]

These new refugees had more difficulty finding jobs than their predecessors. Miami's informal economy of odd jobs and off-the-books employment for minimal pay became the Nicaraguan workers' main means of survival. Flower vendors, a common sight after Mariel, reappeared in every busy intersection. Others took jobs as housepainters, unskilled factory hands, and seamstresses. Lidia Cano, a single mother who fled Nicaragua with two young grandchildren and a draft-dodging son, worked as a seamstress. In Nicaragua she owned a small garment factory. In Miami, she started sewing at home on a machine loaned by a Cuban subcontractor. With her savings, she bought a used Singer and later two other specialized sewing machines. Through expanded homework for Cuban contractors, she was able to earn enough to support her family.[18]

Other Nicaraguan women went to work directly for Miami's numerous apparel factories, replacing the shrinking Cuban labor supply. For Jewish and Cuban factory owners, the arrival of the Nicaraguans was a blessing, as the rapid withdrawal of Cuban women from the garment labor force had already forced the closure of several factories. Ethnic succession in the garment industry neatly reflected the successive immigrant waves shaping the area's economy: from middle-class Cuban women in the sixties and early seventies, to Mariel and Haitian entrants in the early eighties, to poor Central Americans, primarily Nicaraguans, by the end of the decade.[19]

Nicaraguan men had a similar role in Miami's construction industry. The Latin Builders Association—Cuban-owned firms founded in the late sixties and seventies and grouped in a strong guild—confronted a serious labor problem by the mid-eighties. Cuban immigration had virtually stopped after Mariel, and the

builders were reluctant to employ union-prone native labor. Again,
a few Marielitos and Haitians provided a respite, but it was really
the Central Americans who filled the gap. The Nicaraguans' urgent
need for work was obvious, as was their ideological affinity with
their Cuban employers. Increasingly, Nicaraguans became the preferred workers in the Miami building trades.[20]

Others relied on casual work. Between 6:00 and 7:30 A.M. every
weekday from the mid-1980s on, about a hundred men would
gather outside a coffee shop on Calle Ocho, downing Cuban coffee,
waiting and hoping for a day's work from passing cars and pick-up
trucks. Sometimes nearly everyone was hired, but at other times
some thirty men were still waiting at 11:00. Job offers ranged from
gardening to washing dishes. The normal day's wage was $40, paid
in cash at the end of the day when the employer dropped them
back at the coffee shop.[21] As one worker stated, "Sometimes the
employer is conscientious and pays a decent wage, but sometimes
you work eight hours and they pay you $20."[22] In December 1988,
the city of Miami employment office began receiving calls from
people looking for live-in maids. Pay hovered around $100 a month
plus room and board. Although city employees who were helping
the Nicaraguans labeled these jobs "slavery," many Nicaraguans
willingly accepted the offers.[23]

Nicaraguans also followed the Haitians on the trail toward stoop
labor in Florida agriculture. Ana Solis had worked as a cook in a
little eatery near Managua's airport, but she left in 1983 when she
was summoned to train for the local militia. Married with four
children, Solis left her cramped Little Havana apartment at 3:00
A.M. every day for a three-hour bus ride to Immokalee, where she
worked for a produce packer for $4 an hour. Her thoughts on
surviving in the United States were limited to the immediate concerns of earning an income. "It hurt me to see the tomatoes end,
because there was no more work. The lemons are coming, but the
contractor can't take more people."[24]

The arrival of the Nicaraguan working class hence had a significant effect on Miami's economy. All employers of unskilled labor
benefited, especially garment contractors, home builders, farmers,
and middle-class families in search of domestic help. More specifically, the new immigrants helped the Cuban enclave avert a serious problem. Some local economists had worried that the rapid

increase of Latin firms would soon saturate the ethnic market to which they catered. The Nicaraguans, together with other Latin immigrants, expanded that market as well as the labor pool for ethnic firms.

These contributions went unappreciated, however, by other segments of the local population. The Nicaraguans swelled the local informal economy in both low-paying jobs and petty entrepreneurship. The proliferation of street vendors gave to parts of the city a Third World flavor that many natives found distasteful. To overcome this and other consequences of the influx, nativist groups labored mightily to get rid of the new refugees. Like Haitians a few years before, the Nicaraguans found themselves the target of militant hostility by much of the local population. Their weak legal status made them dependent on a few key allies to balance both government hostility and widespread local rejection.

Federal Policy:
Nicaraguans Belong in Nicaragua

In June 1983, President Reagan asserted that if the United States failed to prevail in Central America it would be invaded by refugees. "The result," Reagan said, "could be a tidal wave of refugees—and this time they'll be feet people and not boat people—swarming into our country seeking a safe haven from Communist repression."[25] In many respects, Reagan was correct. The federal government at the time was primarily preoccupied with the Contra war against the Sandinistas. Because Contra leaders resided in Miami, high-level U.S. policymakers frequented the city. This presence, however, did not help the resettlement of ordinary Nicaraguans. Rather, federal officials appeared to encourage these refugees to go back to Nicaragua to battle the Sandinistas. The Reagan and subsequently the Bush administrations thus focused exclusively on the Contra war, ignoring the concerns of the refugee community.

Nowhere is the contrast between Cuban and Nicaraguan exiles more stark than in the U.S. government's differing responses to each. All arriving Cubans, until the 1980 Mariel flow, were automatically extended the right to remain in the country. As a group, they received one of the most generous benefits packages ever offered to arriving foreigners. Secure in the United States, they could plan and debate their designs for overthrowing the Castro regime. But with respect to the Contra war, a different logic was followed as Washington virtually demanded that the Nicaraguans accept the opportunity to confront the Sandinistas on their own terrain. The rebels' base of operations was to be as close as possible to the Sandinistas—in neighboring Honduras, not in Miami. In the eyes of the Reagan administration, Nicaraguans in the United States were too far from the action and were not putting enough pressure on the Sandinistas. Federal officials thus did all they could to deter the arrival and settlement of new Nicaraguan refugees.

Through 1985, only about 10 percent of Nicaraguan applicants were granted political asylum—a figure significantly higher than the approximately 3 percent for Salvadorans and Haitians, but far less than the averages for Cubans (almost 100 percent) or for other nationalities such as Iranians (60 percent).[26] Nicaraguans not granted political asylum were declared illegal aliens, and so not entitled to refugee assistance, resettlement aid, welfare, or government loans. In 1981, they were even kicked out of free English classes for Mariel and Haitian entrants.[27]

Until late 1983, when professionals and other middle-class refugees were arriving, Nicaraguan asylum applicants were at least granted work permits that remained valid until their cases were decided. But then this benefit, too, was withdrawn.[28] At that point, would-be refugees were added to the federal government's Operation Save, which attempted to check the immigration status of every alien who applied for state-administered benefits.[29] If an alien was not properly documented, INS was to initiate deportation proceedings.

Unlike Salvadorans—also unsuccessful asylum-seekers—the Nicaraguans found that some aspects of their plight eventually played in their favor. In the mid-1980s, as the Contra war began to prove more intractable than first imagined, State Department officials toured the country to drum up support. One of their most frequent stops was Miami, where they could be assured of a supportive reception. By this time, the initial waves of Nicaraguan business elite and professionals had become established and had cemented their ties with the Cuban-American community. When

Elliot Abrams, the top Latin American affairs official in the Reagan administration, journeyed to Miami for a celebration of the 165th anniversary of Nicaragua's independence from Spain, he also met with the Nicaraguan Business Council and attended a dinner for one thousand people sponsored by the Nicaraguan-American Bankers Association.[30]

When a group of Cuban-American businessmen organized a $35-a-plate fund-raiser to lobby for more U.S. support to the Contra rebels, guest speakers included Robert Reilly, the special assistant to President Reagan, whose job it was to travel around the country explaining the administration's policies in Central America. Aside from the money contributed to the Contra cause, Washington had good political reasons to pay attention to such events. The focal point of the dinner was a testimonial to Miami's INS district director, Perry Rivkind, who just before the 1984 presidential election had organized a ceremony in which over nine thousand Cubans received U.S. citizenship—and simultaneously registered as Republicans.[31]

Miami under the Cuban-Americans had become a Republican bastion, and administration officials did not want to alienate it. The strong Washington voice of the Cuban-American National Foundation and similar organizations was now heard in support of the Nicaraguans' cause. This effort helped produce the only significant turn in federal policy during the entire Nicaraguan exodus. In April 1986 Rivkind, still INS district director, announced that he had stopped deporting Nicaraguan aliens from Miami. In stating his reasons he said, "I've always had difficulty viscerally with sending back people to a cowardly Communist government. The Sandinistas are exactly that."[32]

Back in Washington, things moved more slowly. The administration appeared to agree implicitly with Rivkind; in any case, his ruling was neither condemned nor reversed. Nicaraguans in Miami were allowed to stay. But neither did the administration welcome all Nicaraguans. Federal policy became utterly ambivalent, allowing Nicaraguans in Miami to remain but deporting others living elsewhere in the country. Only after more than a year did the Department of Justice officially endorse Miami's new policy. In July 1987, Attorney General Meese declared: "No Nicaraguan who has a well-founded fear of persecution will be deported in the absence of a finding by the Justice Department that the individual has either engaged in serious criminal activity or poses a danger to the national security." He further ruled that every qualified Nicaraguan would be entitled to a work permit and encouraged those who had been denied asylum status to reapply.[33]

This major policy shift was reminiscent of President Jimmy Carter's invitation to Cubans to seek freedom in America during the Mariel episode. The Meese memorandum represented a victory for the Nicaraguan refugee community and its Cuban-American allies even as it directly contradicted the logic of the Contra war. The ruling, after all, encouraged Nicaraguans to flee their country, whereas Contra aid tacitly relied on Nicaraguans staying put to increase popular pressure on the Sandinistas. Not surprisingly, Meese's invitation provoked an unprecedented rush that swamped the Miami INS office, prompting it to establish special weekend hours, outreach centers, and rules that dictated when people could apply on the basis of their birth month. In the course of six weekends more than thirty thousand Nicaraguans applied for asylum in Miami. At approximately the same time, the approval rate for Nicaraguan asylum requests climbed from around 10 percent to over 50 percent.[34]

Nicaraguans were still not treated as favorably as Cubans had been. The United States, in its pursuit of the Contra war, still needed some Nicaraguans to remain in Central America to fight the Sandinistas. Moreover, growing sectors of the South Florida community—including some Cuban-Americans—had become alarmed at the rapidly growing Nicaraguan inflow. Finally, a federal government seeking to reduce a gaping deficit was in no mood to assume the cost for new foreign clients. The first response to these contradictory forces was to process the Nicaraguans' asylum applications but deny them access to any special assistance program, such as that organized for Cubans in the early sixties or even that to which Mariel and Haitian entrants eventually became entitled. The same Miami INS official who had claimed he had "visceral" difficulty sending people back to Nicaragua now asserted that Miami's Nicaraguan students did not deserve scholarships because "they may be looking for something they're not entitled to. Why should the public foot the bill?"[35] Off the record, other officials admitted that they feared that providing benefits to Nicaraguans would attract even more.

Federal policy finally shifted again toward repression in the summer of 1988. In the wake of the congressional freeze on military support for the Contras early that year, the flow of Nicaraguans across the Texas-Mexico border increased notably. Too many were coming—nearly thirty thousand applied for asylum between July and December 1988 alone—and the Justice Department went back to treating Nicaraguans as harshly as other illegal aliens. In the fall, Nicaraguans were stripped of their right to work permits and lumped with Salvadoran asylum-seekers. Washington's INS spokesman, Verne Jervis, claimed that "people who make frivolous applications should not win the right to work here."[36] The strategy adopted by the INS at this point was remarkably similar to its various attempts to expel Haitians during the early eighties. As the 1988–89 Nicaraguan refugee crisis unfolded, immigration authorities speeded up the review of asylum applicants, thereby accelerating the process by which they could be deported.[37]

The Justice Department diverted $28 million toward border enforcement in a detain-and-deport policy for Central Americans that included a veritable south Texas blockade of patrols, detention camps, and immigration courts installed at the border. The policy worked. From a peak of 2,400 Central Americans a week crossing into south Texas in July–December 1988, the number dropped to about 150 in January 1989.[38] A few months later, after the Sandinistas scheduled open elections, President Bush called for Contra directors and other Nicaraguans in Miami to go home and test the democratic opening in their country. The State Department followed with a prod in the pocketbook: it announced that it would cut the Contras' monthly $400,000 administration budget by half, which in turn forced a drastic cutback in staffs in Miami.[39]

Federal policy thus reverted to the logic of Reagan's statement at the beginning of the decade. The Contra war had achieved its goals. The Sandinistas were forced into elections that they lost, and hence all Nicaraguans should return to Nicaragua. As the administration saw things, those who had been living and working in Miami for several years were still not a permanent part of any American community. Instead of a resettlement program like that extended to Cubans and other officially recognized refugee groups, the Nicaraguans got a kick in the pants. This official "unwelcoming" was, of course, heartily approved by those sectors of

Miami's population that had sought from the start the refugees' removal.

The Native Response
The Anglos

In 1980, Citizens of Dade United, a grass-roots Anglo organization, placed on the ballot an ordinance that prohibited "the expenditure of any county funds for the purpose of utilizing any language other than English or any culture other than that of the United States."[40] Passage of this ordinance simultaneously galvanized the Cuban community and inaugurated the U.S. English movement nationwide. In 1988, the movement returned to Miami when Citizens of Dade United pushed an English Only amendment to the Florida State constitution. Eighty-four percent of Florida voters approved the amendment in the November election. Support for English Only was not limited to Anglos, but also included much of Dade County's substantial and generally politically liberal Jewish population. In the 1989 Democratic primary to replace Claude Pepper in the U.S. House of Representatives, the Jewish candidate firmly supported English Only, advocating language tests for U.S. citizenship.

By the time of the 1988–89 Nicaraguan refugee crisis, old-time liberal and conservative political positions in Miami seemed to dissolve into either non-Latin anti-immigrant or Latin pro-immigrant views. The first position is illustrated by a letter to the *Miami Herald*:

Most great civilizations in history were brought down by the "barbarians" of their days, whose military conquest of their wealthy neighbors was preceded by insidious invasion in such numbers that it destroyed the fiber of society of their hosts. This newest wave of immigrants to Miami is just the beginning; there are 400 million Latin Americans who are just as desperate as the Nicaraguans.[41]

For most local public officials, the escalating costs of programs for a rapidly increasing population was the concrete issue behind anti-immigrant sentiment. In the mid-1980s, after the large-scale immigration of working-class Nicaraguans had commenced, public officials began to note the extra strain and cost in public services, especially in health and education, created by the new refugees. In 1987, at the Downtown Clinic run by Dade's Public Health Unit, Nicaraguans became the single largest group of patients, accounting for 60 percent of cases.[42] In the same year, Nicaraguan children overtook Cuban children as the largest foreign minority in Dade County public schools, and articles addressing the problem of lack of resources to meet the new demand began appearing with increasing frequency in the *Herald*.[43]

During the 1989 Nicaraguan exodus, a meeting of Dade County's advisory group on the homeless became an angry forum on the impact of Miami-bound immigrants. "This country should open its doors to receive anybody and everybody who wants to come here from a country under Communist rule or dictatorship," said Metro commissioner Sherman Winn, a member of Dade's Immigration Advisory Committee. "Recall, recall," shouted a half-dozen members of Citizens of Dade United.[44] Sporting a button that stated, "Deport Illegals," Pat Keller, a member of Citizens of Dade, asserted that "illegal aliens are encouraged to come here." Another declared that "we cannot afford to take in the Third World excess population."[45] Subsequently, the head of the Immigration Advisory Committee, Commissioner Barbara Carey, urged Dade County to abandon plans to build a trailer-park shelter for Nicaraguan refugees on the grounds that it would only entice more to come.

Most locally elected federal representatives viewed the arriving Nicaraguans in a similar light. Senator Bob Graham, a Miami native who had been governor during the Mariel crisis, sent a letter to U.S. Attorney General Richard Thornburgh on behalf of the local governments. He asserted that America must "regain control of its borders. Those who don't deserve asylum should not be allowed to violate our borders." Florida's other senator, Connie Mack, declared: "We need changes in the law that won't send a message that you can just cross the border, apply for asylum and come to work here."[46]

Congressman Dante Fascell, chair of the House Foreign Affairs Committee and a key figure in obtaining federal funding during the Mariel crisis, stated: "What are we going to do? March six abreast with a gun and shoot the INS commissioner? You're looking at more frustration than can be handled."[47] In the end, they neither had to shoot the commissioner nor open a new trailer park for arriving refugees. The INS's energetic policy at the Texas border deterred new arrivals, and the Nicaraguans already in Miami fended for themselves as well they could as a new source of cheap labor for the local economy.

The Blacks

Black Americans did not lead the fight against Nicaraguan migration, but they did repeatedly express their frustration. When the 1988 Nicaraguan refugee crisis hit Miami, Frank Williams, a Miami-born Black worker who had already spent over a year shifting from one day-labor job to another, claimed: "I'll take anything, any job at all. Five dollars an hour? Some people say that's low, but I'll take it." He directly blamed the newly arrived Nicaraguans, usually hired at $5 an hour, for his not being able to find a steady job. "The bosses should be looking out for the people who have lived here for years. They shouldn't allow these foreigners to come here and take our work," he said.[48]

Most Black Americans, however, did not blame the Nicaraguans for the riots that again convulsed Overtown just before the Miami Super Bowl of January 1989. Instead they pointed to the same issues that had always tormented their community: police brutality, a criminal justice system that repeatedly failed them, and a political system in which nobody listened to them.[49] Nicaraguans did not cause all of this; they were merely the latest manifestations and reminders of where Black Americans stood. Miami's Black leaders compared despairingly their own community's situation with that of the Nicaraguans. For despite all the new refugees' suffering and all the forces arrayed against them, they had a significant advantage that allowed them to survive and even prosper in Miami, while Black Americans continued to struggle.

Comrades-in-Arms: The Enclave at Work

When the Nicaraguan refugee crisis surfaced in late 1988, Cuban-born city of Miami manager Cesar Odio criticized "inhuman" conditions at a private shelter for homeless Nicaraguans, ordered it shut down, and bused more than 150 refugees to Bobby Maduro Stadium—a facility built by wealthy Cubans in the 1950s and the spring training site for the Baltimore Orioles. Odio assured the refugees that they would receive the same consideration given Cuban Mariel refugees in 1980 and told reporters: "Now they understand they have the full support of the city."[50]

The action mobilized squads of city rescue workers, bus drivers, and sanitation employees. Welders fenced off entrances to the baseball field, carpenters built partitions. Cots were placed under the stands, row after row of them along the ramps and the corridors. Outside in center field, the U.S. flag fluttered. In the visitors' on-deck circle, the Nicaraguan flag waved too, from a pole planted by the refugees.[51]

Miami's auxiliary bishop Agustín Román, the same man who had been so decisive during the 1987 Mariel prison riots, dropped by to talk with the new refugees. Doctors from Miami's Pasteur Clinic—run and staffed mostly by Cuban-American doctors—set up an examination room under a stairway. City aides Hiram Gomez and Edgar Sopo raced from a telephone to the parking lot calling names in rapid Spanish: "Centro Vasco, Centro Asturiano, Islas Canarias." They were fielding pledges from restaurants, nearly all Cuban-American, to donate food. Ignacio Martinez, a Cuban exile and retired grocer, showed up with a cigar in his mouth and a sack of clothes in his hand. "We had our time of need, and now it's their turn," he explained. Cuban-American WQBA-AM news director Tomas Garcia Fuste raised $9,000 in one day by calling up local businesses and asking each for a $1,000 donation.[52]

Underneath the stadium seats, two former Cuban political prisoners, Alfredo Menocal and Antonio Candales, manned a green telephone that rang incessantly. As city of Miami employees, they assumed the task of trying to find jobs for the Nicaraguan refugees. A hotel representative inquired about the availability of Nicaraguan maids. A construction foreman asked about refugee day laborers. Some callers, apparently ignorant of the stadium's newest residents, wanted to know when the Baltimore Orioles would be having batting practice.[53]

Two days after Odio promised Miami's "full support" for the homeless Nicaraguans, the Cuban-American manager of Dade

County, Joaquin Aviño, unveiled the plan to build a temporary trailer camp to house 350 to 400 new arrivals. Although the plan was eventually shelved, Aviño persisted in demonstrating unwavering support for the refugees: "We're pulling out all the stops. There are a lot of people in this community who are close to the President. I think it's important for those people to be messengers for us."[54]

Those "close to the President" were not the traditional Anglo establishment of Miami, but Cuban community leaders. Within a week, Odio had flown to Washington to meet with INS commissioner Alan Nelson. Odio requested that INS temporarily reverse its policy of denying work permits to the new Nicaraguans. Despite the pleas of Florida senators to "regain control of the borders," Nelson acceded to Odio's request, promising to process the asylum applications of all Nicaraguans in the baseball stadium in three to five days. Those approved were to be issued permanent work permits, and even those rejected were to get temporary work permits while they appealed their cases. Upon returning from Washington, Odio went directly to the stadium to address the escapees, where he was cheered and had bestowed upon him the title "Father of the Nicaraguan Refugees."[55]

This attitude of the city and county governments did not go unresisted. Aside from the usual nativist cries of anguish, the most effective challenge to local refugee policy came from an unexpected quarter. Advocates of the homeless pointed to the obvious paradox that while the city was stretching itself to provide shelter to newly arrived foreigners, native Americans living in the streets of Miami continued to be woefully neglected. The logic of the argument was unimpeachable, and Odio and his aides had to concede. The city's response was remarkably similar to the policy adopted by the Carter administration ten years earlier after being challenged for discriminating in favor of Mariel Cubans and against Haitians. In both cases, the Solomonic official answer was to treat both groups alike, at least on the surface.

Bobby Maduro Stadium became partitioned: the Nicaraguans occupied right field and, quite appropriately, the visitors' dugout; the homeless were housed in the home-team dugout. Upon arriving in Miami and seeing how their spring training camp had been transformed, the Orioles promptly made arrangements to move to

Sarasota.[56] One firm building prefabricated houses for recent hurricane victims in Jamaica hired from the stadium some hundred Nicaraguans and another hundred homeless Americans. A month later, about eighty of the Nicaraguans were still working for the company, but few of the homeless remained.[57] City officials used this and similar pieces of evidence to cement their obvious bias in favor of the refugees.

In a matter of weeks, Nicaraguan refugees settling in Miami as part of an apparently uncontrollable flow had secured space on the agendas of local governments that had long argued that the refugees were a federal concern. The refugees achieved this recognition not simply because of the magnitude of the migration problem, but because the Cuban-American community had organized a generous welcome. Miami at the end of 1988 was not the same city it had been just eight years earlier during Mariel. Cuban-Americans, now in positions of political power, saw the Nicaraguans as fellow victims of communism. They extended to the new arrivals what is probably the most unique reception for any immigrant group in recent history: not welcomed by the government and the society at large, the new entrants were still granted access to local resources by dint of political kinship with an established refugee community.

As had happened numerous times in the past, events in Miami were the mirror image of those taking place in Havana. Fidel Castro had hailed the arrival to power of the Sandinistas in 1979 and welcomed them as comrades and allies. In reaction, Cuban-American politicians began referring to the new refugees as "our Nicaraguan brothers."[58] The more the Cuban government came to the aid of the beleaguered Sandinistas, the more the Cuban exile community pumped resources into the Contra struggle. In 1983, Cubans and Nicaraguans in Miami created the Central America Pro-Refugee Commission, whose goal was to assist both Nicaraguan refugees and the Contras fighting in Central America. Within a month they amassed 1,000 boxes of clothes, 475 of food, and 350 of medicine, worth $800,000 altogether. While six Cuban and Nicaraguan physicians volunteered to classify the medicines, air transportation for the goods was arranged by the Cuban-American president of the Hialeah Chamber of Commerce.[59]

Spanish-language radio stations in Miami, in cooperation with community organizations, arranged marathons to raise money for the Contras. One such event, in 1983, mobilized about one thousand Cubans and Nicaraguans to man tables throughout Dade County. The Cuban-managed Republic National Bank and General Federal Savings Association opened their drive-in windows to accept donations.[60] In 1985, when the outspoken critic of the Sandinistas Cardinal Miguel Obando y Bravo visited Miami, Cuban-American radio stations broadcast news of the cardinal's visit for an entire week, exhorting all opponents of communism to attend the mass he would deliver. The day the cardinal spoke, three stations announced another radio marathon to raise funds for the Contras.[61] Speakers on local radio and television repeatedly asserted that "the road to Havana runs through Managua."[62]

Beginning in the mid-1980s, Cuban-American representatives to the state legislature also lobbied for support for the Contras as well as lower tuition for Nicaraguans at state universities. They also succeeded in passing a bill to help Nicaraguan doctors quickly get U.S. licenses. Meanwhile, the city of West Miami, led by its Cuban-American mayor, dissolved ties with its sister city, León, Nicaragua—the first time a U.S. city had broken sister city ties for any reason. Miami-Dade Community College, at the suggestion of its Cuban-American vice president, set aside $100,000 in private donations to pay the tuition costs of some hundred Nicaraguan refugees who were not entitled to U.S. government aid.[63]

The incorporation of Nicaraguans into the exile moral community in turn opened the way for their incorporation into the growing business enclave. In both cases, the larger, more established Cuban-American community extended itself to absorb the Nicaraguans, neutralizing the effects of both federal policy and nativist reaction. The partnership was nevertheless one-sided, for Cubans were in complete control. As the Nicaraguan community diversified and the Contra war dragged on, fractures developed in what had so far been a monolithic alliance. Despite their precarious position, Nicaraguans began to chafe under the all-embracing tutelage of their older cousins. For the new refugees, Cuban-Americans had become *the* mainstream in Miami.

In Search of Voice

The first visible Nicaraguan neighborhood in Miami emerged during the early 1980s when middle-class refugees of the second wave purchased condominiums owned by earlier-arriving members of the elite in the suburb of Sweetwater.⁶⁴ Twenty-five years before, Sweetwater had been an enclave of the native white working class—self-styled "rednecks." At that time, one was more likely to hear Greek (from the few Greek immigrants) than Spanish. The Everglades swamps abutted the town on the west, while hundreds of acres of undeveloped land to the east separated it from Miami. During the 1970s, however, metropolitan growth rapidly enveloped Sweetwater as the Cuban-American population spread west along Southwest Eighth Street (Calle Ocho) from its Little Havana hub. The rednecks abandoned Sweetwater, and by the time middle-class Nicaraguans began to arrive in the early 1980s the area was already Latin, with two large Cuban grocery stores, a number of Cuban cafeterias, and assorted other Latin businesses.

As Nicaraguans began to concentrate in Sweetwater, some bought businesses from Cuban-Americans and converted them to the needs of their community. A focal point became Los Ranchos Restaurant, modeled on a Managua favorite. With the Sandinista revolution, the owners of the original had fled and opened a restaurant in Little Havana. As a Nicaraguan neighborhood began to emerge in Sweetwater, co-owner Juan Wong moved the restaurant there and reassumed the name Los Ranchos. He gradually recruited the staff of the old Managua-based establishment, and the restaurant steadily assumed the social importance it had had before the exodus, becoming the most visible gathering place of the refugee community.⁶⁵

The upper- and middle-class Nicaraguans in Miami followed an economic path that closely resembled that of their Cuban brethren. By 1983, when the federal government stopped granting work permits to Nicaraguan asylum applicants, about 100 to 150 Nicaraguan businesses had sprouted in Dade County, including several restaurants, a sprinkling of clothing stores, construction companies, real estate brokers, and florists.⁶⁶ Four years later, after the inflow of Nicaraguan working-class immigrants had commenced, the number of Nicaraguan-owned businesses surpassed 600. A shopping center, Centro Comercial Managua, had opened in Sweetwater; there were also markets, pharmacies, bakeries, clothing stores, restaurants, photo studios, insurance agencies, doctors, and dentists. Wealthy exiles gained a majority interest in the Popular Bank. Tractoamerica, a distributor of tractor parts to Latin America, had gross sales estimated at $7 million. Los Ranchos Restaurant had sprouted five branches in Dade County, employing two hundred Nicaraguans and grossing over $5 million annually.[67]

Like Cubans, Nicaraguan business people maintained high ethnic solidarity: "Wherever I go, to a furniture store or a (car) dealership or insurance company, I always ask, 'Where's the Nicaraguan who works here?' I want to give the commission to a countryman," claimed Maria Cerna, a Nicaraguan who worked as a business development representative for a major Miami savings and loan association. The Nicaraguan-American Bankers Association, with four hundred members in 1987, helped about a hundred fellow Nicaraguans find work and vouched for exiles whose good credit was by now only a memory from before the Sandinista revolution.[68]

The Nicaraguan refugee community did not consist, of course, simply of businesses and job assistance networks. It had many cultural components, including ones that had been dormant back home but assumed a new symbolic significance in exile. These symbols served to distinguish the Nicaraguans not only from "Americans" but also from the Cubans. Nicaraguan stores in Sweetwater sold typical Nicaraguan products such as *cotonas* (cotton shirts usually worn only by Indians) to people who never would have bought them back home. As one Nicaraguan store owner put it, "The people who always wore American brands and European clothes now come shopping for a *cotona* to wear to parties."[69]

Other cultural traditions not highly prized at home found new devotees in Miami as well. Auxiliadora Soriano came to Miami from Managua in 1982. Although she had never been a dancer herself, she immediately began recruiting Nicaraguans between the ages of sixteen and twenty-two to form a folkloric ballet troupe. By 1989, what started with only five dancers had grown into into the nonprofit Ballet Folklórico Nicaragüense with twenty-four members.[70]

All the signs pointed to a repeat performance of the Cuban experience and the eventual emergence of a strong Nicaraguan-American voice in local affairs. This did not happen, however, for other forces conspired against this plausible outcome. First, the Nicaraguan exodus occurred over a far more compressed period of time than the Cuban. The latter had taken place in several well-spaced waves over two decades, allowing the earlier-arriving entrepreneurs and professionals to consolidate positions in the emerging business enclave. By the time of Mariel—twenty years after the first arrivals—there was an economically affluent and socially well established community to absorb the new working-class refugees. By contrast, the Nicaraguan inflow took less than ten years, with the first working-class waves arriving barely five years after the original elites. In 1988–89, when the movement accelerated to a Mariel-like flood, the middle-class Sweetwater ethnic economy was still too recent and too feeble to absorb all the arrivals. The impoverished new refugees thus had to rely on the charity of the Miami and Dade County governments and on the local informal economy for survival. With the influx of working-class immigrants, the image of Nicaraguan-Americans promptly shifted from a group of well-to-do expatriates to that of another impoverished Third World minority putting pressure on local resources.

Second, the hostility of the federal government toward permanent resettlement of Nicaraguans in the United States weakened the group's voice in local affairs. Federal policy rendered the situation of the working-class arrivals still more precarious, forcing them into minimally paid and informal jobs. The struggle to be allowed to remain in the United States also consumed much of the energy of the community, preventing it from articulating a distinct political discourse. The Nicaraguans were just too busy trying to fend off the INS to develop a coherent local profile.

Third, the Nicaraguan exodus lacked finality, with the option of return remaining open to many, even if that meant joining the Contras. After the Sandinistas announced their willingness to hold elections, the option expanded significantly, especially under the prodding of Bush administration officials. Nicaraguan refugees never had the door firmly and permanently closed behind them; thus they were in effect torn between goals to be pursued either in the United States or in their home country. A mythical Nicaragua could not be constructed in exile, as the Cubans had done with their island, because the real Nicaragua was too accessible.

Despite all these difficulties, Nicaraguan exile organizations struggled gamely to be heard. In 1988, the Casa Comunidad organized a Nicaraguan Community Day that attracted four thousand people. Six months later the same organization sponsored a celebration of Nicaraguan culture in the Dade County Auditorium. Stamped on the back of the program was Comunidad's motto: "Unity is our goal."[71] In December 1986, the Centro Comercial Managua held its first exile *gritería*. Nicaraguans filled the parking lot to pray and sing hymns. Little baskets brimming with candy were passed around, and the faithful yelled the refrains that give the religious celebration its name—"The Shouting."[72] By the late 1980s, Nicaraguan fans packed various public parks each Sunday to watch the Nicaraguan national pastime, baseball. Their league's teams had the same names as those back home—Boer, Esteli, Zelaya—and the fierce allegiances remained the same. "In Nicaragua, first you have bread and then you have baseball," said league organizer Carlos Garcia. "It promotes patriotism and unity."[73]

By this time, Nicaraguan immigration to Miami was dominated by the working classes, who were much more visible than the earlier waves. Miami's informal sector was burgeoning, and the stereotype of Nicaraguans had clearly shifted to a definition focusing on poor and unemployed workers. United Nicaraguan Artists was formed in 1989 specifically to improve the image of Nicaraguans in Miami. As one of its founders stated, "People think we're all uneducated, poor people with work-permit problems."[74]

The Rubén Darío Institute, run by a descendant of Nicaragua's most famous poet, concentrated on garnering public recognition of Nicaragua's contributions to South Florida. He convinced the County Commission to rename part of a street that runs through Sweetwater Rubén Darío Avenue. He then persuaded the Dade County School Board to name a new school in the neighborhood the Rubén Darío Middle School. To embellish the recognition, the institute commissioned a sculptor to produce a bust of the poet and a Nicaraguan artist to donate a life-size oil painting of Darío. It also planned to donate a collection of the works of Darío and other Latin American writers to the school's library.[75]

Despite these efforts, the legal and economic precariousness of the refugee community and its contradictory goals conspired against making a lasting local impression. Among the Nicaraguans, no clear leader or position emerged as multiple agendas arose that mixed exile concerns of ousting the Sandinistas in Nicaragua with immigrant concerns of gaining work permits in the United States.

From the Miami-Managua Lions Club to Nicaraguan Democratic Youth, a dozen local groups spoke up, demanding such things as medical supplies for the rebels and legal immigration status.[76] Political issues divided the community more often than immigration problems caused it to coalesce. Roger Blandon, who headed the Ministry of the Economy during the last eighteen months of Anastasio Somoza's regime and then fled to become a car salesman in Miami, declared: "I participated in various groups that were started to unify the exodus but we never arrive at anything. Everybody wants their own ideas to predominate. Some say the Somocistas are to blame. Others say, 'No it's the ones who supported the Sandinistas who are to blame for what happened in Nicaragua.' "[77]

A few months after calling on Senator Connie Mack to allow Nicaraguan refugees to remain in the country, the newly formed Electoral Council of the Nicaraguan Exodus asked more than fifty exile groups to nominate candidates and participate in an election scheduled for early 1990, because "it is important for Miami's community to get behind a leader who will address problems like the need for work permits, refugees detained by the Immigration Service, and the future of Contras living in Honduras."[78] In short, no single political voice had emerged, nor could it. The contradictory goals of remaining in the United States and defeating the Sandinistas pulled at each other at the same time that discord divided the anti-Sandinista militants.

As divisive as political differences, but more insidious, were the latent class divisions separating early and late refugees. The flood of working-class arrivals had erased the relatively positive image of elite exiles, and many responded by distancing themselves from the newcomers: "It's not just a language problem anymore," said Lillian Rios, an elementary school teacher. "Many of the students, like their parents, are barely literate." Oscar Mayorga, a U.S.-educated Nicaraguan exile who ran a plastics plant in Pompano Beach, described the contrast between early and later arrivals in blunter terms. "From what I understand, they're people who are 20 years behind in civilization. It's the effect of the environment and a lack of education and religious training. We have been able to identify with Anglo-Saxon culture, where order and dedication to work has made this country great." Despite a shortage of workers at his factory, Mayorga said he would be reluctant to hire refugees from his country until they were schooled in English and had learned American culture.[79]

Caught up by these contradictions—militant exile group versus struggling immigrant minority, freedom fighters in Nicaragua versus informal workers in Miami—the Nicaraguan exodus could not articulate a distinct voice, much less compete with the discourse of their Cuban-American allies. The Cubans' three-decade plight brought about by a firmly entrenched regime in the island and the impossibility of return gave their presence in Miami a finality that helped consolidate their ethnic economy. The Nicaraguans, in contrast, confronted a feebler and less monolithic adversary, and the option of return to their country confused their local priorities. A second distinct Latin voice in Miami did not emerge in the end.

The "New" *Herald*

As it had done throughout the 1980 Mariel crisis, the *Miami Herald* initially opposed the Nicaraguan inflow and castigated the federal government for creating another immigration mess for which Dade County had to pay. During the early 1980s, the newspaper advocated rigid control over the U.S. borders, preventing new refugees from entering and deporting those who did not meet exacting requirements for political asylum.[80] All of this, however, came before the open confrontation between the paper and Cuban-American leaders that culminated in the full-page paid announcement by the Cuban-American National Foundation in October 1987 proclaiming, "The *Herald* Has Failed Us."[81]

Following this and other related events, the *Herald*'s position began to change rapidly. Anglos were leaving Miami, and Cubans were not buying the newspaper. Market "penetration"—the percentage of households in greater Miami receiving the *Herald*—was declining continuously, as were advertising revenues. Belatedly, *Herald* editors recognized that their town was not just like any other in the United States. Continuing to spout the old Anglo hegemonic message was a sure way of going out of business.

Nowhere was the change of tack more evident than in the editorial positions adopted toward the Nicaraguan exodus in the late 1980s. When, in 1987, Attorney General Meese announced that Nicaraguans would not be deported and that they would receive work permits, the *Herald* endorsed the measure.[82] A year later, it advocated a more stable, permanent status for Nicaraguans.[83] And by late 1988 the newspaper's editorial writers, having apparently forgotten all about their attacks on Mariel, contended that the accelerating Nicaraguan inflow would undoubtedly benefit the community, as had earlier Cuban immigration.[84]

Even more astonishing was the *Herald*'s reaction when Bobby Maduro Stadium opened to shelter the new refugees. This action by the Miami city manager would have triggered howls of protest in the newspaper's editorials only a few years before. In late 1988, however, the recently appointed *Herald* editor congratulated manager Cesar Odio, asserting that "the United States has a moral obligation to take these refugees in and let them work."[85] In a Christmas Day editorial, the *Herald* drew a parallel between the plight of the homeless Nicaraguans in Miami and that of Mary and Joseph in Bethlehem. It declared that politics, economics, and stingy townspeople had caused both situations and called on everyone—but especially the federal government—to live up to the nation's commitment to life, liberty, and the pursuit of happiness.[86]

Miami was very different in 1989 from what it had been ten years earlier. The 180-degree turn in the *Herald*'s position toward supporting the Nicaraguan arrivals signaled no less than a decisive shift in the way local elites thought about their city. Although middle- and working-class Anglo groups continued to embrace the assimilationist discourse and to oppose Latin immigrants as fervently as ever, they had lost their prime channel of expression. Thereafter, Citizens of Dade United and other pronativist groups would be just another minority voice as the Anglo business class distanced itself from them. This singular split came about because corporate leaders realized that the city was not "in transition" to something, but had consolidated a distinct profile, unique in the country. Bilingual Miami was profitable, monolingual Miami was not; as always, the bottom line was what defined corporate policy.

Ironically, the Cuban community was able to do for the Nicaraguans what it had been unable to do for its own co-nationals during the Mariel episode. A decade of investments in U.S.-oriented political organizing made all the difference. Other changes in the *Miami Herald* and its parent Knight-Ridder Corporation, moreover, indicated that the Nicaraguans' sudden welcome was not an isolated event. When the new editor of the newspaper came to Miami in 1990, he took lessons in Spanish and was tutored in the cultural nuances of the Latin community by a Cuban-American professor. Similarly, the same *Herald* columnist who had a few years earlier complained that Castro always called the shots in Miami did not suggest sending the new refugees back. Indeed, he declared that it was "insane" that the Nicaraguans were not being treated as well as the Cubans had been.[87]

More important still was the change in the Spanish edition of the newspaper. The original version, *El Herald*, had remained under the complete editorial control of the English-language editor and relied almost exclusively on translated material. Although costly, the effort did not work; circulation rates among Cuban-American households only declined. Then in 1988, Knight-Ridder took an unprecedented step: it created a brand-new Spanish-language newspaper—*El Nuevo Herald*—that was virtually independent of the English edition. It had its own building, its own reporting staff, and, most important, its own editors, overwhelmingly Cuban-Americans. Not surprisingly, *El Nuevo Herald's* editorial stance came to reflect more closely the conservative discourse of the exile community than the often liberal outlook of its sister English publication. The coexistence of two different versions of the newspaper, each in a different language and with its own editorial line but simultaneously distributed, was a clear evocation of how Miami had been transformed.

The Anglo establishment yielded ground to the Cuban discourse about the city in exchange for social peace and continuing corporate profitability. No matter what the 1980 English Only ordinance and 1988 amendment to the state constitution had mandated, Miami was in fact bilingual and bicultural. The assimilationist discourse receded not only because the business elite toned it down, but also because many of its most fervent native white supporters left the area. Black Americans, on the other hand, stood their ground, and their own interpretation of events became more articulate and urgent. They were well aware that the question of their role and status in this new city, like the role and status of the surging Haitian-American community, remained unresolved.

Chapter Eight

Lost in the Fray

Miami's Black Minorities

Some three hundred anticommunists, mostly Cuban-Americans, were bunched at one end of the esplanade in front of the Miami Beach Convention Center. Amid placards that proclaimed, "Arafat, Gadhafi, and Castro are Terrorists" and "Mr. Mandela, do you know how many people your friend Castro has killed just for asking the right to speak as you do here?" a middle-aged Cuban tile setter asserted, "I'm here because Mandela is a friend of Castro and no friend of Castro is welcome in Miami."[1] Opposing the anticommunists only fifty yards away were three thousand Nelson Mandela supporters, mostly Black, whose placards declared: "Mandela, Welcome to Miami, Home of Apartheid," and "Miami City Council = Pretoria." A tall man waved a cardboard sign: "Anticommunism is no excuse to support racism. Welcome Nelson–Winnie Mandela." A middle-aged Black American woman proclaimed, "I'm here because this [Nelson Mandela] is a great man."[2]

Both sides had been there for about five hours under a searing sun. Planes continuously circled a few thousand feet above, alternately dragging pro- and anti-Mandela banners. Jews against Mandela paraded down the street, followed a few minutes later by Jews for Mandela. A few white supremacists carried racist signs. The main focus of attention, though, was the confrontation between Miami's two largest ethnic groups: Cuban-Americans and Black Americans.[3] Mandela, in the midst of his triumphal tour of the United States, was in town to deliver a speech at the Miami Beach Convention Center before the international convention of the American Federation of State, County, and Municipal Employees (AFSCME). He had already been to New York City, Washington, D.C., and Atlanta, where he had been greeted and warmly welcomed by those cities and by the nation's top elected officials and celebrities.

But things were different in Miami. The city had pointedly refused to honor Mandela because Cuban politicians feared alienating right-wing Cuban radio talk show hosts by welcoming a supporter of Fidel Castro. Even the one Black member of the City Commission had claimed he would not forgo the commission meeting to attend Mandela's speech.[4] Neither he nor the one Black American on the County Commission publicly defended Mandela.[5]

Into the void stepped other Black leaders more willing to confront the Cubans. "Miami may go down in infamy as the only city in America that denounced, criticized, castigated and threw its 'welcome mat' in the face of Nelson Mandela," H. T. Smith, chairman of the Miami Coalition for a Free South Africa, wrote to Miami's Cuban mayor Xavier Suárez.[6] And Patricia Due, one of the founders, three decades earlier, of the Tallahassee chapter of the Congress of Racial Equality, complained: "I feel sick. How dare they do this to us? Mr. Mandela is a symbol. He is a link to our motherland. After all the blood, sweat, and tears of Black Americans, and people are still trying to tell us who we can hear."[7]

In the wake of Mandela's visit, Smith and the Black Lawyers Association brought Black frustration into focus by organizing a boycott of their own city. Over the next four months, at least thirteen national organizations, including the American Civil Liberties Union (ACLU) and the National Organization of Women (NOW), canceled their conventions in Miami.

In July 1990, just a week after Mandela's Miami visit, a Haitian customer got into an argument with a clerk in a Cuban-owned clothing store in the heart of Little Haiti. A fistfight ensued. The following day a Haitian radio announcer related the story and summoned fellow immigrants and "Blacks in Overtown, Liberty City and Opa-Locka to join in protest." Another announcer proclaimed, "We are going to make the Cubans pay for the way they treated Mandela."[8] One thousand protesters blocked access to the store during a nine-hour confrontation, punctuated by street dancing to Haitian *merengue*, occasional eruptions of rocks and bottles aimed at the shuttered store, and screamed epithets at radio reporters from a Spanish-language radio station who visited the scene.

When the merchant reopened his store, a Haitian crowd gathered spontaneously to protest. The merchant spoke peacefully with small groups of protesters, and a Haitian musical group entertained the crowd. About half left the scene during an afternoon downpour, but in the early evening a hundred helmeted police carrying shields surrounded the remaining protesters and began closing in, nightsticks flailing. With television stations broadcasting the melee, police knocked the protesters to the ground and continued to hit many while they were down. Protesters trying to escape were tackled, jabbed with nightsticks, and handcuffed. By late evening, sixty-three who had no immediate proof of their immigration status had been arrested.[9]

The story of Blacks in Miami has always been one of powerlessness, suffering, and frustrated attempts at resistance. Experiences during the 1980s stiffened the community's resolve to improve its lot, while at the same time extending its new double-subordination discourse to Haitians. Yet racial solidarity is not the whole story for either Black Americans or Haitians. A tangle of conflicting and often contradictory perceptions, attitudes, and interactions yielded a confusing scene where racial solidarity alternated with class and ethnic factionalism as well as economic competition. During the decade, Black Americans became increasingly divided by class, as did Haitians; and both immigrant and native Blacks became increasingly ambivalent toward each other. These contradictory tendencies weakened their common voice, making it all the easier for these groups to be lost in the fray.

Color Versus Class

The common reality of color concealed a growing process of differentiation in the Black population of Miami. As in other American cities, the end of segregation and advent of the civil rights era accelerated the growth of a middle class that translated economic success into escape from the ghetto.[10] Unlike in other American cities, this process took place as the minority as a whole was being elbowed aside by an immigrant group. While middle-class Blacks waxed indignant about the symbolic slights meted out to them by the Latins, inner-city ghettos exploded repeatedly for more basic reasons. Miami was the only city during the 1980s to register three urban riots. Each followed the killing of a Black by police, and each was spontaneous and leaderless, a desperate expression of anger.[11]

The suburban Black professionals did not lead these riots, nor did they participate in them, but the local establishment treated them as if they had, addressing them as valid interlocutors in their efforts to prevent the next outburst. Hence, a peculiar dynamic developed in which regular explosions in the ghetto fueled programs that mainly benefited educated Blacks, thereby accentuating the rift between the two segments of the native minority. The process, inaugurated after the 1980 riot, was described explicitly by a Liberty City leader:

The white power structure once again took the easy way out. . . . Once again they listened to the wrong people. They invited the middle-class Black people downtown who did not participate in the riot and asked them, "Why did you all riot?" They didn't know, so what they did was articulate their own frustrations, which were "We're not in business, so if you put us in business we will not riot." And so the white community went out and raised seven million dollars to put us in business . . . but the riots didn't occur because Blacks are not in business and the folks who rioted couldn't go into business tomorrow if they wanted.[12]

The efforts to prevent new urban explosions did produce results that seemed impressive in the aggregate. The $7 million put together by the Greater Miami Chamber of Commerce spawned the Business Assistance Center, which helped launch a number of Black enterprises. In 1989, the center raised $8.3 million on its own. The number of small Black firms in Miami more than tripled between 1977 and 1987, reaching almost seven thousand in the latter year (table 5). In 1980, Dade County did not award a single construction program or purchase order to a Black firm; after establishing a new set-aside program, however, county projects gave work to 158 Black contractors between 1982 and 1990. Black participation peaked in 1985–86 when $12.7 million worth of contracts, or 6.6 percent of the county total, was awarded to these firms.[13]

Similarly, Black participation in the city and county bureaucracies increased steadily (fig. 7). By the end of the 1980s Black officials included one Dade County commissioner, one Miami com-

TABLE 5.   *Growth of Miami's Black Businesses, 1977–87*

	1977	1987
Number of Black firms	2,184	6,747
Number of Black firms with paid employees	380	961
Total number of employees in Black firms	1,579	2,891
Total receipts for Black firms (millions of dollars)	95	276
Total payroll for Black firms (millions of dollars)	10	34

Sources: U.S. Bureau of the Census, *Survey of Minority-owned Business Enterprises, 1977/Blacks* (Washington, D.C.: U.S. Department of Commerce, 1980); idem, *1987/Blacks* (1990).

Note: There were alterations in the procedures used to identify minority firms between the two years. These changes introduce an unknown element of error into the comparison. For details, see the introductory section to the 1990 *Survey.*

missioner, the mayor of one municipality (Opa-Locka), the Miami police chief, the chairman of the board of the area's largest hospital, and numerous lesser functionaries.

Efforts were even made to improve conditions in the poorer Black neighborhoods. In 1981, community developers and the city government sought to attract firms to a new industrial park in Liberty City. A special tax increment district was created to channel new public funds into inner-city areas, and the City began to purchase land for redevelopment in Overtown. In 1984, city government efforts focused on the creation of a new Overtown shopping center, and the following year a Black community-based organization opened another shopping center in the border between Liberty City and Little Haiti. Finally, an enterprise zone was created granting new businesses in Overtown, Liberty City, and other Black neighborhoods tax holidays and rebates.[14]

Although helping to expand public payrolls and giving work to private firms, these initiatives seldom attained their intended purposes. Deterioration of housing in the inner city outpaced construction of new units and rehabilitation of existing dwellings. High-rise apartment buildings built right next to the sparkling new Miami Arena were not affordable to most Overtown residents. Despite legal provisions reserving 20 percent of these units for low-income tenants, managers of the properties readily admitted that they made little effort to rent to locals.[15]

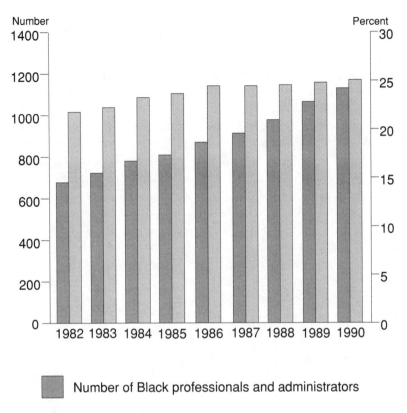

Figure 7. Black professionals and administrators working for Dade County government, 1982–90. *Metro-Dade Affirmative Action Reports*, 1982–90.

The Liberty City Industrial Park had no tenants in 1989, and the Overtown Shopping Center had only two stores in nine spaces. The county's set-aside program was entangled in difficulties stemming from the use of Blacks as "fronts" for white Anglo and Latin contractors. By 1989, Black participation in public construction had plummeted to 1.9 percent, and in April 1990, Dade County discontinued its set-aside program.[16]

The lone success was the Liberty City/Little Haiti Shopping Center, whose Black developer, Otis Pitts, became something of a celebrity in philanthropic circles.[17] But even this success created only 130-odd new jobs. More important, whatever advances Black entrepreneurs and professionals made occurred in the context of a rapid Cuban economic and political advance that threatened to confine Black successes to a mostly symbolic status. In 1987, still less than 2 percent of Dade County's Black population owned businesses, as compared to over 10 percent for the Cubans. Latin firms were much bigger in terms of both sales and employment. Table 6 compares the relative business presence of the two ethnic minorities. The table understates the differences because the data are limited to small unincorporated enterprises, excluding mid-size and large industries, banks, and services firms, a sector overwhelmingly concentrated in the Cuban enclave.

Fueled by the clout of their enterprises and by their sheer numbers, Cuban-Americans moved into local politics and government. Whether or not by intention, these advances were often accomplished by elbowing Blacks aside from positions of real power. For example, the Black Miami city manager, Howard Gary, was fired in 1984 and replaced by Cuban-American Cesar Odio. Black may-

TABLE 6. *Black- and Cuban-owned Firms, 1987*

	United States		Dade County and Miami Metropolitan Area	
	Cuban	Black	Cuban	Black
Number of firms	61,470	424,165	34,771	6,747
Number of firms per 1000 population[a]	76.3	16.2	85.4	24.1
Firms with paid employees	10,768	70,815	5,205	961
Number of firms with paid employees per 1000 population[a]	13.3	2.7	12.8	3.4
Average annual sales (dollars)	89,182	46,592	90,506	40,934

Sources: U.S. Bureau of the Census, *Survey of Minority-owned Business Enterprises*, MB87-1 and -2 (Washington, D.C.: U.S. Department of Commerce, 1991); idem, *1980 Census of Population, General Social and Economic Characteristics—U.S. Summary* (Washington, D.C.: U.S. Department of Commerce, 1983); Metro-Dade Planning Department, *Demographic Profile of Dade County, 1960–1980* (Miami: Dade County Research Division, 1985).
    [a] 1980 Population.

oral candidates were repeatedly defeated, first by Puerto Rican–born Maurice Ferré and then by Cuban-American Xavier Suárez.[18] In 1990, a Cuban-American, Osvaldo Visiedo, again bested a Black American, T. S. Greer, for the job of superintendent of Dade County schools. Greer had been with the system for thirty years, and he served as interim superintendent during the selection process. Many considered him the natural choice for the job. In reaction to his defeat, Black leaders called a one-day boycott of public schools. Over two thousand attended a rally in front of the system's headquarters to protest the decision, 70 percent of school bus drivers stayed away that day, and attendance dropped to as low as 20 percent in some inner-city schools.[19]

Cuban-American elected officials made a number of gestures, such as appointing Blacks to the post of Miami police chief on three consecutive occasions. Yet these gestures were not enough to appease the wary leaders of the native minority. The Black-oriented newspaper *Miami News* flatly asserted that a "Cuban Mafia" controlled Miami, "bullying and threatening all those who do not toe the line."[20] A debate ensued among Black leaders as to whether Cubans had always been as racist as white Americans or if they had become so along their way to social prominence. The latter view was advanced forcefully by one Liberty City activist:

Cubans are afraid of Blacks. Their experience in the United States has made them more racist than they were, and this gets translated into fear. . . . As they go up the totem pole trying to become successful, many Cubans find out that these white Anglos don't like colored folks, so if I'm going to progress, I must take on some of the same behaviors of the Anglos. You don't discriminate, but as a way of doing business you begin to laugh at racist jokes, you talk about those niggers over there in Overtown . . . because you're surrounded by racist people and because it is more important in this moment of your life to pursue your own agenda.[21]

This debate ran roughly parallel with another within the Black leadership. Black leaders who thought their Latin neighbors had brought their racism to America were generally more radical in their opposition to the exiles' rising hegemony; those who argued that Cuban racism was more an adaptive response appeared more inclined to compromise. Hence, the growing class divisions among

Miami Blacks were compounded by increasing disagreement among their leaders. When lawyer H. T. Smith and NAACP local leader Johnnie McMillian called for a boycott of Miami after the Mandela incident, Urban League president T. Willard Fair criticized the move as counterproductive. None of Miami's elected Black officials endorsed either the convention or school boycotts, nor did the one Black county commissioner, the one Black School Board member, or any of the seven Black legislators.[22] The *Miami Herald*'s Black columnist complained that "the boycott is dragging on painfully with little indication that resolution is in sight," and he attacked the *Miami News* for its "Cuban Mafia" comment.[23]

In short, the relative loss of political influence and the growing desperation in the inner city did not produce a unified stance within the Black leadership. More established authority figures saw the future in terms of negotiation and compromise. Newer leaders chose open confrontation, believing that it best interpreted the spontaneous explosions of anger in the streets. In either case, the influence of middle-class leaders was weakened by the widening gulf between their own material situation and that of their brethren left behind in the inner city.

This rift is reflected in the spatial segmentation of Black Miami. As seen in map 2, the Black inner city—Liberty City and Overtown—is completely separate from Black Coconut Grove and the Black middle-class areas located mostly in the south of Dade County. It is in fact impossible to drive from one of these areas to another without crossing large stretches of non-Black population. By contrast, a comparable map (map 3) of Latin Miami depicts it as a virtually seamless web. With the exception of a concentration of Mexican rural workers in Homestead, at the southernmost tip of the county, the rest of the areas with over 50 percent Latin population—from the poorer neighborhoods of East Little Havana to working-class Hialeah and the wealthier areas of Westchester and Coral Gables—are spatially contiguous.

Color Versus Culture

> My name is Herb
> and I'm not poor . . .
> I'm the Herbie that you're looking for,

like Pepsi,
a new generation
of Haitian determination . . .
I'm the Herbie that you're looking for.[24]

A beat tapped with bare hands, a few dance steps, and the Haitian kid was rapping. His song, titled "Straight Out of Haiti," was being performed at Edison High, a school that sits astride the Liberty City–Little Haiti border. His lyrics captured well the distinct outlook of his immigrant community. The panorama of Little Haiti indeed contrasts so sharply with the Black inner city that, by the end of the 1980s, at least one prominent Black leader proclaimed that Haitians had already surpassed Black Americans.[25] In Miami's Little Haiti, the storefronts leap out at the passerby. Bright blues, reds, and oranges vibrate to Haitian *merengue*, blaring from sidewalk speakers. The multilingual signs advertise ethnic products and services—the latest Haitian records, custom-tailored "French-styled" fashions, culinary delights like *lambi* and *griot*, and rapid money transfers to any village in Haiti. Unlike Overtown, the streets are filled with pedestrians.[26]

From very modest beginnings in the 1970s, the Haitian ethnic economy grew to about 120 firms in 1985, and to nearly 300 by the end of the decade. It is still a far cry from Little Havana, especially since most enterprises are small, but it has given Haitians a definite business presence. Underneath the layer of visible firms there is a vast informal economy composed of microbusinesses that bypass official regulation: gipsy cabs, home child care, informal restaurants, unlicensed auto and electric repairs, no-permit residential improvements—all proliferate in Little Haiti and beyond as the black immigrants seek a niche in the local economy.[27]

The number of Haitian professionals increased significantly after the 1960s, when many who had originally migrated to New York came to Florida. Major health and social organizations hired these professionals to serve the expanding immigrant community. Dade Community College and the public adult high school both created classes and professional positions for Haitians. By 1990 there were seventy Haitian teachers and five administrators in the Dade school system and fourteen Haitian officers in Miami's police force. A new public elementary school in Little Haiti was

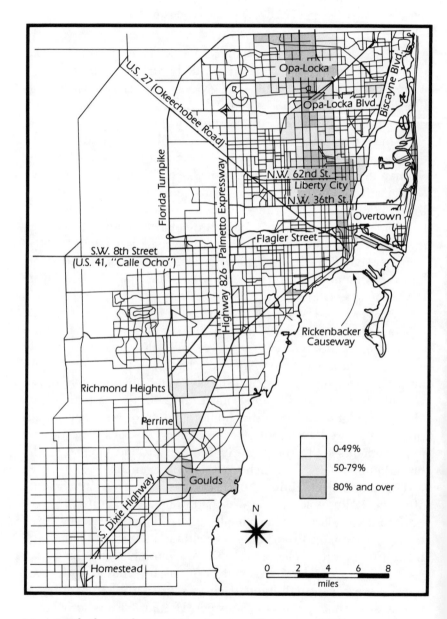

Map 2. Black population, Miami metropolitan area, 1990.

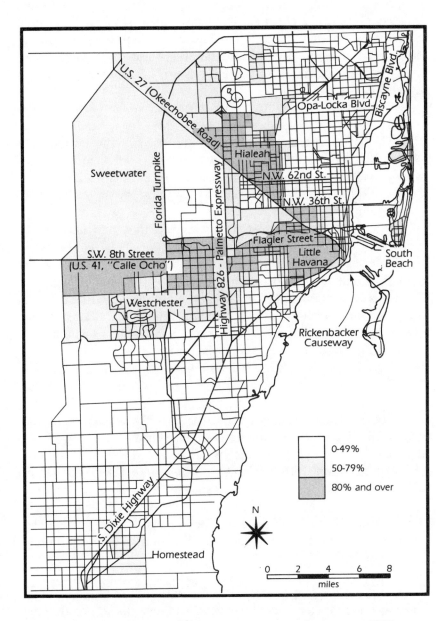

Map 3. Spanish-origin population, Miami metropolitan area, 1990.

renamed in honor of the country's revolutionary hero Toussaint L'Ouverture.[28] Professionals and business people exhibited great energy and optimism, consciously patterning their community on the model of Little Havana. They saw Little Haiti as becoming a cultural and tourist attraction based on their own drive and on Haiti's unique cultural attributes—world-renowned painting, wood crafts, French-inspired cuisine, and numerous skilled trades.[29]

All these signs pointed toward a successful repeat of the Cuban, or at least the Nicaraguan, experience. Like Herbie, many young Haitians saw themselves as "a new generation, filled with determination." Unfortunately, their reception was far different from that which the Latin refugee groups encountered. Unlike Cubans, Haitians could not count on government sympathy or support; unlike Nicaraguans, they could not count on a larger, well-established ethnic community to protect them. Instead they met hostility at every turn. U.S. Coast Guard cutters intercepted Haitian boats on the high seas and returned them to their country. Those who managed to make it ashore were harassed by the Immigration and Naturalization Service. Proportionally, no other would-be refugee group has had so many claims for asylum denied as Haitians. Public health officials repeatedly identified the new refugees as a health threat: in the late 1970s, tuberculosis was declared endemic among Haitians; and in the early 1980s, the Centers for Disease Control (CDC) in Atlanta identified them as a primary group at risk for AIDS.[30]

These and other instances of outside hostility led to the gradual rise of reactive ethnicity among Haitians during the 1980s. True, the CDC later removed them from the AIDS risk list, but the Food and Drug Administration (FDA) continued to refuse to accept blood from Haitian donors. In response, five thousand Haitian protesters rallied in front of the FDA offices in a Miami suburb. Shortly thereafter, the community focused on the INS Krome Detention center on the far west of Dade County, where detained Haitian arrivals are incarcerated and from which many have been deported. This time, twenty-five hundred massed to protest.

The police beating of Haitians in front of the Cuban clothing store was seen by many as the culmination of a decade of growing tension. A Haitian accountant interpreted the police attack as "the result of years of being described as ignorant, as illiterates, of not knowing anything, of not having any skills, of smelling bad, and since 1980 of having imported AIDS here."[31]

The realities of race in America gradually became clear to the Haitians, forcing many to revise their optimistic forecasts. In this southern city, where English- and Spanish-speaking whites controlled business and politics, Creole-speaking blacks had few allies and even fewer avenues for economic mobility. Their plight brought them much closer to the domestic minority, with which they shared a common past of slavery and a common present of discrimination. The "Mandela incident" and the Haitian beatings occurred in quick succession and helped cement an alliance based on color. At a press conference called soon after these events and that included members of both minorities, a Black American leader denounced the police attack against his "brothers," claiming that it would never have happened against Cuban immigrants. Instead of the world-class city it claimed to be, Miami was in his view more like Selma, Alabama; Jackson, Mississippi; and South Africa.[32] Haitians shared his opinion. In the words of one of their leaders: "We have a history of abuse, especially by police officers. I think Blacks and Haitians realize they are in the same boat. The color of our skin all looks the same."[33]

This emergent solidarity led to a series of joint declarations and protests. Haitians felt that Cuban support for the merchant who had allegedly attacked his Haitian customer was akin to Cuban rejection of Mandela. Black Americans agreed and made common cause with the immigrants fighting deportations from Krome and summary interdictions at sea. For Black leaders, the fact that Cubans rescued in the Florida Straits were brought to Miami, but Haitians in the same situation were returned to Haiti, was the clearest evidence of racism.[34] Reactive ethnicity prompted by outside discrimination hence brought the two groups together, temporarily reducing the salience of culture to highlight their common color.

Still, cultural differences did not remain submerged for long. The vast gap in the history and worldviews of immigrants from an impoverished Third World country and long-term citizens of a First World nation could not be entirely papered over. Black Americans did not generally appreciate Haitians' business successes or other manifestations of the immigrant drive to get ahead at any cost. For their part, Haitians accepted Black American support in their struggles against racism, but they did not wish to be identified with what they saw as the poorest and most downtrodden group in the host society. Each group feared and resisted the prospect of *triple* subordination: the double hegemony of Anglos and Latins plus the ascent of another black-skinned group. Black Americans are profoundly ambivalent about Haitians in Miami, who, though "brothers" in color, are regarded as a competitive threat in the labor market and the business world. Haitians, by the same token, resist being pulled down to the economic level of native Blacks and of having their distinct immigrant identity submerged into that of the urban underclass.

The resulting game of mirrors is characterized by each group seeing itself as partly solidary but somehow "above" the other. Haitians view their culture, thrift, and ambitions as giving them a clear advantage over their impoverished neighbors. Haitian business leaders consciously seek to follow the model of the Cuban enclave and to leave the inner city behind. But the political and economic weakness of their community is such that this project is constantly blocked, throwing them back into the less-than-welcome embrace of the domestic minority.

Black Americans, for their part, do not extend their acceptance unconditionally. In their view, Haitians are newcomers who must learn about their new society and adapt to its culture. Just as white Anglos repeatedly preached assimilation to white Cubans, Black Americans push Haitian refugees in the same direction. A Black American student interviewed at Edison High put the matter bluntly: "I can understand people coming over here from other countries . . . I just don't understand why they don't want to be American. . . . They have their privileges. What's the country gonna be called? You have a million different nationalities. Russia is called Russia. They are Russian people. Jamaica is called Jamaica. Hey, if you don't want to be called American . . . get out."[35]

Black American leaders included what they considered to be Haitian issues in the convention boycott without consulting their Haitian counterparts. And no Haitian representative was included on the steering committee of either the convention or the school boycott. Elected Black leaders, in fact, took a notoriously distant stance toward Haitian problems. On the day when community leaders sought to ease tensions after the arrest of more than fifty Haitian demonstrators by the police, Miami's only Black commissioner caught a flight to Jamaica.[36]

Black derision of the immigrants' culture is nowhere more evident than in the schools. In the early 1980s, when Creole-speaking students started to appear in significant numbers in predominantly Black city schools, the word *Haitian* became an epithet, standing for foreign, backward, dirty, unintelligible, and ignorant. On several occasions, school officials had to close down Edison High because of Black student violence against the Haitians.[37]

In response, outnumbered Haitian students learned a pattern of adaptation that was baptized "the cover-up." They learned Black American slang, dress styles, and body language; they publicly denied that they were from Haiti and never spoke Creole at school. This "pressure cooker" assimilation, however, never erased their own concealed sense of identity. By the late 1980s, a few academically outstanding Haitian students, "Herbie" among them, dared to reassert pride in their own heritage—but only in Americanized terms. Rap and similar Black cultural expressions thus became the channels through which disparaged immigrant identities could resurface.[38]

This evolution was clearly seen at Miami's Edison High School. In the mid-1980s, students ridiculed Haitian cultural presentations, such as Haitian dance. Within a few years, however, elements of Haitian culture had infiltrated some school activities. Even so, they were accepted only on Black American terms. The pep rallies were thus for American football and basketball, not for soccer, at which Edison excelled because of the Haitians. Similarly, Black American students enthusiastically received Creole rap songs, but still did not care for traditional Haitian dance.[39]

Assimilation pressures at school also created a painful generational cleavage in the Haitian community. Adult immigrants' pride of culture and hopes for mobility on the basis of Haitian solidarity were shattered by the rapid transformation of their offspring. Unlike Cuban parents across town, who could shelter their children in Catholic, Latin-oriented schools, poor Haitians were financially unable to send their children to private schools, and in any case, there were none that taught in French or promoted Haitian culture.[40] The inner-city public schools were the only option. Hence, "assimilation" was not to the American mainstream, but to Black subculture. This pressured learning of Black American ways brought youth from the two minorities together, but only at the cost of giving up the immigrant dream of economic mobility and a distinct cultural identity. For Haitian kids in public schools, the future became inextricably tied with that of their peers from the impoverished Black inner city.

Class Versus Culture

The unwelcoming reception received by Haitians in Miami and the consequent political and economic weakness of the Little Haiti community also led to a peculiar reproduction among this minority of the class fragmentation that already characterized Miami Blacks. Just as Haitian kids in the inner city were trying to "cover up" their immigrant identity, more fortunate middle-class Haitian professionals were doing the same in the suburbs. Many came from the lighter-skinned mulatto elite of the country, an attribute that facilitated "passing" among Latins and even native whites.[41] These "invisible" Haitians live far from Little Haiti, speak English well, and generally try to find jobs outside the inner city. The loss of this educated element further undermines Haitian attempts to create a viable ethnic economy.

The roots of this segmentation reside in the country of origin. Haiti is a nation of such vast class differences that it has been likened to a caste society.[42] The lighter-skinned mulattoes speak French and try to live as physically apart as possible from the Creole-speaking black masses. Both groups were represented in the U.S.-bound inflow and are now part of the Miami Haitian community. Recently arrived "boat people" tend to come from the impoverished peasantry and laboring classes; they are uniformly black and generally have very low average levels of education and occupational training. Middle-class Haitians, who originally went to New York to escape the François Duvalier regime, started migrating to South Florida in the late seventies. In Miami, they staffed all the professional and managerial positions available to Haitians. They are also responsible for creating most of the formal businesses in the fledgling ethnic economy.

American racism made no distinction between poor and middle-class Haitians. In this situation, the educated segment adopted one of three alternative strategies. Some—the truly "invisible Haitians"—escaped the community altogether, finding jobs outside of it and trying to "pass" as Latins or even native whites. Others run businesses or professional services in Little Haiti but return at night to the suburbs. They admit that they are Haitian, but they speak French and carefully differentiate themselves from the darker, Creole-speaking "boat people." Finally, the third group has chosen to become leaders of the community and identify themselves militantly with its goals. Ministers of religion, like the activist priest Gerard Jean-Juste, are in this category, as are business and professional people who struggle to consolidate a viable ethnic enclave.[43]

In the end, however, there are just too many "invisible Haitians," too much leakage from the community of valuable human resources, to allow the ethnic economy to take off. Trash and peeling storefronts are common in Little Haiti. Many businesses are barely surviving, and the incomes they generate indicate that they are only second-best alternatives to destitution. All of the Haitian enterprises are small: little grocery stores, auto repair shops, and various personal services predominate. In 1985, Haitian businesses in Miami had an average of 1.5 employees, mostly family members; nearly 60 percent had total sales of less than $2,000 a month. There were no Haitian manufacturers or wholesalers. Although some large Haitian import-export businesses exist, they are located mostly outside of Little Haiti and are entirely divorced from the community.[44]

In contrast to the the monolithic political outlook underlying the Cuban enclave, among Haitians political and class divisions overlap. This means that there is no tight, ideologically imbued community to sustain bounded solidarity and enforceable trust. In the 1990s, Haitian immigrant political divisions have become focused on the figure of Jean-Bertrand Aristide, elected and then deposed president of the country. His Miami campaign appearance rallied some seven thousand wildly enthusiastic Haitians. When he returned to Miami in 1991 as elected president, thirteen thousand welcomed him. And in the first two months after he was deposed, five thousand Haitians marched on four separate occasions demanding his reinstatement.[45]

Many middle-class Haitian immigrants, however, especially entrepreneurs and business managers, just as vehemently opposed Aristide. One middle-class woman interviewed shortly after the coup asserted that Aristide intended to "kill" all the better-off Haitians.[46] The owner of a major import-export business claimed that Aristide had used the shantytown mobs to silence the middle class and anyone who opposed him. These groups rallied too, carrying placards supporting the coup and arguing that Haiti could be saved only if Aristide was kept out.[47] Although much smaller, these rallies involved the more influential and wealthier members of the community.

Little Haiti has its business class, but, unlike that running the Cuban enclave, this right-wing elite has not been able to persuade its fellow immigrants as to the merits of its position. Working-class Haitians came to Miami, after all, to escape poverty and oppression, not a communist dictatorship. The absence of a solidary moral outlook compounded premigration class cleavages and accelerated the flight of the better-off immigrants to the suburbs. Weakened by these divisions, having only an uncertain alliance with Black Americans, and subjected to pervasive racism, Haitians in Miami look to a future that is dubious at best. In this context, a partial reproduction of the Black pattern of class segmentation—Haitian kids "covering up" in the inner city, Haitian professionals doing likewise in the suburbs—is an unflattering but realistic alternative to the dreams of a vibrant ethnic economy.

Double Subordination

Miami is a three-legged stool, if one leg is shorter, it will not stand.

Liberty City businessman, 1987

The Anglo-Black Relationship

Despite a rapidly growing Haitian component, the bulk of Miami's black population still comprises the native-born. This group, roughly 20 percent of the metropolitan population, most of it deeply impoverished, continues to pose the greatest challenge to the city's social stability and economic future. Black leaders who articulated the double-subordination perspective in the early eighties continue to blame pervasive racism on the part of both Anglos and Cubans for the plight of their people. Beneath this militant rhetoric, however, some signs of convergence have appeared between their views and those voiced by native whites. Native-born Blacks and whites share, after all, a long history that, despite numerous confrontations, has given rise to certain common outlooks. Under the impact of a rapidly changing situation in which an immigrant group challenges the established order, some of these commonalities have come to the fore.

Three such areas of agreement are apparent in the attitudes of Black and Anglo leaders in Miami: the acknowledgment of the vast gap separating the economic condition of local Blacks from that of the rest of the population; the assignment of responsibility for this situation to the experience of slavery, which undermined the bases for Black solidarity; and the recognition that native-born groups, regardless of color, should resist the inroads of a foreign culture and compel the immigrants' assimilation. The following excerpts— drawn from interviews conducted during the late 1980s—illustrate each of these areas of agreement.

On the Black condition in Miami   Black executive, former city official, and leader of a business promotion association (1988):

It's not so much that the earnings of Blacks are so low but that in comparison to the opportunities for Hispanics and Anglos in this town there is a gulf. . . . In comparison with these communities we are a *developing nation*. If I said that in public, the Governor would want to shoot me but, in reality, all I do now is *development economics*.[48]

White Catholic prelate and community leader (1987):

Basically, Blacks in Miami are an *underdeveloped nation*. It is a situation exactly the same as an island in the Caribbean, and therefore we should be applying the same principles of *economic development* that we would apply there. The relationship of Liberty City to Greater Miami is the same as the relationship of an old colony to the metropolitan power.

On the causes of Black disadvantage   Black businessman and former leader of the Black-oriented Miami Chamber of Commerce (1987):

We've accepted the idea that we're inferior, we can't learn, we can't succeed. A lot of Blacks believe that, they accept it and pass it along to the next generations. Such is the legacy of slavery. . . . I may be biased, but I think that *Bahamians and other foreign blacks are smarter and more hard working* . . . .They come from all-black nations where there was less contrast on the basis of skin color.

Black former city official and business promoter (quoted above with regard to the Black condition):

There used to be a strong Black business in this country, but integration and diminishing reinvestment destroyed the Black entrepreneur. . . . Prior to integration we weren't allowed to go outside. When you tell people they can't do something and they live with that, and then all of a sudden you can, what do you think they do? They do that which they couldn't do before even if it costs more. Over the course of three generations we have lost the common sense and acumen required for business success.

White former chairman of a major local retail corporation (1988):

I guess it is probably *low self-esteem among Black Americans. A Bahamian comes over here and does good, the West Indians, the Haitians.* There is a very successful Jamaican girl in our accounting department, black as could be.

White executive of a major construction company (1987):

We used to have a very good Black business cluster in what is now Overtown, and the Blacks would go to the Black hotel, or store, or whatever and they would be patrons to Black business friends. When we integrated our society, the Blacks started purchasing in shopping centers where they weren't even allowed before. . . . We've had several of our Black leaders say, "Look, the truth of the matter is that our people should be buying from Black businesses." I say, "Absolutely, no question about it."

On Americanism and the Cuban "problem"   Black businessman and Chamber of Commerce leader (quoted above with regard to the causes of Black disadvantage):

There's the fear that they are taking over; *there's still the concern that this is America and that a lot of the older Cubans do and say things that are opposite to what America stands for.* Some of the things those people say and do turn *me* off. It turns me off to have these small-minded zealots tell me what to think. I resent anyone trying to take away my right of free speech. They just got here! We were here before. I don't think they understand the system.

White former chairman of a large retail corporation (quoted above with regard to the causes of Black disadvantage):

We have to preserve us as a country. I'm afraid, I'll tell you, I'm very afraid that the Latin influence in this country is more negative than positive *because they are not really fundamental supporters of pluralism and they are not fundamental supporters of our institutions. . . .* They absolutely are an effective group, actually willing to shut off the democratic system any time it's convenient to them. Pluralism is foreign to Cubans regardless what they say.

Anti-Cuban affinity, in fact, was so strong that one Black informant claimed that native whites, although racist, were more acceptable because at least they "are racist by tradition and they at least know that what they're doing is not quite right. . . . Cubans don't even think there is anything wrong with it. That is the way they've always related, period."

This apparent sense of solidarity between natives of both colors had one important exception, however. Whereas Black leaders blamed the continuously deteriorating condition of the inner city on double subordination and the paucity of resources made available by the establishment to overcome decades of oppression, white leaders stated baldly that they had done all they could to atone for past sins, and now it was the Blacks' turn to shoulder a larger share of responsibility. In a pointed message, the publisher of the *Miami Herald* reminded readers that "after each riot in the past, this community's business and civic leadership raised big dollars for various worthwhile projects in the Black community."[49] One of our informants, a white business executive, put the matter more bluntly: "Most of the successful Blacks ignore the poor Blacks. You find as many white people that try to help the Black as you will see Black people. . . . Blacks in the economic world are not coming back and helping."

Nowhere is the rift more obvious than in the history of the Business Assistance Center (BAC), created in the aftermath of the 1980 riots. The brainchild of Alvah Chapman, chief executive officer of Knight-Ridder Corporation, and other white brahmins, it aimed at encouraging the growth of Black businesses, which in turn would provide jobs for inner-city residents. BAC described itself as a "one-stop technical assistance center servicing established and new Black entrepreneurs."[50] It promoted training courses, consultant assistance, and a seed capital project funded with $6.9 million made available by the Miami business community.

Ten years after the 1980 riot, results of this effort were mixed at best. BAC had certainly provided employment for a number of middle-class Blacks and had stimulated the creation of some businesses, but the record was not outstanding. In the words of a detractor: "An automated factory which provided three jobs opened, and it was considered such a significant event that the Governor came down to open it."[51] Although the criticism is exaggerated, the reality is that the center was caught in a double bind: while trying to administer its limited resources in a "businesslike" manner, it was stymied by the enormous needs and lack of business experience of the population it was intended to serve. As a former BAC staff member reported:

Of the two million dollars we lost, half of that shouldn't be lost. It was lost to poor investments, meaning four hundred thousand of it was lost in one deal, an office supplies company. I knew it was a bad deal. But the board was under so much pressure in this community to make that four hundred thousand dollar loan, they couldn't refuse. . . . It was a Black-owned business, but it is now defunct.[52]

For most BAC critics, however, the key problem was the meager resources invested in this venture relative to its momentous task. White leaders disagreed. They noted that nowhere else in the country had a local chamber of commerce raised such a large sum for minority economic development. They had walked the extra mile and had neither new ideas nor new resources to commit to the cause. Blacks must start helping themselves.[53] It was up to that elusive middle class created by Affirmative Action to start taking the initiative in the inner city. If BAC by itself could not make local entrepreneurship flourish, perhaps some college-educated Blacks could be persuaded to leave the suburbs and provide the hands-on leadership required for entrepreneurial growth in Liberty City and Overtown.

The Black-Cuban Relationship

By 1989, the Cuban average family income had reached $38,497, close to parity with the white non-Hispanic population. The advance during that decade was fueled by an entrepreneurial drive that led one out of every sixteen Cubans to be self-employed and that brought in over $5.4 billion in annual sales by small businesses alone.[54] The contrast with the condition of Miami's Black community could not be starker, and the gap became the source of growing tension. As illustrated by remarks above, the Cuban presence was doubly offensive to many Blacks, both because it was so successful and because it was so foreign. The "un-Americanness" of the exiles emerged as a rallying point for native Anglos and Blacks alike.

For their part, Cubans always disclaimed any intentional racism, and to a certain extent they were sincere. Cuban discrimination operated more by neglect than by deliberate action. Preoccupied with their own economic progress and with the political struggle with Castro, Cubans had little time for the complaints of Blacks. For many, the native minority's rallies and riots were simply a nuisance. Older exiles saw them as an uncomfortable intrusion into their life-style in the "second Havana"; younger Cuban-Americans reacted vehemently at the thought that they or their parents had anything to do with the Blacks' plight. David Rivera, twenty years old and a first-year law student, declared to the *Herald*: "We've pulled ourselves up, why should we restrain ourselves? I don't think the Cuban community in Miami owes anything politically or economically to anyone. The Cuban community succeeded because it's been loyal to itself."[55]

Such youthful outbursts gave way during the 1980s to a more balanced understanding that Blacks were a permanent part of Miami and that there was no shying away from their problems. Cubans also became aware of attempts by Anglo and sometimes

Jewish politicians to win the Black vote on an anti-Cuban platform. They took note that while Anglo elites complained loudly about the exiles' lack of civic spirit and their "clannishness," the same leaders also kept the doors of top corporate offices securely locked.[56]

In 1987, only two of the top twenty-five Dade corporations were run by Cuban-Americans. At about the same time, Cuban-American managers also began to confront a serious "glass ceiling" to advance in such local giants as Southern Bell, Florida Power and Light, Knight-Ridder, Ryder Systems, and Barnett and Southeast Banks. And Cuban membership in local establishment circles such as the Non-Group and the Orange Bowl Committee was minimal.[57] Hence, far from having "taken over," the exiles were still a subordinate group—a fact that created a logical basis for alliance with Black Americans.

Cuban leaders in the late eighties hammered at this theme. They stressed that Cuba was, to a large extent, a black nation and that racism there, if it existed, was much more attenuated than its American counterpart. They also noted that, despite its subordinate position, the Latin community was already doing proportionally more for Blacks than the Anglo elite. A former member of Dade County's Community Relations Board made the point forcefully:

The Black must learn that he needs the Cuban, and vice versa. Increasingly, Cubans offer jobs, personal loans, commercial loans, mortgages. Studies show that, in the last two years, there have been more commercial and personal loans to the Black community by Latin banks than by those owned by Anglos. That is, the Cuban banks have been a source of economic development for Blacks. . . . There is also growing Latin investment in Black areas, and the reason is that Cubans do not object at all to living or working near Blacks. In our own country we had this sort of coexistence, which never existed in the U.S. Racism was never part of our national character.[58]

Black leaders, however, at least by the early 1990s, had not bought the argument. They noted that Cubans invested in Black areas only to exploit the minority market, just as Jewish and other white merchants had done before. Cuban shops were not employing Blacks or providing any special benefits to their Black customers. In the course of field work for this study, we encountered but one notable exception to this pattern of skepticism and distrust: Raul Masvidal, former banker and mayoral candidate, was mentioned repeatedly as a friend of the Black community and as deserving of support. Alone among Cuban leaders, Masvidal visited the Black areas, talked to community representatives, and extended the services of his bank on a favorable basis. When he ran for mayor in 1986, Black voters lined up solidly behind him. One Liberty City activist put it this way:

The Black community supported Masvidal—which may have been a very big mistake—but in political terms they had every reason to support him. He is an active community leader. There was a sense that, given the choices, he would be much more sensitive to the total community. . . . Also, Masvidal campaigned in Black neighborhoods. . . . Raul made a concentrated effort to spend time and money in the Black community. He earned that support. He earned it at the expense of Cuban support.[59]

The Masvidal campaign represented a sort of Cuban counterpart to the Business Assistance Center—a serious initiative to reach across ethnic lines and help the poor. As in the case of the BAC, this initiative did not succeed. In both instances, support from the "donor" community was lacking: not enough money donated by Anglo businessmen to fuel real entrepreneurial development in the inner city; not enough votes among Cubans to promote the one leader who had taken the higher road. As the final statement from the above informant indicates, the Latin vote opted for the more "Cuban" of the two candidates, Mayor Xavier Suárez. For the politically empowered former exiles, preserving the "second Havana" turned out to be more important than building a new multiethnic community.

On the threshold of a new century, Miami's Black population confronts a situation reminiscent of that a hundred years earlier. Just as Flagler's "black artillery" was marched into that founding meeting in 1896 to do its master's bidding and then be shunted aside, Blacks continue to be a major factor in the city but not the builders of their own destiny. Riven by cleavages of class and culture, placed firmly at the bottom of the local hierarchy, Blacks still depend on outside initiatives to determine the future of their community. Colored Town is still there, perhaps more forlorn than ever despite its name change and the legal end of segregation. Its periodic explosions of discontent spark sufficient outside concern to create programs that expand the minority middle class, but the destitute are always left in the same condition as before. Double subordination takes on increasingly ominous hues as the plight of those lost in the fray becomes more intractable.

Chapter Nine

Reprise

*It may be stated with certain confidence that . . .
the prevailing influence in determining the location of cities are facilities for transportation. . . .
The factor of chief importance in the location of
cities is a* break in transportation. *. . . The greatest
centers will be those where the physical transfer of
goods is accompanied with a change of ownership.*
Adna F. Weber, *The Growth of Cities in the
Nineteenth Century* (1899) (emphasis in original)

Since their origins in the nineteenth century, theories about the
growth of cities have emphasized economic causes. Cities arise
out of the imperatives of economic life and develop according to
their importance in the larger economy. Their location can be
analyzed by means of the same logic: urban concentrations
emerge as marketplaces for settled hinterlands, as places where
sources of energy converge with sources of labor, and as "breaks"
in transportation routes requiring the physical transfer of commodities.[1]

This economic emphasis is sufficiently broad to encompass both
mainstream and Marxist theories of the city. The Marxist school
follows the theme of economic determinism and endows it with
greater intentionality than do more conventional theories in sociology and economics. For Marxists, it is not accidents of geography
and prior population settlement, but the deliberate hand of capital
seeking to organize the various factors of production, that accounts
for urban growth. Thus, while the German sociologist Max Weber
referred to the city as a "marketplace" and the American economist Adna Weber portrayed it as a transportation hub, Marxists
have consistently defined it as the site where industrial labor power

is sold and commodities are produced for profit. As François
Lamarche states:

If the city is considered to start with as a market where labour power,
capital, and products are exchanged, it must equally be accepted that the
geographical configuration of the market is not the result of chance.
. . . The main hypothesis underlying our argument can be summarized as
follows: the urban question is first and foremost the product of the capital-
ist mode of production which requires a spatial organization which facili-
tates the circulation of capital, commodities, and information.[2]

Given the vast body of theoretical literature coming from both
sides of the ideological spectrum, the story of Miami is remarkable
indeed. It is not a story that fits "central place" theory very well,
because Miami at its beginnings was not the center of anything; it
did not serve as a "marketplace" for a settled hinterland, of which
there was very little, and it did not sit at the "break" between
alternative transportation routes, because these did not exist at the
time. Certainly, the city was a product of nineteenth-century capitalism, but in a way that deviated significantly from classic orthodox and Marxist theories on the origins of cities. Miami did not
attract industrial capital or industrial labor, and it did not produce
anything of significance. Nor did it serve as a commercial hub for
agricultural products, or for any other good—except one. Its sole
assets were sun and beach, sold by the square foot. Since the
Florida peninsula boasts hundreds of miles of similarly endowed
shoreline, the location of the city was accidental. The metropolis
that grew by Biscayne Bay could equally well have been located in
Palm Beach, by the mouth of the New River in today's Ft. Lauderdale, or even in the Florida Keys.

The origins of the city were hence *economically underdeter-
mined*, more the result of chance and individual wills than of any
geographic or commercial imperative. This accidental birth, added
to the peculiar asset that was the lifeblood of the city, accounted
for Miami's sense of suspension above real life and the feebleness
of its civic organizations. The exotic theme parks dreamed up for
the place by northern entrepreneurs—pseudo-Arab minarets,
mock-Andalusian towers, "Venetian" palaces—did nothing to reduce the feeling of separation from the surrounding landscape or
diminish the city's political fragmentation. Compared to Chicago,

Cincinnati, Cleveland, or Pittsburgh—"real" cities growing at the break points of railroad and water routes and attracting industrial capital—Miami's social organization and civic leadership seemed at best a poor imitation. People came here to retire, enjoy the weather, and play. Apart from the real estate business, few serious economic and civic pursuits could attract their attention.

The poor fit with economic theories about the origins of cities, however, is only the first half of Miami's exceptionality. The flows of men and materials that crisscrossed the Florida peninsula at the turn of the century left their mark on the city, but in different manners and at different times. The Flagler-led feverish building of railroad and hotels gave Miami a distinct profile that, during the first half-century of its existence, separated it from cities up north. The equally busy ferrying of arms to the rebellious Spanish colony of Cuba prefigured its character during the second half. Geography is destiny, but in Miami's case it was not so much economic as political geography that played the determining role.

America in the Caribbean: The Origins of Contemporary Immigration

If the nineteenth-century creation of Miami was due to chance and individual initiative rather than economic imperatives, its late-twentieth-century transformation under the impact of successive waves of migration was without question politically overdetermined. Miami was a choice target for two reasons: first, its geographic proximity and connections to the Caribbean by air and sea routes made the city a logical entry point into the United States; and second, its close ties to Cuba gave it a major role as backstage in Cuban politics.

A more refined understanding of why Caribbean migration arose in the first place and why it came to the United States, however, requires a brief excursus into another body of theory. Explanations of international migration are commonly based on a "push-pull" mechanism that depicts migrants as people encouraged to leave by unfavorable circumstances in their own countries and attracted by conditions in the receiving ones. Although plausible on the surface, these theories do not explain why migrant flows emerge from some countries and not from others at similar levels of disadvantage, or why these flows are directed toward certain receiving countries but not others.³ In short, the theory fails to recognize that decisions to migrate are not made in a social vacuum. Individuals do not simply sit at home and ponder the costs and benefits of going to country X versus country Y. Instead they are guided by precedent, by the experience of friends and relatives, and by the alternative courses of action held to be acceptable and realistic in their own societies.

The social environment of migration is molded, in turn, by the history of prior relationships between the country of origin and those of potential destination. People seldom move to completely unfamiliar places; rather, they seek out those made accessible by past contacts. This is why a great deal of migration from former Third World colonies is directed today to the original *métropoles*— Algerians and Tunisians go to France; Indians, Pakistanis, and West Indians move to Britain; South Americans frequently migrate to Spain; and Koreans go to Japan.⁴

No other region of the world has experienced greater American economic and political penetration than the Caribbean. Although the United States did not become a colonial power in the mold of older European nations, the heavy hand of North American intervention has made itself particularly felt in the smaller countries of its southern fringe. During the last century, U.S. military occupations have been a fact of life throughout the region: Mexico, Puerto Rico, Cuba, the Dominican Republic, Haiti, Nicaragua, Panama, and Grenada have all been, at one time or another, under direct U.S. military rule. In addition, the United States has exercised overwhelming economic dominance in the region and has saturated it with its values, diffused through the media.⁵ Consequences of this historical relationship have been the mass adoption of American consumption patterns and the creation of economic elites that are profoundly "Americanized" in their outlook. Of these, none was more typical than the prerevolutionary Cuban bourgeoisie, molded by the hegemony of North American interests in the island.

A series of grave economic and political crises during the second half of the twentieth century led to enhanced out-migration from a number of Caribbean countries. Migration took place not on the basis of detached calculations of costs and benefits, but along the lines of least resistance opened by the prior history of the region. Hence, when confronted with overwhelming threats to their well-being, Cuban and Nicaraguan elites did not think of going to Japan, Germany, or Canada, but rather to the country whose influence had shaped their own position and mental outlook. Less well-to-do groups followed suit.

The recent waves of Caribbean migration demonstrate how past penetration and molding of weak peripheral societies by a dominant power can turn upon itself. To a large extent, Cubans and Nicaraguans, Haitians and Dominicans, came directly to the United States because they had been socialized in that direction. The same explanation covers the particular destinations of each migrant flow: Caribbean refugees did not distribute themselves evenly across the United States, but concentrated in a few spots. These were the places most salient in the newcomers' mental map as centers of North American influence and power and as logical entry points into the country. For Caribbean immigrants, "America" did not mean Arkansas or North Dakota, but, almost exclusively, New York and Miami.

The 1959 Cuban Revolution was, of course, the decisive event that initiated Miami's politically led transformation. As entire layers of the formerly privileged were forced to leave Cuba, they went to the only country and the only city where, given their history, it made sense to go. And once the defeated Cuban bourgeoisie reestablished itself in Miami, the city became the almost inevitable destination of all major refugee streams fleeing political instability. Nicaraguans crossing the Mexican border caught the bus not to nearby Houston or New Orleans, but to Miami; leaving their desperately poor and repressive country behind, Haitians pointed their boats in the same direction; and less numerous flows from Panama, Colombia, and Honduras followed the same course.

Political migrations then produced a novel economic phenomenon as the rise of the Cuban enclave and the availability of large pools of bilingual labor turned Miami into a major trade entrepôt. The city shed its role as a seasonal resort town to become, as David Rieff put it, a "real" place.[6] Real in the sense that its new economic diversification occurred not by accident, but on the basis of resources that only that city had. While Orlando and other northern locales chipped away at Miami's traditional tourist trade, no other city could outcompete it in the role of "Capital of the Caribbean."

Table 7 illustrates this economic change by showing the decline in the proportion of Dade County's economically active population employed in hotels and restaurants, mainstays of the tourist industry, and the rise in the proportion employed in banking and FIRE (finance, insurance, and real estate) sectors, elements of the city's new economic profile. Also shown is the parallel surge of small businesses, many started by recent immigrants. "Very small" establishments, defined as those employing fewer than ten people, grew more rapidly during the 1970s and 1980s than did business establishments overall, reversing the trend observed in the preceding two decades.

Traversing the Miami River in the direction of Biscayne Bay is a way of gaining firsthand evidence about Miami's Caribbean nexus. Freighters from Honduras, Haiti, Colombia, and the Dominican Republic crowd this working river, loading diverse cargoes for their countries. At the river's mouth, one suddenly leaves Third World trade behind to admire the gleaming silhouettes of the Royal Caribbean pleasure boats anchored in Biscayne Bay. Formerly a tourist destination itself, Miami is now the world's main port of embarkation for vacation cruises, most of them to the Caribbean. Hence, an interesting dynamic sets in as well-heeled tourists depart Miami for enchanted and romantic Caribbean islands, which the native people are often desperately trying to leave . . . for Miami. The freighters in the river also do their part as they haul from Miami the luxuries and conveniences to which tourists are accustomed and which they will consume in their "exotic" Caribbean destinations.

What makes Miami a unique experiment is its peculiar reversal of established patterns of urban growth. Here, politics determines economics rather than vice versa. Almost alone among major American cities, Miami did not originally grow out of economic locational advantages, but acquired them only afterward as an outgrowth of its unplanned political role. The latter did not involve domestic forces, but rather the international dynamics unleashed by the United States' domination of its immediate periphery.

This singularity does not, however, mean that Miami's experiences are not replicable. In this sense, its "uniqueness" may hold important lessons for other cities. The international forces that

TABLE 7. *Employment and Business Establishments in the Miami Metropolitan Area, 1950–87*

	1950	1960	1970	1980	1987
Economically active population (EAP)	157,321	282,774	467,992	788,249	712,568
Percent EAP in services	21.3	25.9	24.8	27.0	30.9
Percent EAP in hotels and restaurants	17.4	13.6	11.0	—	9.1
Percent EAP in banking	1.4	2.4	2.3	2.9	3.6
Percent EAP in finance, insurance, and real estate	6.2	7.6	8.7	7.5	9.4
Total business establishments	14,894	23,051	27,140	42,817	58,036
Percent growth during preceding decade	—	54.8	17.7	57.8	35.5
Business establishments with fewer than 10 employees	11,566	17,178	18,840	32,368	45,617
Percent growth during preceding decade	—	48.5	7.6	75.2	40.9
Banks and finance agencies	141	309	398	671	981
Percent growth during preceding decade	—	119.1	28.8	68.6	46.2

Sources: U.S. Bureau of the Census, *County Business Patterns* (Washington, D.C.: U.S. Department of Commerce, indicated years); idem, *County and City Data Book* (Washington D.C.: U.S. Department of Commerce, indicated years).

transformed Miami are still at play, and have, if anything, grown stronger: people worldwide are increasingly bound together by expanding trade and information networks; consumption expectations diffused from the developed world translate into immigrant flows seeking to satisfy those expectations; the dialectics whereby past colonialism begets refugee movements to the old dominant powers is still very much alive.

For its size, Miami is easily the most "internationalized" of American cities, but others may follow suit as they respond to global social and political dynamics. Today, Boston plays host to a rapidly accelerating Irish immigration, while Los Angeles, San Diego, and San Francisco do the same for the vast Mexican inflow, augmented by refugees from the Central American conflicts.[7] Miami's experience may not reveal to other cities the image of their own future, but the forces that led to its transformation will surely manifest themselves elsewhere, leading to significant social and political outcomes.

Ethnic Discourses

What are some of these outcomes? The arrival of sizable foreign groups necessarily produces a resurgence of ethnicity and, along with it, a transformation in the fabric of local society. Depending on the strength of preexisting elites and the character of the migrant community, newcomers may take their place in the ethnic queue, awaiting their turn to move slowly upward; they may remain entirely outside the playing field as marginal workers; or they may actually transform the rules of the game. In Miami, the politically led transformation of the social structure gave rise to the emergence of alternative discourses about the city and to a rapid shift in local power.

Table 8 presents the evolution of Miami's metropolitan population, providing the background against which the transformation of its political structure must be understood. The table illustrates the dramatic changes in the ethnic composition of the population that led to the shift in elected leadership. Whereas Hispanic (that is, Cuban) political representation was nonexistent in 1950 and 1960, in 1990 it accounted for four mayoral posts in Dade County (including those of the two largest municipalities, Miami and Hialeah),

TABLE 8. *Ethnic Composition of Metropolitan Miami, 1950–90*

	1950	1960	1970	1980	1990
Population total	495,000	935,000	1,268,000	1,626,000	1,937,000
U.S. rank[a]	—	19	17	12	11
Percent increase in preceding decade	—	88.9	35.6	28.2	19.1
White, non-Hispanic	410,000	748,000	779,000	776,000	586,000
Percent of total	82.8	80.0	61.4	47.7	30.3
Percent increase/decrease in preceding decade	—	82.4	4.1	−0.4	−24.5
Hispanic[b]	20,000	50,000	299,000	581,000	953,000
Percent of total	4.0	5.3	23.6	35.7	49.2
Percent increase in preceding decade	—	150.0	498.0	94.3	64.0
Black[c]	65,000	137,000	190,000	280,000	369,000
Percent of total	13.1	14.7	15.0	17.2	19.5
Percent increase in preceding decade	—	110.8	38.7	47.4	31.8

Sources: Metro-Dade Planning Department, Research Division, *Dade County Facts* (Miami: Metropolitan Dade County Government, 1990); idem, *Persons of Hispanic Origin by Race, City, and Census Tract* (Miami: Metropolitan Dade County Government, 1990).

[a] Among standard metropolitan statistical areas.

[b] Hispanics can be of any race.

[c] There is some overlap between the Hispanic and Black categories owing to the presence of black Hispanics. In 1980, the Metro-Dade Research Division reported 11,000 blacks of Hispanic origin; in 1990, there were 28,372 such persons. The table includes them as "Black" for the sake of congruence with earlier figures where this separation was not made.

the majority of the councils of these two cities and several smaller ones, the Miami City and Dade County managers, seven state delegates and two state senators (one-third of the entire county's delegation), and a U.S. congressional representative. Cuban representation among elected officials will only grow further in the coming years. Redistricting required by the 1990 Voting Right Acts will increase the number of "Hispanic" seats in the state House to as many as eleven out of eighteen total; four of the six state senators are likely to be Cuban-American, as well as two out of four members of Dade's congressional delegation. "Politically, we'll hardly recognize the place," writes the *Miami Herald*'s political editor.[8]

This transformation of the political order is taking place in a context where the rupture of the old hegemonic discourse has not yet given rise to a new one. Indeed, the distinct ethnic frames of reference outlined in chapter 1 continue to hold sway, each having its own cogent reading of the principal features of the city and its main problems. This situation has two noteworthy aspects. First, the various frames seldom incorporate points salient to the others but rather slide, as it were, on different planes. The result is that several mutually unintelligible perceptual "maps" coexist in the same physical space. Second, the existence of these separate "maps" plays back on everyday reality, leading to more stereotyped behavior by members of the different communities. Anglos, Blacks, and Latins lead their lives in separate worlds, but when meeting each other in public places they tend to adopt a ritualized stance, influenced by their own particular discourse.

"This microphone has an accent," says the Cuban businessman addressing a meeting of the Miami Chamber of Commerce. But this concession to the cultural sensibilities of his Anglo hosts is followed by a vigorous telling of the familiar "success story."[9] In interethnic public gatherings, Miami Cubans are likely to behave as "up and coming, in-charge Cubans," Anglos as "on the defensive, holding-the-fort Anglos," and Blacks as "entitled and doubly aggrieved citizens of color." This ritualized ballet is guided less by the specific situation of the individual than by his or her perception of the general context, guided by the respective frame of reference.

Every large city possesses a coterie of civic figures who attempt to rise above current problems in order to present the place in the best possible light. The result may be called a "normalizing" narrative that links the city with familiar and valued features of the national culture. Despite its fragmentation, Miami also has a version of this narrative; though its authorship still falls to the editors of the *Miami Herald* and a small group of Anglo business leaders, the content of the message has changed significantly over the last decade. In the 1960s and 1970s, Miami was portrayed as an all-American city, the playground of the nation affected by the "problem" of immigration but ultimately very much in the mainstream. This picture coincided with the then-hegemonic Anglo discourse.

During the eighties, however, the native white population plummeted to just one-third of Dade County's total population. In the city of Miami proper, Anglos shrank in number from an absolute majority in the 1960s to just 10 percent in 1990; in the latter year, meanwhile, Hialeah was over 88 percent Latin.[10] Accompanying this demographic revolution were major changes in local culture. Cuban and to a lesser extent other Latin festivities, music, and cuisine became integral to the city's lore. It was now increasingly common for Anglos and Blacks to learn Spanish, just as Latins were trying to learn English. In response, Miami's "normalizing" narrative shifted to encompass a very different message. Compare the remarks of the Knight-Ridder Anglo executive cited in chapter 1 with those of the new CEO of the same company, James K. Batten, on the occasion of the October 1991 visit of President George Bush to the city:

Those of us who live and work and raise our children in Miami have big aspirations for this vibrant young city. We are only 95 years old, but those 95 years have been jammed with endless change, especially over the last tumultuous three decades. . . . At the beginning of 1959, only a few thousand people of Hispanic descent lived in Dade County. Today the number of Hispanics here has jumped to close to one million or roughly half the population of this community. Their presence here has transformed Miami, and enriched life here in profound and countless ways.[11]

And consider this prediction by presidential son Jeb Bush, cited by Batten: "By the turn of the century, Miami will have completed its evolution into a major world city—a center of international trade, culture, education, health care, and recreation, providing a desirable quality of life for our residents and visitors."[12]

The content of the Anglo elite's portrait of their city thus evolved from one embodying mainstream American customs and traditions to one in which Miami was nothing short of a harbinger of the national future. Immigrants and their foreign languages were transformed from a "problem" into an "enrichment." In a remarkable article entitled "Get on the Ball . . . Learn a Language," *Miami Herald* publisher David Lawrence, Jr., set multicultural Miami as an example to the entire nation and at the "cutting edge" of the America to come. He then urged his fellow Miamians to "get on" and enroll in a foreign language class.[13]

The newer Cuban-American political leadership chimed in with its own tentative attempt at a "normalizing" narrative. Mayor Xavier Suárez regularly raised the "City of the Future" theme, though he tempered it with jabs at the county and state governments for not helping Miami fulfill its destiny. At the City Commission inauguration ceremony in 1989, for example, Suárez declared:

Our own government has been drastically streamlined by our reform-minded city manager. Our own police department has been decentralized under a forward-thinking chief. When are we going to see the same efficiencies in the County which now pays its attorney 50 percent more than we pay ours? And when are we going to see State legislation to provide substantial help to poverty-stricken areas so that commercial growth is fostered and police presence less needed? How long can we remain a high-taxed city in a low-taxed state?[14]

Pursuing the same theme of normalization, a Cuban-American *Herald* columnist went so far as to chide his compatriots for their excessively "Cuban" child-rearing methods. In his view, although the original exiles might remain contentedly within their enclave, their American-born offspring could not afford to do so: "No matter how Latinized Miami continues to become, it is still and always will be in the United States. Thus our children are first generation Americans. That is an important distinction to make if we are to avoid burdening them with identity problems in the future."[15]

Ethnicity in Miami is still paramount, and the fragmentation brought about by the breakup of the old hegemonic discourse remains the city's dominant reality. Anglos, Blacks, and Jews, Nicaraguans, Haitians, and Cubans, tend to stay within their ethnic circles and to greet calls for intermingling with skepticism, if not hostility.[16] Yet at the edges and in the better-educated sectors, there are visible signs of convergence. This trend fits a thus far neglected but fundamental lesson in the history of past immigration and ethnic adaptation in American cities. The story is worth reviewing, for no matter how distinct Miami is at present, it is likely in time to follow a path similar to that taken before by other communities.

Who Rules?

In *Who Governs?* (1961), his classic book on American urban politics, political scientist Robert A. Dahl traced the transformation of New Haven, Connecticut, from a city ruled by its old white Protestant elite to one in which immigrants—in this case Irish, Jews, and Italians—gradually gained the upper hand. He forcefully argued that power had indeed come to be shared between old and new elites rather than being retained by old WASPs behind a façade of ethnic politicians. Not surprisingly, the book became the standard reference for the pluralist perspective on urban community power.

The pluralist-elitist controversy over who "really" rules obscured an important aspect of the book, however, namely its analysis of how the immigrants became integrated into American culture through their participation in politics and management of local institutions. No matter that the first impulse of newly elected Irish mayors was to distribute patronage among their own, the important long-term consequence of institutional participation was to integrate each group firmly into local society:

Hence the politics of New Haven became a kind of ethnic politics; it was a politics of assimilation rather than a politics of reform, a politics that simultaneously emphasized the divisive rather than the unifying characteristics of voters and yet played upon their yearnings of assimilation and acceptance. The very success of politicians who use the ethnic approach leads to the obsolescence of their strategy.[17]

The point of Dahl's analysis, in short, is that ethnic politics provides an effective vehicle for convergence because the achievement of political power socializes immigrants into the functioning of mainstream institutions and gives them the necessary "voice" to feel that they are part of those institutions. Immigrants do not first learn to be "Americans," and only then are freely admitted into the mainstream. Rather, they become Americans by elbowing their way into centers of local power through the political mobilization of ethnic solidarity. The very success of that strategy in turn leads to its gradual dissolution.

The common view of the process of assimilation, unfortunately, tends to reverse this sequence, with acculturation coming before social acceptance. From that perspective, ethnic politics is seen as a looming threat, a fear on which nativist emotions thrive. In a book titled *The Immigration Time Bomb*, former Colorado governor Richard D. Lamm expressed the theme with notable clarity:

The political power of more than fifteen million Hispanics is being used not to support assimilation but to advance "ethnic pride" in belonging to a different culture. The multiplication of outsiders is not a model for a viable society. . . . If immigrants do not feel that they are fully part of this society, as American as everyone else, then we are failing.[18]

First-generation immigrants have seldom felt "as American as anyone else" because natives have repeatedly reminded them of their cultural and linguistic differences. The error in Lamm's formulation is to believe that cultural diversity and ethnic pride must disappear before immigrants can take part in the institutions of society. As Dahl's study suggests, the opposite has often been the case. The process is exemplified not only in New Haven, but in large cities that have been major recipients of immigration. The Irish of Boston, the Italians and Jews of New York, the Poles of Chicago first mobilized around the symbols of a common ethnicity precisely because that was how they had been defined and often ostracized in their places of settlement.

Hence "ethnic pride" arising out of reactive formation is the first and natural rallying point for immigrant groups entering the political system. Through the defense of particularistic goals, they are socialized into national political values. Before politicians of Irish, Greek, and Italian origin learned how to interpret mainstream sentiment and to represent broad constituencies, their predecessors had spent considerable time in ward politics fighting for the narrow interests of their group.[19]

In previous chapters we examined the reactive formation process of Cuban refugees in the aftermath of Mariel, a process that gave rise both to a novel discourse and to strong participation in local politics. The above quotes from the Cuban-American mayor of Miami and the Cuban-American columnist of the *Herald* resemble hundreds that could be used to illustrate how far the process of integration has advanced in a decade. Concerns about a more equitable tax distribution for the city and how to avoid the ghettoization of the next generation are hardly the worries of a refractory minority. Gradual convergence toward the cultural mainstream, however, is attributable more to the entry of former exiles into local political institutions than to the assimilationist sermons of the past.

The extraordinary division of Miami along ethnic lines continues to define its reality, but there are at present a number of Anglo and Cuban leaders who prefer to advance the "Capital of the Caribbean" and "City of the Future" themes over segmented ethnic perspectives. Left out of this endeavor, however, are Miami's black minorities. The double-subordination discourse forged by Black leaders during the last decade represents both an original form of reactive ethnicity and an attempt to gain entry into the city's power structure. So far the attempt has been unsuccessful.

The continuing exclusion of Blacks from true political participation virtually guarantees new episodes of ethnic strife in Miami's future. From the perspective of Dahl's analysis, their position is the precise opposite of the Cubans'. Blacks are thoroughly acculturated, "as American as everyone else"—yet this achievement has yielded nothing near political or economic parity. Indeed, the situation has become so bad in recent years that many Black leaders recall almost wistfully the days of segregation. A principal Black community leader, interviewed in 1987 and whose views were reported in chapter 1, had this to say about Black Miami five years later:

The changes have been for the worse, not for the better; violence is rampant and uncontrollable. . . . What oppression does is that it makes the oppressed group also aspire to be like the oppressor. And if I am able to be like the oppressor, then the things that I was forced to develop by virtue of my oppression are no longer valued. . . . It's a question of emulation having to do with assimilation. Without a doubt, Blacks are the most American people in America. . . .

When things were colored, *when things were colored*, then the same kind of business enclave that exists in the Cuban community, in the Jewish community, also existed in the Black community, because the consumer base was contained.[20]

Lacking an ethnic economy and sufficient political power for effective representation, Black Miami remains marginal to the process of integration-through-participation described by Dahl. Daunted but not beaten, Haitians nevertheless continue striving to build their enclave, and Black leaders still seek a voice in local power circles. If their efforts are not successful, the "Capital of the Caribbean" is in for some tough times no matter how much it has moved toward convergence between its other major groups.

Politics During the Deathwatch

In February 1990, Governor Bob Martinez appointed a twelve-member commission to study the potential effects that a change in government in Cuba would have on the state of Florida. The idea for the commission came from the Cuban-American National Foundation, whose president, Jorge Mas Canosa, was subsequently appointed chair of the panel. Meeting for the first time on the twenty-ninth floor on the Miami-Metro building, the commission discussed such things as preventing widespread absenteeism among Cuban-American workers celebrating the fall of Fidel, controlling the festivities in South Florida, and coping with the influx of Cubans from elsewhere in the United States who would use Miami as a "staging area" to reach Cuba.[21]

The gap between the important-sounding commission and the shallow topics it discussed reflects the fact that neither the participants nor anyone else had the slightest idea of what would happen were Castro's regime to fall. The creation of the panel was, in other words, largely symbolic; it signaled the clout that right-wing exiles had with the Republican governor and their sense that the long-awaited downfall was imminent. That sense permeated the Cuban enclave, being reflected both in the public utterances of its leaders and in street culture. The Cuban-American Foundation, for example, announced with much fanfare a plan for "the future governance of Cuba."[22] So did almost every other exile political group.

Salsa singer Willy Chirino's hit song of 1990 proclaimed, "Ya viene llegando" (It's just around the corner); another popular rap singer, perhaps with a keener instinct about the future, announced that "soon in Cuba, English will be spoken."

In 1990, Cuban Miami embarked on the deathwatch for its enemy. Events in Europe had converted Cuba into the single Western country still governed by orthodox communism. The fall of East European regimes and the end of the Soviet Union left the island nation bereft of allies and protectors, and the defeat of the Sandinista regime in Nicaragua and the end of the Salvadoran insurgency entirely isolated Cuba in the Western Hemisphere. Widespread domestic scarcities and rising popular discontent made it clear to many that the end was near.[23] After three decades, the revolutionary episode that had transformed Miami appeared to be near an end, and not only Cubans, but the entire city, watched with both anticipation and foreboding. What new surprises did the convulsed island hold in store? Would the "City of the Future" be suddenly abandoned by half its population, as militant exile leaders promised? Or would it, on the contrary, be inundated by a still larger inflow of post-Castro refugees?

Both scenarios are probably overdrawn. A massive return to Cuba is unlikely because of the roots established during three decades of settlement and the growing process of social convergence. Few well-established former exiles are likely to pack up and leave all they have accomplished behind. A recent survey on the topic by researchers at Florida International University shows that only a third of adult Cuban residents (38 percent) in Dade County would consider returning to the island to live in the event of Castro's downfall. Such a move is even less probable among U.S.-born Cuban-Americans. Only the most recent refugees, those with the least social roots and smallest economic assets, are likely to find the return option attractive.[24]

And although a new refugee influx is more likely because of widespread material scarcities in Cuba, it would probably be checked by the end of the island's special status as America's main adversary in the Western Hemisphere. With the conversion of Cuba into just another Caribbean country, new arrivals would necessarily be labeled conventional immigrants rather than political refugees.

If the downfall of Castroism would not lead to a major demographic movement, it could have a subtler but still far-reaching effect, namely, the end of the monolithic ideological outlook that undergirds the Cuban ethnic economy. For more than three decades, ideological fervor and tight social controls have been maintained on the strength of a single theme: irreconcilable opposition to Castro and communism. This has been the message hammered out daily by the Cuban exile media, and it has furnished the frame according to which all other domestic and world events are interpreted.[25] Castro's end would remove the raison d'être of this fierce preaching and put the bellicose radio commentators and militant activists on the spot: either they move back to Cuba as announced for so long, or they accept their role as regular immigrants and, hence, the inevitable reality of assimilation.

The same is true, in fact, for the entire community. Among those former exiles who choose to remain in Miami—easily the majority—the claim of a unique status based on principled opposition to a dictatorial regime would dissolve. The social mechanisms that underlie business success in the enclave may remain, on the strength of habit and past practice, but would weaken over time because of the loss of social controls rooted in exile ideology. In these circumstances, the most likely prognosis is the gradual end of the ethnic economy and the acceleration of the process of cultural convergence, already under way.

Yet Miami will never return to what it was before its transformation. The former exiles will still be there, and new Caribbean and South American inflows will replace them in number, if not in ideological fervor. Even today, in the midst of the deathwatch, the process of acculturation-in-reverse continues. Every year, new parts of Miami become more like Havana, or at least like the nostalgic image that Cubans have of their capital city. In an article entitled "Miami's Crossroads of the Vanities," *Herald* columnist Howard Kleinberg lamented that the streets in the "Latin quarter" were being named for "Latin American militarists and romantics who never had been to Miami and whose names barely made it into any encyclopedia."[26] He proposed instead that the City Commission name a street for John Reilly, the city's first mayor, and another for Francisco Villareal, the Spanish friar who in 1567 established the first Catholic mission on the site of today's Hyatt Regency.

Despite his otherwise keen observations, Kleinberg failed to understand the driving force behind all this name changing. The intention was not to memorialize Miami as it had been until 1959, but rather to celebrate pre-Castro Havana. In their symbolic reenactment of a lost past, Cubans and their elected leaders could not be counted on to know much about the Merricks, the Reillys, and the Deerings, though these were prominent men in the city's modest history. Instead a much older past was imported, so that the friars, scholars, and soldiers whose names now adorned the streets of Miami were also those who gave their names to streets and schools in Cuba.

With or without Castro's downfall, a long-term trend toward integration and cultural convergence appears inevitable. In the short to medium term, however, Miami will continue to be characterized by ethnic fragmentation, strife, lack of a hegemonic discourse, and the nostalgic reproduction of a foreign past. For Karl Marx, great historical dramas are often enacted twice, the second time as farce. There are indeed tragicomic aspects to the exiles' single-minded attempt to reenact past lives in South Florida. There is nothing farcical, however, in the depths of the transformation that they have wrought and in the unique urban experiment that their presence, along with that of natives and newer immigrants, have forged in their adopted city.

In the Eye of the Storm

Waiting for a political cataclysm, and disaster of a very different kind struck. Not the end of Castroism, but a huge storm that swept away everything in its path. The same fearful natural event that has been the curse of these lands for centuries made its reappearance to remind everyone of the banality of human conflicts and the frailty of their outcomes. For centuries, storms have wreaked havoc on civilization in the tropics. They have done so with notable impartiality to the contenders of the day, scattering and sinking Spanish gold galleons and their French and English pursuers; trampling with equal fury on the colonizing ventures of competing European powers. The great wind of 1992 behaved in this time-honored way, impartially spreading destruction among peoples of different color, language, and political creed.

It is not the first time a storm has brought Miami to its knees. Forty-seven thousand residents were left homeless by the hurricane of 1926. It killed 113 people and flattened five thousand Miami dwellings.[1] That storm blew away not only the palm trees planted with so much care by Collins and his successors, but also the reputation of the city as a carefree playground. For the next few years, it was not possible to give away the same land that, until then, had sold for millions. But every time, as calm returned and a new generation came of age, Miami renewed its illusion that disasters of such a magnitude could not happen there.

The first thing that strikes the observer in the aftermath of the August 1992 storm is how psychologically unprepared the city and its inhabitants were. Worried by everyday concerns, many people could not conceive that a catastrophe of an altogether different magnitude would hit them. Boats and houses were left unattended, utterly exposed to the wind's fury. Dade County did not even have an emergency evacuation plan for the hundreds of small craft in its docks and marinas. As a result, a good number ended up in the streets. Taught a lesson by Hurricane Hugo three years earlier, the Charleston, South Carolina, police department came barreling down Interstate 95 hours before the storm and managed to be in place in the worst-hit areas ahead of Dade County's own dazed officers.[2]

The vast destruction was not media hype. It was real. Eighty thousand homes destroyed or rendered uninhabitable; 160,000 people left homeless; 82,000 businesses destroyed or damaged; $20 billion in property losses. The miles and miles of wrecked properties and instant poverty added up to a defining moment in the history of the city. Thereafter, being a Miamian would mean having lived through the "worst wind."[3] Consequences will not be short-lived or easily forgotten. Yet, as with natural disasters elsewhere, they will not reverse but most likely will accelerate the social and demographic trends under way. Disasters of this order do not seem to stop social change; instead, they throw it into high gear.[4]

In the case of Miami, several such trends are apparent and have been noted in the preceding chapters. The most important is the incipient progress toward a convergence of some sort between the city's polarized ethnic communities. Cultural and linguistic fragmentation is still dominant, but, as noted above (chapter 9), there are signs of a narrowing distance. The aftermath of the storm can accelerate this process. Two types of poststorm convergences must be carefully distinguished, however. The first is the well-publicized outburst of compassion, solidarity, and neighborliness in the immediate wake of the disaster. Articles in the *Miami Herald* have made much of how class and race barriers came tumbling down in the rush to rebuild half-destroyed neighborhoods and help hundreds of victims.[5]

The new blue-ribbon local committee put together at the initiative of President Bush has been baptized We Will Rebuild and has also focused on the themes of unity and community solidarity.[6] The temporary suspension of ethnic animosities and heightened community spirit is a natural response, given the magnitude of the calamity. It would be risky to bet, however, that such altruistic behavior will be long lived. As things return to normal, established patterns invariably reassert themselves, and with them the social fragmentation and competing outlooks that have been dominant in the past.

There is, however, a more profound process of convergence. It is linked to the "defining" character of the cataclysm, the fact that hereafter the identity of the area will incorporate this experience. As San Francisco was marked by shaking earth and fire in the century's first decade, so have the winds imprinted Miami in its last. To local identities built on the successive and competing images described in the preceding chapters must now be added that of a land regularly ravaged by one of the most fearsome natural forces. The people who inhabit the land will incorporate this element into their outlook, whether they came originally from New York or Havana, or were born in South Florida itself. As in other places similarly afflicted, the sense of identity derived from disaster cuts across ethnic lines.

It is this natural introjection of the experience into people's self-image, rather than any display of immediate solidarity, that can have the greater effect on long-term community building. This is because the new shared identity of formerly segmented groups can create a basis for forging a more unified discourse. The question remains, however, of what direction such a convergence will take, since the process can incorporate, to varying degrees, elements from the competing definitions of the situation prevalent in the past.

Here the evidence is mixed. In an article published in the *Miami Herald* shortly after the disaster, a Florida International University sociologist argues that its demographic consequences will be significant:

South Dade (the area hardest hit by hurricane Andrew) has been one of the few remaining areas of the county with an "Anglo" population majority. It has also been one of the few areas within Dade with affordable suburban housing. Other areas have experienced fast suburban growth. . . . But those are predominantly Hispanic. . . . For "Anglos" choosing to leave the hurricane-stricken zones, the areas that will prove attractive, in terms of housing prices and ethnicity, are not in Dade.[7]

If this analysis is correct, it would mean the acceleration of the process of Latinization of the area, as the outflow of the Anglo population to Ft. Lauderdale and points north is augmented by the South Dade victims of Andrew. This trend would consolidate the political power of the Cuban-American community. At the time of this writing, some changes in this direction, anticipated as the outcome of electoral reapportionment, have already materialized: Lincoln Diaz-Balart, a former state senator, has become the second Cuban-American elected to Congress; the expected increases in Cuban representation to the state legislature have also occurred, to the detriment of Anglo politicians.

Such a trend suggests that the process of convergence will have a strong Latin undertone. *Acculturation-in-reverse* may spearhead the transition to a discourse focused on the city's unique Caribbean roots. Although participation in the political system will inevitably socialize Cubans into the institutions of the American mainstream, their local dominance can influence decisively the pace and character of the convergence process.

Hurricane Andrew also created a powerful countertrend, however. It is perhaps best symbolized by those Charleston policemen directing traffic in devastated South Dade: the aid pouring into Miami came from the rest of the country, not from the Caribbean. Baptist sects set up instant soup kitchens, the U.S. Red Cross and the Salvation Army distributed desperately needed water and clothing, caravans of volunteers came from as far north as Philadelphia and New York, and, a few days after the storm, the U.S. Army was setting up emergency tents for thousands.[8] This outpouring of national solidarity took Miami as by a second storm. It made evident that, whatever its quirks and foibles, it remained firmly an American town. "Miami, U.S.A.," not "Capital of the Caribbean," was the theme under which reconstruction was launched.

Reenergized, the old Anglo leadership took charge of directing the task. That perennial local brahmin, Alvah Chapman, was appointed chairman of the We Will Rebuild Committee, with other Anglo leaders occupying key posts. Ethnic figures were relegated to secondary positions, a fact that prompted Black attorney H. T. Smith, leader of the Black boycott, to remark, "We must have the face of Miami, which is culturally diverse, making and executing the decisions."[9] To be sure, the Cuban-American National Foundation launched a vigorous relief effort, and thousands of Miami Cubans and other Latins contributed funds and worked as volunteers in the affected areas. But there was nothing in the "success story" discourse that could effectively integrate the tragedy and its aftermath. Instead, the themes of voluntarism and solidarity-in-crisis, so close to the core of American culture and so thoroughly practiced over many similar experiences, became dominant. The flattened Miami landscape was an American, not a pan-Caribbean, reality.

The storm made the city even more unique, if that was possible, and simultaneously brought it back into the national mainstream. Cubans and Latins will become increasingly influential, but in the storm's aftermath, it seemed evident that their local hegemony would be securely ensconced in a broader American framework. Undoubtedly, the cadences of Spanish, the sights and sounds of the Caribbean, and the ritual denunciations of Castro and his henchmen will be heard for a long time to come. But none of this will prevent a process of convergence, given renewed impulse and a strong national focus by the natural catastrophe.

Notes

1. Change Without a Blueprint

1. Christopher Marquis and Andres Viglucci, "Some Cuban Exiles Decry Plan to Deport Detainees," *Miami Herald*, November 21, 1987; Doug Struck, "Hostages Set Free, Oakdale Inmates Yield," *Baltimore Sun*, November 30, 1987; "Agreement Signed After Cubans Hear Plea from Bishop," *Baltimore Sun*, November 30, 1987; Dianna Solís and José de Córdoba, "Mariel Firestorm," *Wall Street Journal*, December 1, 1987.

2. Jacob V. Lamar, "A Brightly Colored Tinderbox," *Time*, January 30, 1989; Robert L. Steinback, "For Black Miami, a Sense of Justice," *Miami Herald*, December 8, 1989; Sandra Dibble and Karen Branch, "Colombians Angered by Conviction," *Miami Herald*, December 8, 1989; Christine Evans and Peggy Rogers, "Lozano Gets 7 Years," *Miami Herald*, January 25, 1990; Rachel L. Swarns, "Lozano Wins a Manslaughter Retrial," *Miami Herald*, June 26, 1991.

3. Floyd Hunter, *Community Power Structure* (Chapel Hill: University of North Carolina Press, 1953); Robert A. Dahl, *Who Governs? Democracy and Power in an American City* (New Haven: Yale University Press, 1961); C. Wright Mills, *The Power Elite* (New York: Oxford University Press, 1956); idem, "The Middle Classes in Middle-sized Cities," *American Sociological Review* 11 (October 1946): 520–29. For a succinct review of the literature on American community power, see Charles M. Bonjean and David M. Olson, "Community Leadership: Directions of Research," *Administrative Science Quarterly* 9 (December 1964): 278–300.

4. Harvey Molotch, "The City as a Growth Machine," *American Journal of Sociology* 82 (1976): 309–30; John Logan and Harvey Molotch,

Urban Fortunes: The Political Economy of Place (Berkeley and Los Angeles: University of California Press, 1987).

5. C. Wright Mills and Melville J. Ulmer, "Small Business and Civic Welfare," in U.S. Congress, Senate, *Report of the Smaller War Plants Corporation to the Special Committee to Study Problems of American Small Business*, 79th Cong., 1946, S. Rept. 135. For a critique of Mills's position, see Irvin A. Fowler, "Local Industrial Structures, Economic Power, and Community Welfare," *Social Problems* 6 (Summer 1958): 41–51.

6. W. Lloyd Warner and Paul S. Lunt, *The Status System of a Modern Community* (New Haven: Yale University Press, 1942).

7. W. Lloyd Warner and Leo Srole, *The Social Systems of American Ethnic Groups* (New Haven: Yale University Press, 1945).

8. Nathan Glazer and Daniel P. Moynihan, *Beyond the Melting Pot: The Negroes, Puerto Ricans, Jews, Italians, and Irish of New York City* (Cambridge, Mass.: MIT Press, 1970); Andrew Greeley, *Why Can't They Be Like Us? America's White Ethnic Groups* (New York: E. P. Dutton, 1971).

9. Following the prison takeover, Román led a coalition of Cuban-American political leaders and clergy that lobbied the federal government for leniency as well as careful review of individual appeals. The subsequent slow pace of deportations to Cuba and the release of a number of former prisoners to their families are due to Román's activism.

10. M. Janowitz, ed., *W. I. Thomas on Social Organization and Social Personality* (Chicago: University of Chicago Press, 1969); see also Leon Festinger, *A Theory of Cognitive Dissonance* (Stanford: Stanford University Press, 1957).

11. The statements are drawn from interviews, conducted between 1983 and 1988, with approximately sixty of Miami's most prominent business, political, and religious leaders as a complement to a large survey of the recently arrived immigrant population in the area. Results from this survey have been published in several articles, including Alejandro Portes and Alex Stepick, "Unwelcome Immigrants: The Labor Market Experiences of 1980 (Mariel) Cuban and Haitian Refugees in South Florida," *American Sociological Review* 50 (August 1985): 493–514; and Alejandro Portes, Juan M. Clark, and Robert D. Manning, "After Mariel: A Survey of the Resettlement Experiences of 1980 Cuban Refugees in Miami," *Cuban Studies* 15 (Summer 1985): 35–59.

12. Joan Didion, *Miami* (New York: Simon & Schuster, 1987), 51.

13. David Rieff, *Going to Miami: Exiles, Tourists, and Refugees in the New America* (Boston: Little, Brown, 1987), 164–65.

2. A Year to Remember: Mariel

1. Dianna Solís and José de Córdoba, "Cuban Prison Riots Followed Seven Years of U.S. Ambivalence," *Wall Street Journal*, December 1, 1987.

2. Florida, Department of Health and Rehabilitative Services (DHRS), *Refugees and Entrants in Florida: Background and Current Issues* (Tallahassee: DHRS, March 1982); J. Franklin, *Cuban Foreign Relations: A Chronology, 1959–1982* (New York: Center for Cuban Studies, 1983).

3. Rafael Hernandez and Redi Gomis, "Retrato del Mariel: el ángulo socio-económico," *Cuadernos de nuestra America* 3 (January–June 1986): 138–39.

4. This and other statements presented in this chapter are excerpts from interviews with community leaders conducted during a panel study of Mariel and Haitian refugees in South Florida between 1983 and 1988. Sixty interviews with government officials, entrepreneurs, and religious leaders were completed during this period.

5. Robert L. Bach, Jennifer B. Bach, and Timothy Triplett, "The Flotilla 'Entrants': Latest and Most Controversial," *Cuban Studies* 11 (1981): 29–48; Portes, Clark, and Manning, "After Mariel."

6. Alejandro Portes and Rafael Mozo, "The Political Adaptation Process of Immigrants and Other Refugee Minorities in the United States: A Preliminary Analysis," *International Migration Review* 19 (Spring 1985): 35–63.

7. Cited in Guillermo Martínez, "Mariel Myths Feed Venom Across Nation," *Miami Herald*, November 18, 1982, 31A.

8. Eric Fehrnstrom, "Confession of a Killer," *Boston Herald*, April 17, 1987, 1, 20.

9. A day-by-day account of these events was produced as part of our study of post-1980 immigration to South Florida; see Yohel Camayd-Freixas, *Crisis in Miami*, Report to the Project on "Help-Seeking and Services Use Among Recent Latin American Refugees," conducted by the Sociology Department and School of Public Health, Johns Hopkins University (Boston: Boston Urban Research and Development Group, 1988).

10. Ibid., III-33–48.

11. Ibid., III-37.

12. The vast majority of these businessmen and elected officials, including many of the richest Cubans, were unknown to Miami's Anglos, for whom Cubans generally were simply a mass of foreigners, speaking an unintelligible language and obsessed with their homeland politics. See Alejandro Portes, "The Rise of Ethnicity: Determinants of Ethnic Perceptions Among Cuban Exiles in Miami," *American Sociological Review* 49 (June 1984): 383–97.

13. Charles Whited, "Castro Always Seems to Call the Shots Here," *Miami Herald*, November 24, 1987.

14. "Cuban Success Story: In the United States," *U.S. News & World Report*, March 20, 1967, 104–6; "Flight from Cuba—Castro's Loss is U.S. Gain," *U.S. News & World Report*, May 31, 1971, 74. Similar reports were published in the 1980s, though less frequently than before; see, for example, "Florida's Latin Boom: Hispanics Are the Only Spark in a Somnolent Economy," *Newsweek*, November 11, 1985, 55–56; and Sonia L. Nazario, "After a Long Holdout, Cubans in Miami Take a Role in Miami Politics; Economic Success Spurs Steps to Assimilate," *Wall Street Journal*, June 7, 1983, 1, 23.

15. For descriptions of the broader study and its results, see Portes and Stepick, "Unwelcome Immigrants"; Portes, Clark, and Manning, "After Mariel."

16. Camayd-Freixas, *Crisis in Miami*, III-33.

17. Nathan Glazer, "Ethnic Groups in America: From National Culture to Ideology," in *Freedom and Control in Modern Society*, ed. M. Berger, T. Abel, and C. Page (New York: Van Nostrand, 1954), 158–73; Greeley, *Why Can't They Be Like Us?*; Portes, "Rise of Ethnicity."

18. Frederic Tasker, "Anti-Bilingualism Measure Approved by Dade County," *Miami Herald*, November 5, 1980, 1A, 11A.

19. Rieff, *Going to Miami*, 71.

20. Luis J. Botifoll, *Introducción al futuro de Miami* (Miami: Laurenty, 1988), 3, 10.

21. Sergio Pereira (Assistant County Manager, Dade County), Presentation at conference sponsored by Strategy Research, Miami, May 1981.

3. A Year to Remember: The Riot and the Haitians

1. Cited in Bruce Porter and Marvin Dunn, *The Miami Riot of 1980: Crossing the Bounds* (Lexington, Mass.: D. C. Heath, 1984), 193.

2. Community leaders, both Latin and Black, commented on this to us during fieldwork in Miami between 1983 and 1989. See also Portes, "Rise of Ethnicity."

3. J. E. Buchanan, *Miami: A Chronological and Documentary History, 1513–1977* (New York: Oceana, 1977), 53–57.

4. Field Interview, January 1987.

5. Porter and Dunn, *Miami Riot of 1980*, 195.

6. Metro-Dade County Planning Department, *Profile of the Black Population* (Miami: Research Division, Metro-Dade County Planning Department, 1984), 84.

7. Porter and Dunn, *Miami Riot of 1980*, 195–96. Alejandro Portes, "The Social Origins of the Cuban Enclave Economy of Miami," *Sociological Perspectives* 30 (October 1987): 340–72.

8. Portes, "Social Origins of the Cuban Enclave Economy"; Marvin Dunn and Alex Stepick, "Blacks in Miami," in *Miami Now! Immigration, Ethnicity, and Social Change*, ed. G. J. Grenier and A. Stepick (Gainesville: University Press of Florida, 1992), 41–56.

9. Porter and Dunn, *Miami Riot of 1980*, 196–97. Only 1.4 percent of Miami's Black population owned businesses in 1982. Of the 3,385 Black businesses in the area, only 450 had paid employees. See Max Castro and Timothy Yeaney, *Documenting Dade's Diversity: An Ethnic Audit of Dade County* (Miami: Greater Miami United, January 1989).

10. Cited in Porter and Dunn, *Miami Riot of 1980*, 48.

11. Didion, *Miami*, 41.

12. "Dade Fears Refugee Wave," *Miami Herald*, May 11, 1980.

13. Ibid., 129–30.

14. Ibid., 47–60; Didion, *Miami*, 45.

15. Porter and Dunn, *Miami Riot of 1980*, 60–68.

16. Field interview with head of a major social services agency in Liberty City, 1985.

17. Porter and Dunn, *Miami Riot of 1980*, 68.

18. Stanley Lieberson and Arnold R. Silverman, "The Precipitants and Underlying Conditions of Race Riots," *American Sociological Review* 30 (December 1965): 887–98.

19. See field interviews excerpted in chapter 1. By the time of the Overtown uprising of January 1989, the distinct positions of the Miami Black community had become well articulated. See, for example, Dorothy

Gaiter, "Lozano Verdict Brought Relief and Long-delayed Justice," *Miami Herald*, December 8, 1989, 31A.

20. *Tonton macoutes* is the name given by Haitians to the bands of thugs hired by the successive Duvalier regimes to intimidate the population.

21. This story is an amalgamation of affidavits of Haitian refugees who testified in *Haitian Refugee Center v. Civiletti*, 503 F. Supp. 442 (S.D. Fla 1980), modified *Sub nom. Haitian Refugee Center v. Smith*, 676 F. 2d 1023 (5th Cir. 1982), including especially the case of Odilius Jean. Parts were also derived from Stevan Petrow, "What Did the Haitians Do?" *St. Petersburg Times*, November 11, 1979, 8ff.; and Bruce Keldan, "Tales of the Tonton Macoutes from Haitians Who Fled," *Philadelphia Inquirer*, October 8, 1979, A1, 10A.

22. Alex Stepick, *Haitian Refugees in the U.S.*, Minority Rights Group (MRG) no. 52 (London: MRG, 1986), 11.

23. Alex Stepick and Alejandro Portes, "Flight into Despair: A Profile of Recent Haitian Refugees in South Florida," *International Migration Review* 20 (Summer 1986): 329–50.

24. The combination was sanctioned officially by the creation of the federal Cuban-Haitian Interagency Task Force in mid-1980. This agency is described below.

25. Stepick, *Haitian Refugees*, 14.

26. Task Force on Immigration and Refugee Policy, "Issue Paper—Subject: What Policy Should the United States Adopt with Regard to Foreign Persons Who Enter South Florida Without Visas?" (June 26, 1981), Memorandum to President Reagan from task force established by him March 6, 1981. Subsequently, the policy became formal and legal via U.S. Department of State, "Migrants—Interdiction," Agreement Between the United States of America and Haiti, Effected by Exchange of Notes, Signed at Port-au-Prince, September 23, 1981, Treaties and Other International Acts Series, 10241, pursuant to PL 89–497, approved July 8, 1966 (80 Sta. 271; 1 U.S.C. 113).

27. Stepick, *Haitian Refugees*, 14–15.

28. John Silva, "Court Told of Living Death in Haitian Prison," *Miami News*, April 9, 1980, 4A.

29. Fred Grimm and Ellen Bartlett, "Political Heavyweights Bring Bout Here," *Miami Herald*, March 9, 1980, 1B, 7B.

30. Kathy Sawyer, "Refugee Policy Draws Fire in Hearing," *Washington Post*, May 13, 1980, A6.

31. In December 1980, the task force was moved to the Department of Health and Human Services. Its first coordinator was Ambassador Victor Palmieri. See White House, "New Cuban-Haitian Plan," *Fact Sheet #114* (Washington, D.C., July 1980).

32. The above information comes from field observation and interviews conducted with Haitian community leaders as part of the Cuban/Haitian immigration project, June–August 1983. Informants included Mr. Yves Savain, then head of the Haitian Task Force; the Reverend Gerard Jean-Juste, director of the Haitian Refugee Center; and officials of HACAD.

33. See Fredric Tasker, "Dade Neighborhoods Stay Segregated as Residents Seek American Dream," *Miami Herald*, November 1, 1982, D1; "Miami: America's Casablanca," *Newsweek*, January 25, 1988.

34. Field interview conducted as part of the Cuban/Haitian immigration project, August 1983.

35. This sample is statistically representative of adult Haitians arriving between 1980 and 1982 and settling in the principal areas of Haitian concentration in South Florida. The methodology and initial results of the survey are summarized in Stepick and Portes, "Flight into Despair"; and in Portes and Stepick, "Unwelcome Immigrants."

36. Stepick and Portes, "Flight into Despair"; Portes and Stepick, "Unwelcome Immigrants."

37. Camayd-Freixas, *Crisis in Miami*, chaps. 5 and 6.

4. The Early Years

1. Polly Redford, *Billion-Dollar Sandbar: A Biography of Miami Beach* (New York: E. P. Dutton, 1970), chap. 2.

2. Cited in Howard Kleinberg, "A Wistful Eye Back to Young Coconut Grove," *Miami Herald*, March 6, 1990.

3. Marjory S. Douglas, *Florida, the Long Frontier* (New York: Harper & Row, 1967), 147–49.

4. Helen Muir, *Miami, U.S.A.* (Miami: Pickering Press, 1990), 47–53.

5. Cited in Kleinberg, "A Wistful Eye."

6. Douglas, *Florida*, 47–48; William R. Gillaspie, "Ponce de Leon," in *Encyclopedia of World Biography*, vol. 8 (New York: McGraw-Hill, 1973), 521–22.

7. Howard Kleinberg, "Ponce de Leon's Landing in Chequescha (Miami), Fla.," *Miami Herald*, March 22, 1990.

8. Douglas, *Florida*, 49–50.

9. Ibid., 51–53.

10. William R. Gillaspie, "De Soto," in *Encyclopedia of World Biography*, vol. 3 (New York: McGraw-Hill, 1973), 352–53; "Soto, Hernando de," *New Encyclopaedia Britannica*, 15th ed. (Chicago: Encyclopaedia Britannica, 1989), 11:23; Emil Ludwig, *Biografía de una isla* (i.e., Cuba) (Mexico City: Editorial Centauro, 1948), 75–78.

11. Gillaspie, "De Soto."

12. One other colonizing effort occurred in 1558–61, led by Don Tristán de Luna y Arellano who, with a party of 1,500, established a small settlement on Pensacola Bay in the Florida panhandle. It failed, however, and on September 23, 1561, Philip II issued a cedula barring further colonizing efforts in Forida. See Richard B. Morris, ed., *Encyclopedia of American History* (New York: Harper & Row, 1976), 59.

13. "St. Augustine," in *The Columbia Lippincott Gazetteer of the World*, ed. L. E. Seltzer (New York: Columbia University Press, 1962), 1627; Douglas, *Florida*, 69–70.

14. Douglas, *Florida*, 75–80.

15. Ibid., 86–90; "St. Augustine."

16. "St. Augustine"; T. Walter Wallbank and Alastair M. Taylor, *Civilization, Past and Present*, 4th ed., vol. 2 (Chicago: Scott, Foresman, 1961), 36–37; A. Malet and J. Isaac, *Los tiempos modernos* (Mexico City: Editora Nacional, 1961), 278–79.

17. Douglas, *Florida*, 100–103; Luis J. Botifoll, *The Conspiracy of Silence: Hispanics' Vital Role in the American Revolution* (Miami: Laurenty, 1986), 4–5.

18. Wallbank and Taylor, *Civilization*, 105–11; Malet and Isaac, *Los tiempos modernos*, 283–86.

19. Douglas, *Florida*, 105. Douglas traces the word *cimarrón* to Jamaica, although it is a Spanish term imported originally from Cuba.

20. Ibid., 129. Gloria Jahoda, *Florida: A Bicentennial History* (New York: W. W. Norton, 1976), 47.

21. T. D. Allman, *Miami: City of the Future* (New York: Atlantic Monthly Press, 1987), 148; Jahoda, *Florida*, 54.

22. Douglas, *Florida*, 130–32.

23. Allman, *Miami*, 152–53. Jahoda, *Florida*.

24. Douglas, *Florida*, 146.

25. Ibid., 146–47.

26. Allman, *Miami*, 153; Jahoda, *Florida*, 143, 158.

27. Muir, *Miami, U.S.A.*, 15.

28. Douglas, *Florida*, 148, 165.

29. V. O. Key, *Southern Politics* (New York: Alfred A. Knopf, 1950), 86.

30. Douglas, *Florida*, 143–69.

31. Key, *Southern Politics*, 82–83.

32. Redford, *Billion-Dollar Sandbar*, 27.

33. Ibid., chap. 2; Muir, *Miami, U.S.A.*, 55–65.

34. Edward Sofen, *The Miami Metropolitan Experiment* (Bloomington: Indiana University Press, 1963), 11.

35. Paul S. George, "Colored Town: Miami's Black Community, 1896–1930," *Florida Historical Quarterly* 16 (April 1978): 432–47; Redford, *Billion-Dollar Sandbar*, chaps. 4, 5, 8; Douglas, *Florida*, 251.

36. Redford, *Billion-Dollar Sandbar*, chap. 4; Rieff, *Going to Miami*, 6.

37. Rieff, *Going to Miami*; Redford, *Billion-Dollar Sandbar*, chaps. 5–8, 20.

38. Redford, *Billion-Dollar Sandbar*, 95.

39. Rieff, *Going to Miami*, 10–11; Sofen, *Miami Metropolitan Experiment*, 13.

40. Allman, *Miami*, 170; Muir, *Miami, U.S.A.*, 47–65; Douglas, *Florida*, 244.

41. Douglas, *Florida*, 244–45.

42. Rieff, *Going to Miami*, 10.

43. Allman, *Miami*, 207–10; Redford, *Billion-Dollar Sandbar*, 149–50.

44. Redford, *Billion-Dollar Sandbar*; Allman, *Miami*, 219–21.

45. Rieff, *Going to Miami*, chap. 1; Muir, *Miami, U.S.A.*, 131–42.

46. Redford, *Billion-Dollar Sandbar*, 148.

47. Karl Marx, *The Eighteenth Brumaire of Napoleon Bonaparte* (New York: International Publishers, 1963).

48. Paul S. George, "Policing Miami's Black Community, 1896–1930," *Florida Historical Quarterly* 17 (April 1979): 434–50.

49. George, "Colored Town," 444.

50. Ibid.

51. Quoted in ibid., 441

52. Porter and Dunn, *Miami Riot of 1980*, 12.

53. Ibid., 10.

54. Cited in Allman, *Miami*, 156.

55. Statement of a Black Episcopal pastor, cited in Porter and Dunn, *Miami Riot of 1980*, 193.

56. George, "Colored Town," 440.

57. Ibid., pp. 438–40.

58. Porter and Dunn, *Miami Riot of 1980*, 9–13.

59. Raymond A. Mohl, "Trouble in Paradise: Race and Housing in Miami During the New Deal Era," *Prologue* 8 (Spring 1987): 7–20.

60. Ibid., 13.

61. George, "Policing Miami's Black Community."

62. Redford, *Billion-Dollar Sandbar*, chap. 14; Sofen, *Miami Metropolitan Experiment*, 14–15; Allman, *Miami*, 211.

63. Allman, *Miami*, 224–26; Sofen, *Miami Metropolitan Experiment*.

64. Sofen, *Miami Metropolitan Experiment*, 16; Metro-Dade Planning Department, selected tabulations from the 1990 Census made available to the authors.

65. Key, *Southern Politics*, 87.

66. Ibid., 85.

67. Ibid.; Sofen, *Miami Metropolitan Experiment*, 3–10.

68. Sofen, *Miami Metropolitan Experiment*, 99.

69. Allman, *Miami*, 210–15; Muir, *Miami, U.S.A.*, 127, 218.

70. Redford, *Billion-Dollar Sandbar*, 214.

71. Ibid.; Rieff, *Going to Miami*, 26; Miami Design and Preservation League, "Miami Beach Architecture" (1989).

72. Sofen, *Miami Metropolitan Experiment*, 8–10, 216–17.

73. Ibid., 23.

74. Ibid., 34–35.

75. Ibid., chaps. 4, 7.

76. Ibid., 71; Redford, *Billion-Dollar Sandbar*, chap. 1.

77. Key, *Southern Politics*, 103–4; Samuel Proctor, *Napoleon Bonaparte Broward, Florida's Fighting Democrat* (Gainesville: University of Florida Press, 1950).

78. Allman, *Miami*, 223–27; Sofen, *Miami Metropolitan Experiment*, 216–17.

5. Enter the Cubans

1. The foregoing information is based on the authors' field work. Information on the construction of the San Carlos was obtained on site.

2. Muir, *Miami, U.S.A.*, 27.

3. Hugh Thomas, *Cuba: The Pursuit of Freedom* (New York: Harper & Row, 1971), 305.

4. Ibid.

5. Muir, *Miami, U.S.A.*, 47–49.

6. Proctor, *Napoleon Bonaparte Broward*, 97–99.

7. Ibid., 103–11.

8. Ibid., 114.

9. Ibid., 124.

10. Ibid., 131–32.

11. Muir, *Miami, U.S.A.*, 59–62; Proctor, *Napoleon Bonaparte Broward*, 117.

12. Thomas, *Cuba*, 356–66; Proctor, *Napoleon Bonaparte Broward*, 135–37.

13. Thomas, *Cuba*, 328–37; Muir, *Miami, U.S.A.*, 61; Redford, *Billion-Dollar Sandbar*, 30.

14. Muir, *Miami, U.S.A.*, 67–69; George, "Policing Miami's Black Community, 1896–1930," 435.

15. Thomas, *Cuba*, 453–54.

16. Sidney W. Mintz, "The Industrialization of Sugar Production and Its Relationship to Social and Economic Change," in *Background to Revolution: The Development of Modern Cuba*, ed. R. F. Smith (New York: Alfred A. Knopf, 1966), 178.

17. Redford, *Billion-Dollar Sandbar*, 249, 269.

18. Thomas, *Cuba*.

19. Jorge Garcia Montes and Antonio Alonso Dávila, *Historia del Partido Comunista de Cuba* (Miami: Ediciones Universal, 1970), chap. 6; Justo Carrillo, *Cuba 1933: estudiantes, yankis y soldados* (Miami: Institute of Ibero-American Studies, University of Miami, 1985), 37–50.

20. Carrillo, *Cuba 1933*, 587.

21. Thomas, *Cuba*, 625.

22. Muir, *Miami, U.S.A.*, 173–75; Redford, *Billion-Dollar Sandbar*, 183–91; Mohl, "Trouble in Paradise."

23. Fulgencio Batista, *Respuesta* (Mexico City: Impresora Manuel Leon Sánchez, 1960), 43.

24. Not only Prío but many other major Cuban political figures as well resided in Miami during the struggle against Batista. Jose Miró Cardona, prime minister–designate of the first revolutionary government, was awakened in his Miami home on January 1, 1959, with the news of Batista's fall and had to be flown to Oriente Province for the swear-in ceremony. See Andrés Suarez, *Cuba: Castroism and Communism, 1959–1966* (Cambridge, Mass.: MIT Press, 1967), 30.

25. Thomas, *Cuba*, 876.

26. Suarez, *Cuba*, 23; Thomas, *Cuba*, 891.

27. Thomas, *Cuba*, 968–69.

28. Suarez, *Cuba*, 25, 31; Thomas, *Cuba*, 978–79.

29. Fidel Castro, *Manifesto of the Sierra Maestra*, cited in ibid., 969.

30. In January 1958, the U.S. yacht *Corinthia* left Miami and landed revolutionaries on the north coast of Camaguey Province; they eventually succeeded in establishing a "second front" of guerrilla warfare. See Thomas, *Cuba*, 978–79.

31. William Wieland, cited in ibid., 977.

32. Field interviews with former Cuban government officials in 1983–84. Their statements agreed independently on the frequency and habitual character of these trips.

33. For comparison on the difficulties of adaptation confronted by other recent refugee groups, see Alejandro Portes and Rubén G. Rumbaut, "A Foreign World: Immigration, Mental Health, and Acculturation," in *Immigrant America: A Portrait* (Berkeley and Los Angeles: University of California Press, 1990).

34. Field interviews, Miami immigration project, 1984.

35. Muir, *Miami, U.S.A.*, 239–40.

36. Alejandro Portes and Robert L. Bach, *Latin Journey: Cuban and Mexican Immigrants in the United States* (Berkeley: University of California Press, 1985), 84–90.

37. Ibid.

38. John F. Thomas and Earl E. Huyck, "Resettlement of Cuban Refugees in the United States" (Paper presented at the meetings of the American Sociological Association, San Francisco, August 1967).

39. Portes and Bach, *Latin Journey*, 86.

40. Alejandro Portes, Juan M. Clark, and Robert L. Bach, "The New Wave: A Statistical Profile of Recent Cuban Exiles to the United States," *Cuban Studies* 7 (January 1977): tables 4–7.

41. Thomas and Huyck, "Resettlement of Cuban Refugees."

42. Sergio Diaz-Briquets and Lisandro Perez, "Cuba: The Demography of Revolution," *Population Bulletin* 36 (April 1981): 2–41.

43. Ibid.

44. See Michael Piore, *Birds of Passage: Migrant Labor and Industrial Societies* (New York: Cambridge University Press, 1979); and Portes and Bach, *Latin Journey*, 7–10.

45. Juan M. Clark, Jose I. Lasage, and Rose S. Reque, *The 1980 Mariel Exodus: An Assessment and Prospect* (Washington, D.C.: Council for Inter-American Security, 1981); and Portes and Stepick, "Unwelcome Immigrants."

46. The episode, a true story, took place during preliminary field work for a study on post-1970 Cuban emigration and its adaptation to U.S. society. Final results of this study are presented in Portes and Bach, *Latin Journey*.

47. Carlos Forment, "Political Practice and the Rise of an Ethnic Enclave: The Cuban-American Case, 1959–1979," *Theory and Society* 18 (1989): 47–81.

48. The expression was first used by David Rieff; see his *Going to Miami*.

6. How the Enclave Was Built

1. "Ascenso de IMC despertó controversia," *El Miami Herald*, March 28, 1986, 9; "Recarey pagó millones a cabilderos," *El Nuevo Herald*, December 20, 1987, 6A. The present section is based on these two sources.

2. *Miami Herald*, December 20, 1987.

3. Didion, *Miami*, 90–91.

4. Ibid., 83, 86–98.

5. Ivan Light, "Immigrant and Ethnic Enterprise in North America," *Ethnic and Racial Studies* 7 (April 1984): 195–216; Portes, "Social Origins of the Cuban Enclave Economy."

6. Field interview, January 15, 1986.

7. Ibid.

8. Luis J. Botifoll, "How Miami's New Image Was Created," Occasional Paper no. 1985-1, Institute of Inter-American Studies, University of Miami, 1985, 13.

9. Ibid.; and field interview with officials of the Latin Builders Association in Miami, January 21, 1986.

10. See Forment, "Political Practice and the Rise of an Ethnic Enclave," 47. This article maintains that CIA ties played a pivotal role in the rise of the first Cuban enterprises in Miami.

11. "Florida's Latin Boom."

12. Dory Owens, "Her Faith in Hispanics Paid Off Big," *Miami Herald*, "Profile" sec., October 1, 1988.

13. Field interview with Diego R. Suarez, January 30, 1986; cited with permission.

14. Ivan Light, "Asian Enterprise in America: Chinese, Japanese, and Koreans in Small Business," in *Self-Help in Urban America*, ed. S. Cummings (New York: Kennikat Press, 1980), 33–57.

15. Field interview in Miami, February 7, 1989.

16. Field interview in Miami, January 14, 1987.

17. Field interview in Hialeah, August 15, 1984.

18. Field interview, January 14, 1987.

19. Field interviews in Miami, January 30, 1986, and January 22, 1991; Portes, "Social Origins of the Cuban Enclave Economy."

20. Portes, "Social Origins of the Cuban Enclave Economy"; U.S. Bureau of the Census, *Survey of Minority-owned Business Enterprises, 1977/Hispanic* (Washington, D.C.: U.S. Department of Commerce, 1980).

21. Field interviews with Cuban-American bankers, January 2, 21, 1986; February 7, 1989; February 12, 1991; also Owens, "Her Faith in Hispanics Paid Off."

22. Clifford Geertz, *Peddlers and Princes* (Chicago: University of Chicago Press, 1963), 123.

23. Field interviews with garment manufacturer, January 14, 1987; owner of restaurants and liquor shops, January 9, 1986; executives of Inter-American Transport, January 30, 1986; and local union organizer, August 15, 1984.

24. Heberto Padilla, "Miami: el mundo en blanco y negro," *El Miami Herald*, January 18, 1986, 5.

25. Joanna Wragg, "The Boycott, Blacks, and Cubans," *Miami Herald*, December 30, 1990, 2C; Sergio Lopez-Miro, "Where the 'Cuban' Ends and the 'American' Begins," *Miami Herald*, February 1, 1990.

26. Field interview, January 14, 1987.

27. "The Cuban-American Community and the Miami Herald" (paid political announcement), *Miami Herald*, October 19, 1987, 11A.

28. The statement in Spanish is usually read by WQBA news director Tomas Garcia Fusté; field visits, 1989–90.

29. Forment, "Political Practice and the Rise of an Ethnic Enclave."

30. Ibid. Also field interviews with Cuban-American industrialist, January 14, 1987; banker, February 7, 1987; and community organizer, December 22, 1987.

31. "Deportar a un ciudadano no existe," *El Nuevo Herald*, January 10, 1988, 2A.

32. Wragg, "The Boycott, Blacks, and Cubans."

33. "The Quiet Riot," *New Times*, September 26–October 2, 1990, 12–22.

34. See Richard F. Fagen, Richard A. Brody, and Thomas J. O'Leary, *Cubans in Exile: Disaffection and the Revolution* (Stanford: Stanford University Press, 1968), chaps. 3, 7.

35. Herbert Matthews, *Revolution in Cuba* (New York: Charles Scribner's Sons, 1975), 195–200; Herminio Portell-Vila, *Nueva historia de la República de Cuba* (Miami: La Moderna Poesia, 1989), 793–806.

36. Richard E. Welch, *Response to Revolution: The United States and the Cuban Revolution, 1959–1961* (Chapel Hill: University of North Carolina Press, 1985), 81–84; Forment, "Political Practice and the Rise of an Ethnic Enclave."

37. See Allman, *Miami*, chap. 14; Didion, *Miami*, chap. 7.

38. Forment, "Political Practice and the Rise of an Ethnic Enclave," 65.

39. Interview with Monsignor Walsh, Director of Catholic Community Services of the Archdiocese of Miami, January 12, 1987; cited with permission.

40. Portes and Bach, *Latin Journey*, tables 61, 65.

41. Ibid., tables 59, 60, 63, 64, 68.

42. Ibid., table 70.

43. U.S. Bureau of the Census, *Survey of Minority-owned Business Enterprises, 1987/Hispanics* (Washington, D.C.: U.S. Department of Commerce, 1991), tables C, D, and 6.

44. Field interview in Miami, May 3, 1981.

45. Field interviews with SALAD leaders, May 3 and June 16, 1981.

46. Luis J. Botifoll, Chairman of the Republic National Bank, manuscript, 1990.

47. Field interview with José (Pepe) Hernandez, President of CANF, February 14, 1991; cited with permission.

7. A Repeat Performance?
The Nicaraguan Exodus

1. Christopher Marquis, "Miami Grapples with Influx of Nicaraguans," *Miami Herald*, December 15, 1988, 1A.

2. Christopher Marquis and Frank Cerabino, "Dade on Edge over Nicaraguans," *Miami Herald*, January 14, 1989, 1A.

3. Dave Von Drehle and Christopher Marquis, "Nicaraguan Stream into Miami; Many Find They Must Fend for Themselves," *Miami Herald*, January 13, 1989, 1A.

4. Christopher Marquis, "Nicaraguan Exile Community Forges New Life in S. Florida," *Miami Herald*, July 16, 1989, 1A.

5. Christopher Marquis, "Refugees Find Exiles Thriving," *Miami Herald*, January 22, 1989, 1B.

6. Ana Veciana-Suarez and Sandra Dibble, "Miami's Nicaraguans: Remaking Their Lives" (pt. 1 of 2 pts.), *Miami Herald*, September 13, 1987, 1G.

7. Marquis, "Nicaraguan Exile Community Forges New Life."

8. Barbara Gutierrez, "We're 'Invisible' Exiles, Nicaraguans Say," *Miami Herald*, February 5, 1984, 1B.

9. Veciana-Suarez and Dibble, "Miami's Nicaraguans."

10. Ibid.

11. Ana Veciana-Suarez, "Nicaraguan Exiles Begin to Climb the Ladder," *Miami Herald*, March 28, 1983, 10BM.

12. "Exiled Nicaraguans Reflect," *Miami Herald*, July 16, 1989, 11A.

13. Carlos Briceno, "Nicaraguan Plea for 'Sanctuary' Doubles in Year," *Miami Herald*, February 5, 1985, 1D.

14. Gutierrez, "We're 'Invisible.' "

15. Jaime Suchlicki and Arturo Cruz, "The Impact of Nicaraguans in Miami: The Nicaraguan Exodus to Miami Under the Sandinistas, and the Future Outlook Following Their Electoral Defeat," Study for the City Manager of Miami prepared by the Institute of Interamerican Studies, University of Miami, March 1990.

16. Sandra Dibble, "Nicaraguan Exiles Find Homes in Little Havana," *Miami Herald*, February 10, 1986, 2B; Gutierrez, "We're 'Invisible.' "

17. Gutierrez, "We're 'Invisible' "; Dibble, "Nicaraguan Exiles Find Homes"; Veciana-Suarez and Dibble, "Miami's Nicaraguans"; Rodrigo Lazo, "There Is So Little Money, but There Is Peace of Mind," *Miami Herald*, December 25, 1989, 2D.

18. Veciana-Suarez and Dibble, "Miami's Nicaraguans."

19. Increased international competition in the 1980s also affected the industry as it began to contract for the first time, lessening demand for workers.

20. Interview with Carpenters' Union organizer, Miami, June 9, 1988.

21. Karen Branch, "Immigrants Jam Street Corner, Hoping for a Job," *Miami Herald*, March 15, 1989, 1B.

22. Rodrigo Lazo, "Without Work Permit, Day Jobs Sustain Him," *Miami Herald*, December 25, 1989, 2D.

23. Rodrigo Lazo, "A Year Later, Panacea Turns to Struggle for Nicaraguans," *Miami Herald*, December 25, 1989, 1D.

24. "Exiled Nicaraguans Reflect."

25. Quoted in Alfonso Chardy, "Much of Blame for Influx Put on Failed Reagan Policy," *Miami Herald*, January 22, 1989, 16A.

26. Sandi Wisenberg, "An Unlikely Champion," *Miami Herald*, April 26, 1985, 1C. At the same time, barely over fifty Nicaraguans were

deported and fewer than five hundred who faced deportation left voluntarily; see Briceno, "Nicaraguan Plea for Sanctuary."

27. Fabiola Santiago and Barbara Gutierrez, "Dade's Little Managua: Bastion of Uncertainty," *Miami Herald*, July 19, 1984, 16A.

28. Sandra Dibble, "Nicaraguans in Miami: Living in Limbo, Most Refugees Denied Work Permits, Welfare," *Miami Herald*, December 23, 1985, 1A.

29. Yves Colon, "State-INS Plan Aims to Take away Aliens' Incentives to Stay," *Miami Herald*, December 26, 1984, 1D.

30. "U.S. Official Joins Celebration of Nicaragua's Independence," *Miami Herald*, September 10, 1986, 2B.

31. Fabiola Santiago, "Dinner for INS Chief to Fund Contra Lobby," *Miami Herald*, June 27, 1985, 1D.

32. Sandra Dibble, "INS Halts Deportation of Nicaraguan Aliens," *Miami Herald*, April 11, 1986, 1A.

33. "At Last, Work Permits," *Miami Herald*, July 10, 1987, 24A. Meese's directive was based on a 1986 Supreme Court ruling that loosened standards for granting political asylum, itself based on a provision of the Refugee Act of 1980, which states that a refugee must show a "well-founded fear of persecution" to be granted asylum. Administration officials had interpreted that clause to mean that refugees must prove "a clear probability" of persecution if they returned to their home country. But the Supreme Court ruling relaxed the standard by ruling that asylum claims are valid if "persecution is a reasonable possibility" (*INS v. Cardoza-Fonseca*). Even though the court decision on asylum applied to all refugees, Meese specifically ordered INS to halt deportation of Nicaraguans from the United States. He made no mention of other groups, however, such as Salvadorans and Haitians. See Tina Montalvo, "Nicaraguans Are Only Immigrants Benefitting from New Asylum Aid," *Miami Herald*, September 11, 1987. 6C.

34. R. A. Zaldívar, "Vague Laws Spur Refugee Movements," *Miami Herald*, January 15, 1989, 1A; Richard Wallace, "Nicaraguans Jam INS Offices for Work Papers," *Miami Herald*, August 23, 1987, 1B; Tina Montalvo, "Job Permits Going Fast at INS Offices; 10,200 Nicaraguans Processed in 4 Days," *Miami Herald*, September 6, 1987, 1B.

35. Rodrigo Lazo, "Lacking Aid, Immigrants Wait to Learn," *Miami Herald*, October 12, 1988, 1B.

36. Christopher Marquis, "In Miami, Confusion Reigns for Applicants," *Miami Herald*, December 17, 1988, 1A.

37. David Hancock, "U.S. Denies Policy Shift on Handling Nicaraguans," *Miami Herald*, December 15, 1988, 1D.

38. Zaldívar, "Vague Laws Spur Refugee Movements"; Chardy, "Much of Blame for Influx Put on Failed Reagan Policy"; Marquis, "Nicaraguan Exile Community Forges New Life."

39. Christopher Marquis, "Many Nicaraguans Reject Call to Go Home," *Miami Herald*, April 3, 1989, 1B.

40. Michael Browning, "Antibilingual Backers Celebrate Early," *Miami Herald*, November 5, 1980, 1B.

41. "Nicaraguan Refugees: How the Community Feels," *Miami Herald*, January 20, 1989, 24A.

42. Luis Feldstein Soto, "Nicaraguan Influx Strains Schools, Services," *Miami Herald*, July 5, 1987, 2B.

43. Ibid.; Richard J. Feinstein, "Why Public Hospitals Are Ailing," *Miami Herald*, February 10, 1985, 3E; Christopher Marquis, "Dade Unprepared for Refugee Influx," *Miami Herald*, October 23, 1988, 1A; Charles Whited, "Washington Is Guilty of Big, Fat Blunder over Refugees," *Miami Herald*, January 14, 1989, 1B; Marquis, "Nicaraguan Exile Community Forges New Life."

44. Quoted in Sandra Dibble, "Immigration Debate Erupts," *Miami Herald*, December 22, 1988, 1C.

45. Ibid. Of course, there were some who still ignored the newest arrivals in their city. During the 1988–89 Nicaraguan refugee crisis and just before Miami's hosting of the Super Bowl, Tom Ferguson, president of the Beacon Council, a group of businessmen devoted to promoting Miami's image, declared: "I hate to say it, but because of the Super Bowl, people's energies are focused in another direction now."

46. Ibid.

47. "How the Community Is Responding," *Miami Herald*, January 13, 1989, 19A.

48. Geoffrey Biddulph, "Blacks Feel Left Out as Refugees Get Jobs," *Miami Herald*, January 20, 1989, 1D.

49. Bea Hines, "Overtown Feels Pain, Frustration," *Miami Herald*, January 18, 1989, 1A.

50. Marquis, "Miami Grapples with Influx."

51. Ibid.

52. Ibid.

53. Joe Starita, "Nicaraguans Stream into Miami Stadium, an Unlikely Refuge," *Miami Herald*, January 13, 1989, 1A.

54. "How the Community Is Responding."

55. Rodrigo Lazo, "Mass Offers Ray of Hope for Refugees," *Miami Herald*, December 26, 1988, 1B.

56. Richard Capen, "Hand Is Out to the Tempest-tossed," *Miami Herald*, January 1, 1989, 3C; Liz Balmaseda, "The New Nicaragua," *Miami Herald*, February 5, 1989, 1–6G.

57. Biddulph, "Blacks Feel Left Out."

58. Fred Strasser, "Nicaraguans Share Fight for Freedom at Cubans' Rally," *Miami Herald*, May 21, 1984, 1B.

59. Barbara Gutierrez, "Supplies to Be Ferried to Refugees," *Miami Herald*, June 26, 1983, 4B.

60. Barbara Gutierrez, "Cubans Hold Marathon to Raise Money for Nicaraguan Guerrillas," *Miami Herald*, August 1, 1983, 3B. Over four months later the aid, however, was still undelivered; see "Aid for Rebels Undelivered," *Miami Herald*, April 29, 1984, 6B.

61. Sandra Dibble, "Nicaraguan Cardinal Brings Peace Message," *Miami Herald*, June 14, 1985, 1A; Lourdes Meluza, "Spanish Radio Marathon to Raise Nicaraguan Aid Funds," *Miami Herald*, June 14, 1985, 2C. The Cuban American radio stations conduct marathons for a variety of causes, most related to the Latin community and a good number concerned specifically with anticommunism; see Sandra Dibble, "Latin Listeners Open Hearts to Airwave Appeals," *Miami Herald*, December 15, 1985, 1A.

62. Strasser, "Nicaraguans Share Fight for Freedom."

63. Fabiola Santiago, "$100,000 Fund to Pay Tuition for 100 Exiles," *Miami Herald*, January 9, 1985, 6B.

64. Veciana-Suarez, "Nicaraguan Exiles Begin to Climb the Ladder"; Ben Barber, "Open Three: Enclave for Exiles," *Miami Herald*, "Neighbors S.E." sec., December 29, 1983, 14.

65. Lawrence Josephs, "Ranchos Carries on Tradition," *Miami Herald*, "Neighbors S.E." sec., July 7, 1983, 31.

66. Veciana-Suarez, "Nicaraguan Exiles Begin to Climb the Ladder."

67. Veciana-Suarez and Dibble, "Miami's Nicaraguans."

68. Ibid.

69. Ibid.

70. Karen Branch, "Nicaraguan Culture: Alive and Growing in Dade," *Miami Herald*, "Neighbors" sec., May 25, 1989, 20.

71. Karen Branch, "Nicaraguans Try to Help Their Own," *Miami Herald*, "Neighbors Kendall" sec., June 4, 1989, 10.

72. Veciana-Suarez and Dibble, "Miami's Nicaraguans."

73. Ibid.

74. Branch, "Nicaraguan Culture."

75. Ibid.

76. Santiago and Gutierrez, "Dade's Little Managua," 16A; Sandra Dibble, "Nicaraguans Lobbying to Stay in U.S. Legally, *Miami Herald*, August 15, 1985, 2D; Jay Gayoso, "Nicaraguan Flights for Refugees' Aid," *Miami Herald*, "Neighbors S.E." sec., January 18, 1987, 16; idem, "Battle Unites Nicaraguan Refugees," *Miami Herald*, "Neighbors S.E." sec., February 8, 1987, 3; Karen Branch, "Nicaraguan Exile Groups Unite in Appeal to Mack," *Miami Herald*, July 1, 1989, 3B.

77. Santiago and Gutierrez, "Dade's Little Managua."

78. "Nicaraguan Exiles Seek Overall Leader," *Miami Herald*, September 12, 1989, 3B.

79. Marquis, "Refugees Find Exiles Thriving."

80. "Immigration: How to Control It; A Legal Limbo" (5th of a series), *Miami Herald*, December 30, 1983, 28A.

81. "The Cuban-American Community and the Miami Herald," *Miami Herald*, October 19, 1987, 11A.

82. "At Last, Work Permits."

83. "Mercy for Refugees," *Miami Herald*, June 26, 1988, 2C.

84. "Nicaraguan Exodus," *Miami Herald*, October 20, 1988, 24A.

85. "Immoral Policy," *Miami Herald*, December 17, 1988, 34A.

86. "Room at the Infield," *Miami Herald*, December 25, 1988, 2C.

87. Whited, "Washington Is Guilty of Big, Fat Blunder."

8. Lost in the Fray: Miami's
Black Minorities

1. Scott Kraft and Barry Bearak, "After Miami, Mandela Finds Hero's Welcome in Detroit," *Los Angeles Times*, June 29, 1990, A18–19.

2. Elinor Burkett and Sharony Andrews, "Rhythms of African Pride Pulsate in Miami Streets," *Miami Herald*, June 29, 1990, 13A.

3. Kraft and Bearak, "After Miami, Mandela Finds Hero's Welcome."

4. Kimberly Crockett, Elinor Burkett, and Karen Branch, "Grassroots Welcome Counters Official Snub," *Miami Herald*, June 29, 1990, 1A, 12A. The Black commissioner subsequently did go to the convention to greet Mandela. Unfortunately, Mandela was late, and the commissioner had to leave before Mandela arrived.

5. Carl Goldfarb, "Mandela's Visit Prompts Rerun of Old Ethnic Battles," *Miami Herald*, July 1, 1990, 1B, 4B.

6. Carl Goldfarb, "Mandela Backers, Critics Brace for Momentous Visit," *Miami Herald*, June 28, 1990, 4A, 4B.

7. Margaria Fichtner, "Still Far to Go, Sisters Who Led Sit-ins in Sixties Still Seek Dignity. 'Isn't That Ridiculous?' " *Miami Herald*, July 3, 1990, 1C, 2C.

8. Charles Strouse and David Hancock, "1,000 Haitians Trap Storeowner," *Miami Herald*, July 1, 1990, 1B, 2B. It is impossible to assign responsibility in this incident. The Haitian customer apparently had a police record for violence, while the Cuban employee had a reputation for being surly and at times verbally abusive of customers.

9. Kimberly Crockett, David Hancock, and Carlos Harrison, "Police Crush Haitian Protest," *Miami Herald*, July 6, 1990, 1A, 12A.

10. William J. Wilson, "The Underclass: Issues, Perspectives, and Public Policy," *Annals of the American Academy of Political and Social Sciences* 516 (January 1989): 182–92; Carole Marks, "The Urban Underclass," *Annual Review of Sociology* 17 (1991): 445–66.

11. See Martin M. Marger, *Race and Ethnic Relations* (Belmont, Calif.: Wadsworth, 1991), 5. Marger starts his textbook with the story of these repeated incidents.

12. Field interview, January 8, 1987.

13. Gail Epstein, "Contracts Still Scarce for Blacks," *Miami Herald*, September 29, 1991, 1B, 3B.

14. Joint Center for Environmental and Urban Problems, *An Evaluation of Redevelopment in Overtown* (Miami: Florida International University, October 1991), 3 and 9 (table 1).

15. Interviews with Professor Rick Tardanico and Kevin Yelvington of Florida International University, who conducted research for the Joint Center for Environmental and Urban Problems; see ibid.

16. Epstein, "Contracts Still Scarce."

17. Andres Viglucci, "Liberty City Rises like the Phoenix; Group Accomplishes Change Few Envisioned," *Miami Herald*, July 22, 1990, 1B, 7B.

18. Heather Dewar and Mike Ward, "Teele: Jobs Would Heal Miami's Woes," *Miami News*, October 16, 1987, 1A, 7A.

19. Kimberly Crockett and Patrick May, "Black Protests Draw on Past, Look to Future," *Miami Herald*, November 12, 1990, 1B, 2B.

20. "Page One Comment—Miami Run by Cuban Mafia," *Miami Times*, December 20, 1990, 1.

21. Field interview, January 8, 1987.

22. Goldfarb, "Mandela Visit Prompts Rerun."

23. Robert L. Steinback, "Tensions Push Miami to Brink of Its Own War," *Miami Herald*, December 28, 1990, 1B.

24. The research from which this quote comes is reported in Alex Stepick, Max Castro, Marvin Dunn, and Guillermo Grenier, "Newcomers and Established Residents: The Case of Miami," Final Report to the Ford Foundation for the Changing Relations Project (Miami: Center for Labor Research and Study, Florida International University, 1989).

25. Field interview, January 1987.

26. See Alex Stepick, "The Business Community of Little Haiti," Dialogue no. 32, Occasional Paper Series, Latin American and Caribbean Center (Miami: Florida International University, February 1984), 1–45; idem, "Little Haiti," in *Miami: Insight City Guides*, ed. Joann Biondi (London: APA Publications, 1991), 209–16; and Integrated Advertising, *S & R Haitian Telephone Directory, 1987* (Miami: Integrated Management Group, 1987).

27. Alex Stepick, "The Haitian Informal Sector in Miami," *City and Society* 5 (June 1991): 10–22; idem, "Miami's Two Informal Sectors," in *The Informal Economy: Studies in Advanced and Less Developed Coun-*

tries, ed. A. Portes, M. Castells, and L. Benton (Baltimore: Johns Hopkins University Press, 1989), 111–31.

28. David Hancock, Sandra Dibble, and Kimberly Crockett, "Haitians: We Want Respect in S. Florida," *Miami Herald*, July 22, 1990, 1A, 17A; Nancy San Martin, "Haitians Struggle for Unity in New Land," *Miami Herald*, "Neighbors North" sec., September 23, 1990, 16–17.

29. See, for example, 1983–87 issues of *Pótparól*, published by the Haitian Task Force, Miami.

30. Thomas Monnay, "Haitians Are Still Smarting from the Effects of Blood Ban Stigma," *Miami Times*, January 3, 1991, 1A.

31. Kimberly Crockett and Sandra Dibble, "New Tensions Seizing Dade: Haitians Vent Long-still Anger," *Miami Herald*, July 3, 1990, 1B, 2B.

32. Ana Santiago and Ivan Román, "Haitianos denuncian brutalidad policial," *El Nuevo Herald*, July 7, 1990, 1A, 6A.

33. Nancy San Martin, Andres Viglucci, and David Hancock, "Peaceful Rally Ends Days of Divisiveness," *Miami Herald*, July 8, 1990, 1B, 2B.

34. Marjorie Valburn and Sharony Andrews, "Aristide Saw Haitians, U.S. Blacks as One," *Miami Herald*, September 28, 1991, 1B, 4B; Barry Bearak, "Ethnic Relations in Miami Unravel," *Los Angeles Times*, July 8, 1990, A21.

35. Stepick, Castro, Dunn, and Grenier, "Newcomers and Established Residents."

36. Carl Goldfarb, "Dawkins Leaves Town, Turmoil Behind," *Miami Herald*, July 7, 1990, 1B.

37. Marvin Dunn, Florida International University, personal communication.

38. Stepick, Castro, Dunn, and Grenier, "Newcomers and Established Residents."

39. Ibid.

40. Results of preliminary field work in Miami for a project entitled "Children of Immigrants, the Adaptation Process of the Second Generation," supported by the Spencer Foundation and National Science Foundation; Alejandro Portes and Lisandro Perez, principal investigators, 1990.

41. Nancy San Martin and Xose Alvarez-Alfonso, "Haitian Families Are Moving out to the Suburbs," *Miami Herald*, "Neighbors North-

west" sec., October 14, 1990, 20, 21. For similar processes with Haitians in other cities, see Tekle Woldemikael, *Becoming Black American: Haitians and American Institutions in Evanston, Illinois* (New York: AMS Press, 1989); Susan Buchanan, "Scattered Seeds: The Meaning of Migration for Haitians in New York City" (Ph.D. diss., New York University, 1980); idem, "The Cultural Meaning of Social Class for Haitians in New York City," *Ethnic Groups* 5 (1983): 7–30; and Loretta J. P. Saint-Louis, "Migration Evolves: The Political Economy of Network Process and Form in Haiti, the U.S., and Canada" (Ph.D. diss., Boston University, 1988).

42. All analyses of Haitian society emphasize its class and color divisions. Among the most insightful is Michel-Rolph Trouillot, *Haiti, State Against Nation: The Origins and Legacy of Duvalierism* (New York: Monthly Review Press, 1990).

43. Alex Stepick, "The Refugees Nobody Wants: Haitians in Miami," in Grenier and Stepick (eds.), *Miami Now!*, 57–82.

44. Stepick, "Business Community of Little Haiti"; idem, "Little Haiti."

45. Nancy San Martin and Karen Branch, "Miami Haitians March," *Miami Herald*, October 3, 1991, 18A; Harold Maass, " 'We're Not Going to Stop,' Haitians Cry in 6th Protest," *Miami Herald*, October 6, 1991, 1B, 2B; David Hancock and Jon O'Neill, "5,000 to U.S.: Back Aristide, Take Refugees," *Miami Herald*, November 17, 1991, 1B, 2B.

46. Field interview by authors, October 1991.

47. Nancy San Martin, "Miami's Haitians Not All of One Mind on the Aristide Presidency," *Miami Herald*, October 5, 1991, 2B.

48. In this and the following citations, italics are used to indicate common themes expressed by Black and white informants.

49. David Lawrence, Jr., "Find a Way to the Future for Everyone," *Miami Herald*, December 2, 1990, 3G.

50. Miami's Business Assistance Center, promotional brochure, 1987; courtesy of N. Daughtrey, BAC's former executive director.

51. Field interview, January 12, 1987.

52. Field interview, January 8, 1992.

53. Field interviews with white business leaders in Miami, January 1987 and January 1992.

54. U.S. Bureau of the Census, *The Hispanic Population of the United*

States, 1989 (Washington, D.C.: U.S. Department of Commerce, 1990); idem, *Survey of Minority-owned Business Enterprises, 1987/Hispanics*.

55. Cited during interview with Guillermo Martinez, then Latin affairs columnist of the *Miami Herald*, January 13, 1987.

56. Field interviews with Cuban community and business leaders in Miami, January and December 1987.

57. Ibid.; data on Cuban business and civic participation were provided by our informants.

58. Field interview, December 22, 1987.

59. Field interview, January 8, 1987.

9. Reprise

1. Adna F. Weber, *The Growth of Cities in the Nineteenth Century: A Study in Statistics* (Ithaca, N.Y.: Cornell University Press, 1967), 172. See also the classic essay on the origins of European urbanization by Henri Pirenne, *Medieval Cities: Their Origins and the Revival of Trade* (Princeton: Princeton University Press, [1925] 1970); and Max Weber, *The City* (New York: Free Press, [1921] 1966), chap. 1.

2. François Lamarche, "Property Development and the Economic Foundations of the Urban Question," in *Urban Sociology: Critical Essays*, ed. C. G. Pickvance (New York: St. Martin's Press, 1976), 86.

3. A more detailed critique of this argument is presented in Alejandro Portes, "Unauthorized Immigration and Immigration Reform: Present Trends and Prospects," in *Determinants of Emigration from Mexico, Central America, and the Caribbean*, ed. S. Diaz-Briquets and S. Weintraub (Boulder, Colo.: Westview Press, 1991), 76–97.

4. Ibid.; Aristide Zolberg, "The Next Waves: Migration Theory for a Changing World," *International Migration Review* 23 (Fall 1989): 403–30; Abdelmalek Sayad, "Immigration in France: An 'Exotic' Form of Poverty" (Paper presented at the conference on Urban Poverty, Migration, and Marginality, Maison Suger, Paris, May 1991).

5. J. H. Parry, Philip Sherlock, and Anthony Maingot, *A Short History of the West Indies*, 4th ed. (New York: St. Martin's Press, 1987); Franklin W. Knight and Colin A. Palmer, *The Modern Caribbean* (Chapel Hill: University of North Carolina Press, 1989), chaps. 1, 4, 6, 7, 8, 12; Sidney W. Mintz and Sally Price, *Caribbean Contours* (Baltimore: Johns Hopkins University Press, 1985), chaps. 1, 7; André Corten, Carlos M. Vilas, Mercedes Acosta, and Isis Duarte, *Azucar y política en la República Dominicana* (Santo Domingo: Taller, 1976).

6. Rieff, *Going to Miami.*

7. For a description of the places of destination of major U.S.-bound immigrant and refugee flows, see Portes and Rumbaut, *Immigrant America*, chap. 2.

8. Tom Fielder, "Politically, We'll Hardly Recognize the Place," *Miami Herald*, October 6, 1991, 5C.

9. Field observations by the authors, Miami, 1989. The speaker went on to become a prominent member of the Miami Chamber of Commerce.

10. Richard Wallace, "South Florida Grows to a Latin Beat," *Miami Herald*, March 6, 1991, 1–2Z; Carl Goldfarb, "Alienation Keeps Miami's Anglos away from Polls," *Miami Herald*, November 19, 1989, 1–2B.

11. James K. Batten, "Miami's Can-Do Spirit Remains Strong Even in Tough Times," *Miami Herald*, October 10, 1991.

12. Ibid.

13. David Lawrence, Jr., "Get on the Ball . . . Learn a Language," *Miami Herald*, March 24, 1991, 2C.

14. Xavier L. Suárez, "Miami Is Poised to Fulfill 'City of the Future' Role," *Miami Herald*, December 6, 1989.

15. Lopez-Miró, "Where the 'Cuban' Ends."

16. A seven-year-old girl alluded to in the above column replied to Lopez-Miró saying, "I perfectly know where I come from and who I am. My identity and my image are very clear: I am from the United States and I know it. But my Cuban heritage I cannot ignore." See Roxanne Valdés, "American—With Cuban Blood," *Miami Herald*, February 15, 1990, 26A.

17. Dahl, *Who Governs?*, 33–34.

18. Richard D. Lamm and Gary Imhoff, *The Immigration Time-Bomb: The Fragmenting of America* (New York: E. P. Dutton, 1985), 123–24.

19. The classic statement about the enduring significance of ethnicity for urban politics is Nathan Glazer and Daniel P. Moynihan, *Beyond the Melting Pot: The Negroes, Puerto Ricans, Jews, Italians, and Irish of New York City* (Cambridge, Mass.: MIT Press, 1970). See also Andrew Greeley, *Why Can't They Be Like Us? America's White Ethnic Groups* (New York: E. P. Dutton, 1971); and Richard D. Alba, *Italian Americans: Into the Twilight of Ethnicity* (Englewood Cliffs, N.J.: Prentice Hall, 1985).

20. Field interview, January 7 and 8, 1992.

21. Sandra Dibble, "Think Tank Seeks Wide-ranging Plan for Life After Castro," *Miami Herald*, February 23, 1990, 1–3B.

22. Pablo Alfonso, "Panel Offers a Plan for Governing New Cuba," *Miami Herald*, March 3, 1990.

23. See Carmelo Mesa-Lago, "Cuba's Economic Counter-Reform: Causes, Policies, and Effects," *Journal of Communist Studies* 5 (December 1989): 98–139; and Peter T. White, "Cuba at a Crossroads," *National Geographic*, August 1991, 94–121. For an analysis of the internal contradictions undermining the revolutionary regime, see Ariel Hidalgo, *Cuba: el estado marxista y la nueva clase* (Miami: General Printing, 1988).

24. Guillermo J. Grenier, Hugh Gladwin, and Douglas McLaughen, *Views on Policy Options Toward Cuba Held by Cuban-American Residents of Dade County, Florida: The Results of the Second 1991 Cuba Poll* (Miami: Cuban Research Institute, Florida International University, 1991).

25. An illustration can be found in coverage of the 1991 Gulf War. Saddam Hussein was consistently likened to Fidel Castro in the Cuban exile media. One commentator after another suggested that, after Hussein's defeat, the logical thing to do was to transport the mobilized troops to the Caribbean and thus do away with the remaining threat to national security.

26. Howard Kleinberg, "Greater Miami's Crossroads of the Vanities; City Renames History Streets at the Whim of Politicians," *Miami Herald*, July 31, 1990.

Postscript

1. Muir, *Miami, U.S.A.*, 149–50.

2. Sean Rowe, "Hugo's Homeboys," *New Times*, September 2–8, 1992, 13–14.

3. "The Worst Wind," *New Times*, September 2–8, 1992 (special issue).

4. This common pattern has been noted by specialists on the field in the past; see Frederick L. Bates and Walter G. Peacock, "Disasters and Social Change," in *The Sociology of Disasters*, ed. R. R. Dynes and C. Pelanda (Gorizia, It.: Franco Angeli Press, 1987), 291–330.

5. These articles consistently focused on the theme that people who barely spoke to each other before came together to share what little they had in the days after the hurricane. One such article announced in its

headline: "At Long Last, Neighbors: The Storm That Tore South Dade Apart Has Brought Many of Its People Together" (by Curtis Morgan, in the *Miami Herald*, September 5, 1992, 1–2F).

6. David Satterfield, "We Will Rebuild Hits $11 Million," *Miami Herald*, September 19, 1992, 1A, 20A.

7. Lisandro Perez, "Hurricane Has Severely Tilted Community Demographics," *Miami Herald*, September 27, 1992, 4M.

8. "Worst Wind."

9. Satterfield, "We Will Rebuild," 20A.

Bibliography

"Agreement Signed After Cubans Hear Plea from Bishop." *Baltimore Sun*, November 30, 1987.

"Aid for Rebels Undelivered." *Miami Herald*, April 29, 1984, 6B.

Alba, Richard D. *Italian Americans: Into the Twilight of Ethnicity*. Englewood Cliffs, N.J.: Prentice-Hall, 1985.

Alfonso, Pablo. "Panel Offers a Plan for Governing New Cuba." *Miami Herald*, March 3, 1990, 1B, 4B.

Allman, T. D. *Miami: City of the Future*. New York: Atlantic Monthly Press, 1987.

"Andrew by the Numbers." *Miami Herald*, September 24, 1992, 24A.

"Ascenso de IMC despertó controversia." *El Miami Herald*, March 28, 1986, 9.

"At Last, Work Permits." *Miami Herald*, July 10, 1987, 24A.

Bach, Robert L., Jennifer B. Bach, and Timothy Triplett. "The Flotilla 'Entrants': Latest and Most Controversial." *Cuban Studies* 11 (1981): 29–48.

Balmaseda, Liz. "The New Nicaragua." *Miami Herald*, February 5, 1989, 1–6G.

Barber, Ben. "Open Three: Enclave for Exiles." *Miami Herald*, "Neighbors S.E." sec., December 29, 1983, 14.

Bates, Frederick L., and Walter G. Peacock. "Disasters and Social Change." In *The Sociology of Disasters*, edited by R. R. Dynes and C. Pelanda, 291–330. Gorizia, It.: Franco Angeli Press, 1987.

Batista, Fulgencio. *Respuesta*. Mexico City: Impresora Manuel León Sánchez, 1960.

Batten, James K. "Miami's Can-Do Spirit Remains Strong Even in Tough Times." *Miami Herald*, October 10, 1991, 23A.

Bearak, Barry. "Ethnic Relations in Miami Unravel." *Los Angeles Times*, July 8, 1990, A21.

Biddulph, Geoffrey. "Blacks Feel Left Out as Refugees Get Jobs." *Miami Herald*, January 20, 1989, 1D.

Bonjean, Charles M., and David M. Olson. "Community Leadership: Directions of Research." *Administrative Science Quarterly* 9 (December 1964): 278–300.

Botifoll, Luis J. "How Miami's New Image Was Created." Occasional Paper no. 1985-1, Institute of Inter-American Studies, University of Miami, 1985.

————— *Introducción al futuro de Miami*. Miami: Laurenty, 1988.

————— *The Conspiracy of Silence: Hispanics' Vital Role in the American Revolution*. Miami: Laurenty, 1986.

Branch, Karen. "Immigrants Jam Street Corner, Hoping for a Job." *Miami Herald*, March 15, 1989, 1B.

————— "Nicaraguan Culture: Alive and Growing in Dade." *Miami Herald*, "Neighbors" sec., May 25, 1989, 20.

————— "Nicaraguan Exile Groups Unite in Appeal to Mack." *Miami Herald*, July 1, 1989, 3B.

————— "Nicaraguans Try to Help Their Own." *The Miami Herald*, "Neighbors Kendall" sec., June 4, 1989, 10.

Briceno, Carlos. "Nicaraguan Plea for 'Sanctuary' Doubles in Year." *Miami Herald*, February 5, 1985, 1D.

Browning, Michael. "Antibilingual Backers Celebrate Early." *Miami Herald*, November 5, 1980, 1B.

Buchanan, J. E. *Miami: A Chronological and Documentary History, 1513–1977*. New York: Oceana, 1977.

Buchanan, Susan. "The Cultural Meaning of Social Class for Haitians in New York City." *Ethnic Groups* 5 (1983): 7–30.

————— "Scattered Seeds: The Meaning of Migration for Haitians in New York City." Ph.D. diss., New York University, 1980.

Burkett, Elinor, and Sharony Andrews. "Rhythms of African Pride Pulsate in Miami Streets." *Miami Herald*, June 29, 1990, 13A.

Camayd-Freixas, Yohel. *Crisis in Miami*. Report to the project on "Help-Seeking and Services Use Among Recent Latin American Refugees," conducted by the Sociology Department and School of Public Health, Johns Hopkins University. Boston: Boston Urban Research and Development Group, 1988.

Capen, Richard. "Hand Is Out to the Tempest-tossed." *Miami Herald*, January 1, 1989, 3C.

Carrillo, Justo. *Cuba 1933: estudiantes, yankis y soldados*. Miami: Institute of Ibero-American Studies, University of Miami, 1985.

Castro, Max, and Timothy Yeaney. *Documenting Dade's Diversity: An Ethnic Audit of Dade County*. Miami: Greater Miami United, January 1989.

Chardy, Alfonso. "Much of Blame for Influx Put on Failed Reagan Policy." *Miami Herald*, January 22, 1989, 16A.

Clark, Juan M., Jose I. Lasage, and Rose S. Reque. *The 1980 Mariel Exodus: An Assessment and Prospect.* Washington, D.C.: Council for Inter-American Security, 1981.

Colon, Yves. "State-INS Plan Aims to Take away Aliens' Incentives to Stay." *Miami Herald*, December 26, 1984, 1D.

Corten, André, Carlos M. Vilas, Mercedes Acosta, and Isis Duarte. *Azucar y política en la República Dominicana.* Santo Domingo: Taller, 1976.

Crockett, Kimberly, Elinor Burkett, and Karen Branch. "Grass-roots Welcome Counters Official Snub." *Miami Herald*, June 29, 1990, 1A, 12A.

Crockett, Kimberly, and Sandra Dibble. "New Tensions Seizing Dade: Haitians Vent Long-still Anger." *Miami Herald*, July 3, 1990, 1B, 2B.

Crockett, Kimberly, David Hancock, and Carlos Harrison. "Police Crush Haitian Protest." *Miami Herald*, July 6, 1990, 1A, 12A.

Crockett, Kimberly, and Patrick May. "Black Protests Draw on Past, Look to Future." *Miami Herald*, November 12, 1990, 1B, 2B.

"The Cuban-American Community and the Miami Herald" (paid political announcement). *Miami Herald*, October 19, 1987, 11A.

"Cuban Success Story: In the United States." *U.S. News & World Report*, March 20, 1967, 104–6.

"Dade Fears Refugee Wave." *Miami Herald*, May 11, 1980, 1A, 20A.

Dahl, Robert A. *Who Governs? Democracy and Power in an American City.* New Haven: Yale University Press, 1961.

"Deportar a un ciudadano no existe." *El Nuevo Herald*, January 10, 1988, 2A.

Dewar, Heather, and Mike Ward. "Teele: Jobs Would Heal Miami's Woes." *Miami News*, October 16, 1987, 1A, 7A.

Diaz-Briquets, Sergio, and Lisandro Perez. "Cuba: The Demography of Revolution." *Population Bulletin* 36 (April 1981): 2–41.

Dibble, Sandra. "Immigration Debate Erupts." *Miami Herald*, December 22, 1988, 1C.

——— "INS Halts Deportation of Nicaraguan Aliens." *Miami Herald*, April 11, 1986, 1A.

——— "Latin Listeners Open Hearts to Airwave Appeals." *Miami Herald*, December 15, 1985, 1A.

——— "Nicaraguan Cardinal Brings Peace Message." *Miami Herald*, June 14, 1985, 1A.

———— "Nicaraguan Exiles Find Homes in Little Havana." *Miami Herald*, February 10, 1986, 2B.

———— "Nicaraguans in Miami: Living in Limbo, Most Refugees Denied Work Permits, Welfare." *Miami Herald*, December 23, 1985, 1A.

———— "Nicaraguans Lobbying to Stay in U.S. Legally." *Miami Herald*, August 15, 1985, 2D.

———— "Think Tank Seeks Wide-ranging Plan for Life After Castro." *Miami Herald*, February 23, 1990, 1–3B.

Dibble, Sandra, and Karen Branch. "Colombians Angered by Conviction." *Miami Herald*, December 8, 1989, 25A.

Didion, Joan. *Miami*. New York: Simon & Schuster, 1987.

Douglas, Marjory S. *Florida, the Long Frontier*. New York: Harper & Row, 1967.

Dunn, Marvin, and Alex Stepick. "Blacks in Miami." In *Miami Now! Immigration, Ethnicity, and Social Change*, edited by G. J. Grenier and A. Stepick, 41–56. Gainesville: University Press of Florida, 1992.

Epstein, Gail. "Contracts Still Scarce for Blacks." *Miami Herald*, September 29, 1991, 1B, 3B.

Evans, Christine, and Peggy Rogers. "Lozano Gets 7 Years." *Miami Herald*, January 25, 1990, 1A, 3A.

"Exiled Nicaraguans Reflect." *Miami Herald*, July 16, 1989, 11A.

Fagen, Richard F., Richard A. Brody, and Thomas J. O'Leary. *Cubans in Exile: Disaffection and the Revolution*. Stanford: Stanford University Press, 1968.

Fehrnstrom, Eric. "Confession of a Killer." *Boston Herald*, April 17, 1987, 1–20.

Feinstein, Richard J. "Why Public Hospitals Are Ailing." *Miami Herald*, February 10, 1985, 3E.

Feldstein Soto, Luis. "Nicaraguan Influx Strains Schools, Services." *Miami Herald*, July 5, 1987, 2B.

Festinger, Leon. *A Theory of Cognitive Dissonance*. Stanford: Stanford University Press, 1957.

Fichtner, Margaria. "Still Far to Go, Sisters Who Led Sit-ins in Sixties Still Seek Dignity. 'Isn't That Ridiculous?' " *Miami Herald*, July 3, 1990, 1C, 2C.

Fielder, Tom. "Politically, We'll Hardly Recognize the Place." *Miami Herald*, October 6, 1991, 5C.

"Flight from Cuba—Castro's Loss Is U.S. Gain." *U.S. News & World Report*, May 31, 1971, 74.

Florida. Department of Health and Rehabilitative Services (DHRS). *Refugees and Entrants in Florida: Background and Current Issues*. Tallahassee: DHRS, March, 1982.

"Florida's Latin Boom; Hispanics Are the Only Spark in a Somnolent Economy." *Newsweek*, November 11, 1985, 55–56.

Forment, Carlos. "Political Practice and the Rise of an Ethnic Enclave: The Cuban-American Case, 1959–1979." *Theory and Society* 18 (1989): 47–81.

Fowler, Irvin A. "Local Industrial Structures, Economic Power, and Community Welfare." *Social Problems* 6 (Summer 1958): 41–51.

Franklin, J. *Cuban Foreign Relations: A Chronology, 1959–1982*. New York: Center for Cuban Studies, 1983.

Gaiter, Dorothy. "Lozano Verdict Brought Relief and Long-delayed Justice." *Miami Herald*, December 8, 1989, 31A.

García Montes, Jorge, and Antonio Alonso Dávila. *Historia del Partido Comunista de Cuba*. Miami: Ediciones Universal, 1970.

Gayoso, Jay. "Battle Unites Nicaraguan Refugees." *Miami Herald*, "Neighbors S.E." sec., February 8, 1987, 3.

——— "Nicaraguan Flights for Refugees' Aid." *Miami Herald*, "Neighbors S.E." sec., January 18, 1987, 16.

Geertz, Clifford. *Peddlers and Princes*. Chicago: University of Chicago Press, 1963.

George, Paul S. "Colored Town: Miami's Black Community, 1896–1930." *Florida Historical Quarterly* 16 (April 1978): 432–47.

——— "Policing Miami's Black Community, 1896–1930." *Florida Historical Quarterly* 17 (April 1979): 434–50.

Gillaspie, William R. "De Soto." In *Encyclopedia of World Biography* 3:352–53. New York: McGraw-Hill, 1973.

——— "Ponce de Leon." In *Encyclopedia of World Biography* 8:521–22. New York: McGraw-Hill, 1973.

Glazer, Nathan. "Ethnic Groups in America: From National Culture to Ideology." In *Freedom and Control in Modern Society*, edited by M. Berger, T. Abel, and C. Page, 158–73. New York: Van Nostrand, 1954.

Glazer, Nathan, and Daniel Moynihan. *Beyond the Melting Pot: The Negroes, Puerto Ricans, Jews, Italians, and Irish of New York City*. Cambridge, Mass.: MIT Press, 1970.

Goldfarb, Carl. "Alienation Keeps Miami's Anglos away from Polls." *Miami Herald*, November 19, 1989, 1–2B.

——— "Dawkins Leaves Town, Turmoil Behind." *Miami Herald*, July 7, 1990, 1B.

——— "Mandela Backers, Critics Brace for Momentous Visit." *Miami Herald*, June 28, 1990, 4A, 4B.

——— "Mandela's Visit Prompts Rerun of Old Ethnic Battles." *Miami Herald*, July 1, 1990, 1B, 4B.

Greeley, Andrew. *Why Can't They Be Like Us? America's White Ethnic Groups*. New York: E. P. Dutton, 1971.

Grenier, Guillermo J., Hugh Gladwin, and Douglas McLaughen. *Views on Policy Options Toward Cuba Held by Cuban-American Residents of Dade County, Florida: The Results of the Second 1991 Cuba Poll*. Miami: Cuban Research Institute, Florida International University, 1991.

Grimm, Fred, and Ellen Bartlett. "Political Heavyweights Bring Bout Here." *Miami Herald*, March 9, 1980, 1B, 7B.

Gutierrez, Barbara. "Cubans Hold Marathon to Raise Money for Nicaraguan Guerrillas." *Miami Herald*, August 1, 1983, 3B.

———— "Supplies to Be Ferried to Refugees." *Miami Herald*, June 26, 1983, 4B.

———— "We're 'Invisible' Exiles, Nicaraguans Say." *Miami Herald*, February 5, 1984, 1B.

Hancock, David. "U.S. Denies Policy Shift on Handling Nicaraguans." *Miami Herald*, December 15, 1988, 1D.

Hancock, David, Sandra Dibble, and Kimberly Crockett. "Haitians: We Want Respect in S. Florida." *Miami Herald*, July 22, 1990, 1A, 17A.

Hancock, David, and Jon O'Neill. "5,000 to U.S.: Back Aristide, Take Refugees." *Miami Herald*, November 17, 1991, 1B, 2B.

Hernandez, Rafael, and Redi Gomis. "Retrato del Mariel: el ángulo socio-económico." *Cuadernos de nuestra America* 3 (January–June 1986): 138–39.

Hidalgo, Ariel. *Cuba: el estado marxista y la nueva clase*. Miami: General Printing, 1988.

Hines, Bea. "Overtown Feels Pain, Frustration." *Miami Herald*, January 18, 1989, 1A.

"How the Community Is Responding." *Miami Herald*, January 13, 1989, 19A.

Hunter, Floyd. *Community Power Structure*. Chapel Hill: University of North Carolina Press, 1953.

"Immigration: How to Control It; A Legal Limbo" (5th of a series). *Miami Herald*, December 30, 1983, 28A.

"Immoral Policy." *Miami Herald*, December 17, 1988, 34A.

Integrated Advertising. *S & R Haitian Telephone Directory, 1987*. Miami: Integrated Management Group, 1987.

Jahoda, Gloria. *Florida: A Bicentennial History*. New York: W. W. Norton, 1976.

Janowitz, M., ed. *W. I. Thomas on Social Organization and Social Personality*. Chicago: University of Chicago Press, 1969.

Joint Center for Environmental and Urban Problems. *An Evaluation of Redevelopment in Overtown*. Miami: Florida International University, October 1991.

Josephs, Lawrence. "Ranchos Carries on Tradition." *Miami Herald*, "Neighbors S.E." sec., July 7, 1983, 31.

Keldan, Bruce. "Tales of the Tonton Macoutes from Haitians Who Fled." *Philadelphia Inquirer*, October 8, 1979, 1A, 10A.

Key, V. O. *Southern Politics*. New York: Alfred A. Knopf, 1950.

Kleinberg, Howard. "Greater Miami's Crossroads of the Vanities; City Renames History Streets at the Whim of Politicians." *Miami Herald*, July 31, 1990, 15A.

———. "Ponce de Leon's Landing in Chequescha (Miami), Fla." *Miami Herald*, March 22, 1990, 25A.

———. "A Wistful Eye Back to Young Coconut Grove." *Miami Herald*, March 6, 1990, 15A.

Knight, Franklin W., and Colin A. Palmer. *The Modern Caribbean*. Chapel Hill: University of North Carolina Press, 1989.

Kraft, Scott, and Barry Bearak. "After Miami, Mandela Finds Hero's Welcome in Detroit." *Los Angeles Times*, June 29, 1990, A18–19.

Lamar, Jacob V. "A Brightly Colored Tinderbox." *Time*, January 30, 1989, 28–29.

Lamarche, François. "Property Development and the Economic Foundations of the Urban Question." In *Urban Sociology: Critical Essays*, edited by C. G. Pickvance, 85–118. New York: St. Martin's Press, 1976.

Lamm, Richard D., and Gary Imhoff. *The Immigration Time-Bomb: The Fragmenting of America*. New York: E. P. Dutton, 1985.

Lawrence, David, Jr.. "Find a Way to the Future for Everyone." *Miami Herald*, December 2, 1990, 3G.

———. "Get On the Ball . . . Learn a Language." *Miami Herald*, March 24, 1991, 2C.

Lazo, Rodrigo. "Lacking Aid, Immigrants Wait to Learn." *Miami Herald*, October 12, 1988, 1B.

———. "Mass Offers Ray of Hope for Refugees." *Miami Herald*, December 26, 1988, 1B.

———. "There Is So Little Money, but There Is Peace of Mind." *Miami Herald*, December 25, 1989, 2D.

———. "Without Work Permit, Day Jobs Sustain Him." *Miami Herald*, December 25, 1989, 2D.

———. "A Year Later, Panacea Turns to Struggle for Nicaraguans." *Miami Herald*, December 25, 1989, 1D.

Lieberson, Stanley, and Arnold R. Silverman. "The Precipitants and Underlying Conditions of Race Riots." *American Sociological Review* 30 (December 1965): 887–98.

Light, Ivan. "Asian Enterprise in America: Chinese, Japanese, and Koreans in Small Business." In *Self-Help in Urban America*, edited by S. Cummings, 33–57. New York: Kennikat Press, 1980.

———— "Immigrant and Ethnic Enterprise in North America." *Ethnic and Racial Studies* 7 (April 1984): 195–216.

Logan, John R., and Harvey L. Molotch. *Urban Fortunes: the Political Economy of Place*. Berkeley and Los Angeles: University of California Press, 1987.

Lopez-Miró, Sergio. "Where the 'Cuban' Ends and the 'American' Begins." *Miami Herald*, February 1, 1990, 19A.

Ludwig, Emil. *Biografía de una isla* (Cuba). Mexico City: Editorial Centauro, 1948.

Maass, Harold. " 'We're Not Going to Stop,' Haitians Cry in 6th Protest." *Miami Herald*, October 6, 1991, 1B, 2B.

Malet, A., and J. Isaac. *Los tiempos modernos*. Mexico City: Editora Nacional, 1961.

Marger, Martin M. *Race and Ethnic Relations*. Belmont, Calif.: Wadsworth, 1991.

Marks, Carole. "The Urban Underclass." *Annual Review of Sociology* 17 (1991): 445–66.

Marquis, Christopher. "Dade Unprepared for Refugee Influx." *Miami Herald*, October 23, 1988, 1A.

———— "In Miami, Confusion Reigns for Applicants." *Miami Herald*, December 17, 1988, 1A.

———— "Many Nicaraguans Reject Call to Go Home." *Miami Herald*, April 3, 1989, 1B.

———— "Miami Grapples with Influx of Nicaraguans." *Miami Herald*, December 15, 1988, 1A.

———— "Nicaraguan Exile Community Forges New Life in S. Florida." *Miami Herald*, July 16, 1989, 1A.

———— "Refugees Find Exiles Thriving." *Miami Herald*, January 22, 1989, 1B.

Marquis, Christopher, and Frank Cerabino. "Dade on Edge over Nicaraguans." *Miami Herald*, January 14, 1989, 1A.

Marquis, Christopher, and Andres Viglucci. "Some Cuban Exiles Decry Plan to Deport Detainees." *Miami Herald*, November 21, 1987, 1A, 22A.

Martínez, Guillermo. "Mariel Myths Feed Venom across Nation." *Miami Herald*, November 18, 1982, 31A.

Marx, Karl. *The Eighteenth Brumaire of Napoleon Bonaparte.* New York: International Publishers, 1963.

Matthews, Herbert. *Revolution in Cuba.* New York: Charles Scribner's Sons, 1975.

Meluza, Lourdes. "Spanish Radio Marathon to Raise Nicaraguan Aid Funds." *Miami Herald,* June 14, 1985, 2C.

"Mercy for Refugees." *Miami Herald,* June 26, 1988, 2C.

Mesa-Lago, Carmelo. "Cuba's Economic Counter-Reform: Causes, Policies, and Effects." *Journal of Communist Studies* 5 (December 1989): 98–139.

Metro-Dade County Planning Department. *Profile of the Black Population.* Miami: Research Division, Metro-Dade County Planning Department, 1984.

"Miami: America's Casablanca." *Newsweek,* January 25, 1988, 22–29.

Miami Design and Preservation League. "Miami Beach Architecture." 1989.

Mills, C. Wright. "The Middle Classes in Middle-sized Cities." *American Sociological Review* 11 (October 1946): 520–29.

———— *The Power Elite.* New York: Oxford University Press, 1956.

Mills, C. Wright, and Melville J. Ulmer. "Small Business and Civic Welfare." In U.S. Congress, Senate, *Report of the Smaller War Plants Corporation to the Special Committee to Study Problems of American Small Business,* 79th Cong., 1946, S. Rept. 135. Reprinted in abbreviated form in *The Structure of Community Power,* ed. M. Aiken and P. E. Mott, 124–54. New York: Random House, 1970.

Mintz, Sidney W. "The Industrialization of Sugar Production and Its Relationship to Social and Economic Change." In *Background to Revolution: The Development of Modern Cuba,* edited by R. F. Smith, 176–86. New York: Alfred A. Knopf, 1966.

Mintz, Sidney W., and Sally Price. *Caribbean Contours.* Baltimore: Johns Hopkins University Press, 1985.

Mohl, Raymond A. "Trouble in Paradise: Race and Housing in Miami During the New Deal Era." *Prologue* 8 (Spring 1987): 7–20.

Molotch, Harvey. "The City as a Growth Machine." *American Journal of Sociology* 82 (1976): 309–30.

Monnay, Thomas. "Haitians Are Still Smarting from the Effects of Blood Ban Stigma." *Miami Times,* January 3, 1991, 1A.

Montalvo, Tina. "Job Permits Going Fast at INS Offices; 10,200 Nicaraguans Processed in 4 Days." *Miami Herald,* September 6, 1987, 1B.

———— "Nicaraguans Are Only Immigrants Benefiting from New Asylum Aid." *Miami Herald,* September 11, 1987, 6C.

Morgan, Curtis. "At Long Last, Neighbors." *Miami Herald*, September 5, 1992, 1–2F.

Muir, Helen. *Miami, U.S.A.* Miami: Pickering Press, 1990.

Nazario, Sonia L. "After a Long Holdout, Cubans in Miami Take a Role in Miami Politics; Economic Success Spurs Steps to Assimilate." *Wall Street Journal*, June 7, 1983, 1, 23.

"Nicaraguan Exiles Seek Overall Leader." *Miami Herald*, September 12, 1989, 3B.

"Nicaraguan Exodus." *Miami Herald*, October 20, 1988, 24A.

"Nicaraguan Refugees: How the Community Feels." *Miami Herald*, January 20, 1989, 24A.

Owens, Dory. "Her Faith in Hispanics Paid Off Big." *Miami Herald*, "Profile" sec., October 1, 1988.

Padilla, Heberto. "Miami: el mundo en blanco y negro." *El Miami Herald*, January 18, 1986, 5.

"Page One Comment—Miami Run by Cuban Mafia." *Miami Times*, December 20, 1990, 1.

Parry, J. H., Philip Sherlock, and Anthony Maingot. *A Short History of the West Indies.* 4th ed. New York: St. Martin's Press, 1987.

Perez, Lisandro. "Hurricane Has Severely Tilted Community Demographics." *Miami Herald*, September 27, 1992, 4M.

Petrow, Stevan. "What Did the Haitians Do?" *St. Petersburg Times*, November 11, 1979, 8.

Piore, Michael. *Birds of Passage: Migrant Labor and Industrial Societies.* New York: Cambridge University Press, 1979.

Pirenne, Henri. *Medieval Cities: Their Origins and the Revival of Trade.* Princeton: Princeton University Press, [1925] 1970.

Portell-Vila, Herminio. *Nueva historia de la República de Cuba.* Miami: La Moderna Poesia, 1989.

Porter, Bruce, and Marvin Dunn. *The Miami Riot of 1980: Crossing the Bounds.* Lexington, Mass.: D. C. Heath, 1984.

Portes, Alejandro. "The Rise of Ethnicity: Determinants of Ethnic Perceptions Among Cuban Exiles in Miami." *American Sociological Review* 49 (June 1984): 383–97.

——— "The Social Origins of the Cuban Enclave Economy of Miami." *Sociological Perspectives* 30 (October 1987): 340–72.

——— "Unauthorized Immigration and Immigration Reform: Present Trends and Prospects." In *Determinants of Emigration from Mexico, Central America, and the Caribbean*, edited by S. Diaz-Briquets and S. Weintraub, 76–97. Boulder, Colo.: Westview Press, 1991.

Portes, Alejandro, and Robert L. Bach. *Latin Journey: Cuban and Mexican Immigrants in the United States.* Berkeley and Los Angeles: University of California Press, 1985.

Portes, Alejandro, Juan M. Clark, and Robert L. Bach. "The New Wave: A Statistical Profile of Recent Cuban Exiles to the United States." *Cuban Studies* 7 (January 1977): 1–32.

Portes, Alejandro, Juan M. Clark, and Robert D. Manning. "After Mariel: A Survey of the Resettlement Experiences of Cuban Refugees in Miami." *Cuban Studies* 15 (Summer 1985): 35–59.

Portes, Alejandro, and Rafael Mozo. "The Political Adaptation Process of Immigrants and Other Refugee Minorities in the United States: A Preliminary Analysis." *International Migration Review* 19 (Spring 1985): 35–63.

Portes, Alejandro, and Rubén G. Rumbaut, *Immigrant America: A Portrait*. Berkeley and Los Angeles: University of California Press, 1990.

Portes, Alejandro, and Alex Stepick. "Unwelcome Immigrants: The Labor Market Experiences of 1980 (Mariel) Cuban and Haitian Refugees in South Florida." *American Sociological Review* 50 (August 1985): 493–514.

Proctor, Samuel. *Napoleon Bonaparte Broward, Florida's Fighting Democrat*. Gainesville: University of Florida Press, 1950.

"The Quiet Riot." *New Times*, September 26–October 2, 1990, 12–22.

"Recarey pagó millones a cabilderos." *El Nuevo Herald*, December 20, 1987, 6A.

Redford, Polly. *Billion-Dollar Sandbar: A Biography of Miami Beach*. New York: E. P. Dutton, 1970.

Rieff, David. *Going to Miami: Exiles, Tourists, and Refugees in the New America*. Boston: Little, Brown, 1987.

"Room at the Infield." *Miami Herald*, December 25, 1988, 2C.

Rowe, Sean. "Hugo's Homeboys." *New Times*, September 2–8, 1992, 13–14.

"St. Augustine." In *The Columbia Lippincott Gazetteer of the World*, edited by L. E. Seltzer, 1627. New York: Columbia University Press, 1962.

Saint-Louis, Loretta J. P. "Migration Evolves: The Political Economy of Network Process and Form in Haiti, the U.S., and Canada." Ph.D. diss., Boston University, 1988.

San Martin, Nancy. "Haitians Struggle for Unity in New Land." *Miami Herald*, "Neighbors North" sec., September 23, 1990, 16–17.

——— "Miami's Haitians Not All of One Mind on the Aristide Presidency." *Miami Herald*, October 5, 1991, 2B.

San Martin, Nancy, and Xose Alvarez-Alfonso. "Haitian Families Are Moving out to the Suburbs." *Miami Herald*, "Neighbors Northwest" sec., October 14, 1990, 20, 21.

San Martin, Nancy, and Karen Branch. "Miami Haitians March." *Miami Herald*, October 3, 1991, 18A.

San Martin, Nancy, Andres Viglucci, and David Hancock. "Peaceful Rally Ends Days of Divisiveness." *Miami Herald*, July 8, 1990, 1B, 2B.

Santiago, Ana, and Ivan Román. "Haitianos denuncian brutalidad policial." *El Nuevo Herald*, July 7, 1990, 1A, 6A.

Santiago, Fabiola. "$100,000 Fund to Pay Tuition for 100 Exiles." *Miami Herald*, January 9, 1985, 6B.

——— "Dinner for INS Chief to Fund Contra Lobby." *Miami Herald*, *Local*, June 27, 1985, 1D.

Santiago, Fabiola, and Barbara Gutierrez. "Dade's Little Managua: Bastion of Uncertainty." *Miami Herald*, July 19, 1984, 16A.

Satterfield, David. "We Will Rebuild Hits $11 Million." *Miami Herald*, September 19, 1992, 1A, 20A.

Sawyer, Kathy. "Refugee Policy Draws Fire in Hearing." *Washington Post*, May 13, 1980, A6.

Sayad, Abdelmalek. "Immigration in France: An 'Exotic' Form of Poverty." Paper presented at the conference on Urban Poverty, Migration, and Marginality, Maison Suger, Paris, May 1991.

Silva, John. "Court Told of Living Death in Haitian Prison." *Miami News*, April 9, 1980, 4A.

Sofen, Edward. *The Miami Metropolitan Experiment*. Bloomington: Indiana University Press, 1963.

Solís, Dianna, and José de Córdoba. "Cuban Prison Riots Followed Seven Years of U.S. Ambivalence." *Wall Street Journal*, December 1, 1987, 1.

——— "Mariel Firestorm." *Wall Street Journal*, December 1, 1987.

"Soto, Hernando de." *New Encyclopaedia Britannica*. 15th ed. Vol. 11. Chicago: Encyclopaedia Britannica, 1989.

Starita, Joe. "Nicaraguans Stream into Miami Stadium, an Unlikely Refuge." *Miami Herald*, January 13, 1989, 1A.

Steinback, Robert L. "Tensions Push Miami to Brink of Its Own War." *Miami Herald*, December 28, 1990, 1B.

Stepick, Alex. "The Business Community of Little Haiti." Dialogue no. 32, Occasional Paper Series, Latin American and Caribbean Center, 1–45. Miami: Florida International University, February 1984.

——— "The Haitian Informal Sector in Miami." *City and Society* 5 (June 1991): 10–22.

——— *Haitian Refugees in the U.S.* Minority Rights Group Publication no. 52. London: MRG, 1986.

——— "Little Haiti." In *Miami: Insight City Guides*, edited by Joann Biondi, 209–16. London: APA Publications, 1991.

——— "Miami's Two Informal Sectors." In *The Informal Economy: Studies in Advanced and Less Developed Countries*, edited by A. Portes, M. Castells, and L. Benton, 111–31. Baltimore: Johns Hopkins University Press, 1989.

———— "The Refugees Nobody Wants: Haitians in Miami." In *Miami Now! Immigration, Ethnicity, and Social Change*, edited by G. J. Grenier and A. Stepick, 57–82. Gainesville: University Press of Florida, 1992.

Stepick, Alex, Max Castro, Marvin Dunn, and Guillermo Grenier. "Newcomers and Established Residents: The Case of Miami." Final Report to the Ford Foundation for the Changing Relations Project. Miami: Center for Labor Research and Study, Florida International University, 1989.

Stepick, Alex, and Alejandro Portes. "Flight into Despair: A Profile of Recent Haitian Refugees in South Florida." *International Migration Review* 20 (Summer 1986): 329–50.

Strasser, Fred. "Nicaraguans Share Fight for Freedom at Cubans' Rally." *Miami Herald*, May 21, 1984, 1B.

Strouse, Charles, and David Hancock. "1,000 Haitians Trap Storeowner." *Miami Herald*, July 1, 1990, 1B, 2B.

Struck, Doug. "Hostages Set Free, Oakdale Inmates Yield." *Baltimore Sun*, November 30, 1987, 1A.

Suarez, Andrés. *Cuba: Castroism and Communism, 1959–1966*. Cambridge, Mass.: MIT Press, 1967.

Suárez, Xavier L. "Miami Is Poised to Fulfill 'City of the Future' Role." *Miami Herald*, December 6, 1989, 17A.

Suchlicki, Jaime, and Arturo Cruz. "The Impact of Nicaraguans in Miami: The Nicaraguan Exodus to Miami Under the Sandinistas, and the Future Outlook Following Their Electoral Defeat." Study for the City Manager of Miami prepared by the Institute of Interamerican Studies, University of Miami, March 1990.

Swarns, Rachel L. "Lozano Wins a Manslaughter Retrial." *Miami Herald*, June 26, 1991, 1A, 10A.

Task Force on Immigration and Refugee Policy. "Issue Paper—Subject: What Policy Should the United States Adopt with Regard to Foreign Persons Who Enter South Florida Without Visas?" Memorandum to President Ronald Reagan. June 26, 1981.

Tasker, Frederic. "Anti-Bilingualism Measure Approved by Dade County." *Miami Herald*, November 5, 1980, 1A, 11A.

———— "Dade Neighborhoods Stay Segregated as Residents Seek American Dream." *Miami Herald*, November 1, 1982, D1.

Thomas, Hugh. *Cuba: The Pursuit of Freedom*. New York: Harper & Row, 1971.

Thomas, John F., and Earl E. Huyck. "Resettlement of Cuban Refugees in the United States." Paper presented at the meetings of the American Sociological Association, San Francisco, August 1967.

Trouillot, Michel-Rolph. *Haiti, State Against Nation: The Origins and Legacy of Duvalierism*. New York: Monthly Review Press, 1990.

U.S. Bureau of the Census. *The Hispanic Population of the United States, 1989*. Washington, D.C.: U.S. Department of Commerce, 1990.

———— *Survey of Minority-owned Business Enterprises, 1977/Hispanics*. Washington, D.C.: U.S. Department of Commerce, 1980.

———— *Survey of Minority-owned Business Enterprises, 1987/Hispanics*. Washington, D.C.: U.S. Department of Commerce, 1991.

"U.S. Official Joins Celebration of Nicaragua's Independence." *Miami Herald*, September 10, 1986, 2B.

Valburn, Marjorie, and Sharony Andrews. "Aristide Saw Haitians, U.S. Blacks as One." *Miami Herald*, September 28, 1991, 1B, 4B.

Valdés, Roxanne. "American—With Cuban Blood." *Miami Herald*, February 15, 1990, 26A.

Veciana-Suarez, Ana. "Nicaraguan Exiles Begin to Climb the Ladder." *Miami Herald*, March 28, 1983, 10BM.

Veciana-Suarez, Ana, and Sandra Dibble. "Miami's Nicaraguans: Remaking Their Lives" (pt. 1 of 2 pts.). *Miami Herald*, September 13, 1987, 1G.

Viglucci, Andres. "Liberty City Rises Like the Phoenix; Group Accomplishes Change Few Envisioned." *Miami Herald*, July 22, 1990, 1B, 7B.

Von Drehle, Dave, and Christopher Marquis. "Nicaraguan Stream into Miami; Many Find They Must Fend for Themselves." *Miami Herald*, January 13, 1989, 1A.

Wallace, Richard. "Nicaraguans Jam INS Offices for Work Papers." *Miami Herald*, August 23, 1987, 1B.

———— "South Florida Grows to a Latin Beat." *Miami Herald*, March 6, 1991, 1–2Z.

Wallbank, T. Walter, and Alastair M. Taylor. *Civilization, Past and Present*. 4th ed. Vol. 2. Chicago: Scott, Foresman, 1961.

Warner, W. Lloyd, and Paul S. Lunt. *The Status System of a Modern Community*. New Haven: Yale University Press, 1942.

Warner, W. Lloyd, and Leo Srole. *The Social Systems of American Ethnic Groups*. New Haven: Yale University Press, 1945.

Weber, Adna F. *The Growth of Cities in the Nineteenth Century: A Study in Statistics*. Ithaca, N.Y.: Cornell University Press, 1967.

Weber, Max. *The City*. New York: Free Press, [1921] 1966.

Welch, Richard E. *Response to Revolution: The United States and the Cuban Revolution, 1959–1961*. Chapel Hill: University of North Carolina Press, 1985.

White, Peter T. "Cuba at a Crossroads." *National Geographic*, August 1991, 94–121.

Whited, Charles. "Castro Always Seems to Call the Shots Here." *Miami Herald*, November 24, 1987, 1B.

——— "Washington Is Guilty of Big, Fat Blunder over Refugees." *Miami Herald*, January 14, 1989, 1B.

White House. "New Cuban-Haitian Plan." *Fact Sheet #114*. Washington, D.C., July 1980.

Wilson, William J. "The Underclass: Issues, Perspectives, and Public Policy." *Annals of the American Academy of Political and Social Sciences* 516 (January 1989): 182–92.

Wisenberg, Sandi. "An Unlikely Champion." *Miami Herald*, April 26, 1985, 1C.

Woldemikael, Tekle. *Becoming Black American: Haitians and American Institutions in Evanston, Illinois*. New York: AMS Press, 1989.

"The Worst Wind." *New Times*, September 2–8, 1992 (special issue).

Wragg, Joanna. "The Boycott, Blacks, and Cubans." *Miami Herald*, December 30, 1990, 2C.

Zaldívar, R. A. "Vague Laws Spur Refugee Movements." *Miami Herald*, January 15, 1989, 1A.

Zolberg, Aristide. "The Next Waves: Migration Theory for a Changing World." *International Migration Review* 23 (Fall 1989): 403–30.

Index

Abrams, Elliot, 158
Acculturation-in-reverse, 8, 17, 220, 225
African-Americans. *See* Blacks
AIDS among Haitian immigrants, 188, 189
American Civil Liberties Union (ACLU), 177
American Federation of State, County, and Municipal Employees (AFSCME), 176
American International Container, 130–131
Anglos. *See* Whites
Anticommunism among Cuban immigrants, 143, 176
Aristide, Jean-Bertrand, 138, 193–194
Artime, Manuel, 101
Assimilation: biculturalism and, 8; ethnicity and, 5–7; ethnic politics and, 215–218; speed of,6,7
Auténtico party, 98
Aviño, Joaquin, 165

Bahamians, 76
Ballet Folklórico Nicaragüense, 169
Batista, Fulgencio, 97–99, 102
Batten, James K., 213
Bay of Pigs invasion, 30, 102, 106, 126, 127
Biculturalism, 175; and assimilation, 8
Big Five Club, 131
Bilingualism: employment and, 12; opposition to, 34, 35, 147, 161; social relations and, 12. *See also* English Only movement; Language
Biscayne Bay, 74
Black Lawyers Association, 177
Blacks: Black-owned businesses and, 43, 78, 179–180, 182, 196, 197–199, 233 n. 9; boycott of Miami and, 141, 177, 184, 190; boycott of public schools

and, 183, 184, 190; compared to foreign blacks, 196; discrimination against, 77–78; divisions among leaders, 183–184; double subordination of, 10, 47, 50, 194–195, 197, 202, 217; in early Florida, 72, 76–80; economic development and, 195; employment of, 39–46, 179–181; income of, 40–42, 44; local economy and, 14; local politics and, 182–184, 199; Lozano case and, 2–3; middle class, 40, 42, 78, 178–180, 181–184; New Deal and, 78; police violence against, 2–3, 47–48, 50, 178, 179, 189; relations with Cuban immigrants, 12, 13, 14, 16, 38–39, 140–141, 176–177, 182–184, 196–197, 199–202; relations with Haitian immigrants, 177–178, 185, 189–192; relations with whites, 14, 195–199; residence patterns of, 184, 186; residential segregation of, 77, 79–80; segregation and, 38; self-employment of, 199; violence against, 77–78, 80; visit of Mandela and, 141, 176–177
Boat people. *See* Haitian immigrants
Bobby Maduro Stadium, 164–166
Botifoll, Luis, 36
Bounded solidarity: among Cuban immigrants, 135, 136, 137, 139; among Haitian immigrants, 193; among Nicaraguan immigrants, 169
Broward, Napoleon Bonaparte, 87, 91
Bush, George, 213, 224
Bush, Jeb, 123, 124, 213
Business Assistance Center (BAC), 179, 198–199, 201

Camarioca, Cuba, 103–104
Camayd-Freixas, Yohel, 27
Carey, Barbara, 162

Caribbean migration to U.S., 206–207
Carter, Jimmy, 24, 25, 26, 29, 159
Carter administration: Cuban-American
    voters and, 22, 24; policy toward
    Haitian immigrants, 54; policy toward
    Mariel boatlift, 22, 24
Casa Comunidad, 170
Castro, Fidel, 18; anticipated demise of,
    218–221; as anti-imperialist symbol,
    143; description of Mariel refugees,
    21; movement against Batista and,
    97–99; support for Sandinistas, 166;
    visit of Mandela and, 141, 176
Center for Study of the Americas, 20
Centers for Disease Control, 188
Central America Pro-Refugee
    Commission, 166
Central Intelligence Agency (CIA):
    Cuban businesses and, 129, 242 n. 10;
    JM-Wave and, 126, 127; support of
    anti-Castro exiles, 101, 126–127, 129,
    142
Chamber of Commerce, Greater Miami,
    35, 179, 212
Chapman, Alvah, 198, 226
Character loans, 132–135
Charles I (Holy Roman Emperor), 64
Chisholm, Shirley, 54
Citizens of Dade United, 161, 162, 174
Civic League of Colored Town, 79
Class: divisions among Blacks, 178–184,
    197; divisions among Haitian
    immigrants, 178, 192–194; divisions
    among Nicaraguan immigrants,
    172–173; in "Yankee City," 5
Coast Guard, U.S.: Haitian immigrants
    and, 52, 188; Mariel boatlift and, 24,
    53
Cocoanut Grove, 62, 72, 76, 90
Coconut Grove, 184
Collins, John S., 72–73
Colored Board of Trade, 79
"Colored Town," 76–80, 93, 202
Community power, theories of, 4
Congressional Black Caucus, Haitian
    immigrants and, 54
Congress of Racial Equality (CORE),
    177
Construction industry: Cuban
    immigrants in, 133–134; ethnic groups
    in, 40–41; Nicaraguan immigrants in,
    154
Convergence of ethnic communities, 221,
    224–225, 227
Coral Gables, Fla., 74–75, 84, 128;
    incorporation of, 81

Corporate control: of cities, 4–5; in
    Miami, 8
Council of National Liberation, 98
Creole (language), 52, 54, 59, 189, 191,
    193
Cuba: anticipated demise of Castro and,
    218–221; independence movement in,
    89–94; Kennedy administration policy
    toward, 103; national identity of, 94;
    new migration from, 218; relations
    with U.S., 93–96, 106
Cuban-American: use of term, 148. *See*
    Cuban immigrants
Cuban-American National Foundation
    (CANF), 132; founding of, 35, 148;
    future of Cuba and, 218; Hurricane
    Andrew relief and, 226; influence in
    Washington, 158; *Miami Herald* and,
    15, 138, 173; political action branch
    of, 148
Cuban ethnic economy: apprenticeship
    in, 145–146; character loans and,
    132–135; credit in, 132–135;
    development of, 126, 144–147; future
    of, 220; hegemony of conservatism
    and, 144; origins of, 127–129; role of
    social capital in, 135–137;
    self-employment in, 146; social
    networks in, 135–137
Cuban-Haitian Interagency Task Force,
    54, 234 n. 24
Cuban immigrants: conflict with *Miami
    Herald*, 15–16; Cuban-owned
    businesses and, 43, 46, 182;
    discrimination against, 135, 147, 200;
    electoral power of, 141; involvement
    in local politics, 29–30, 35, 37,
    148–149, 182–183, 201, 210–211, 225;
    Johnson administration policy toward,
    103, 142; Kennedy administration
    and, 30, 142; middle class, 40–42,
    100; as moral community, 137–144,
    145; as political exiles in U.S., 63–67,
    89–99, 101–102; political intolerance
    of, 137–144; prospect of returning to
    Cuba and, 218–219; public opinion
    toward, 31; as refugees from Castro
    regime, 102–105, 106–107, 126–127;
    relations with Blacks, 12, 13, 14, 16,
    38–39, 140–141, 176–177, 182–184,
    196–197, 199–202; relations with
    Haitian immigrants, 177–178;
    relations with whites, 17; resettlement
    of, 103–105; residence patterns of,
    184, 187; response to Mariel refugees,
    21, 29, 30–37; self-employment of, 40,

199; as success story, 30–36; upper
class, 207; women workers, 127–128.
See also Mariel refugees
Cuban immigration: compared to
Haitian immigration, 51–54, 188;
compared to Nicaraguan immigration,
151–152, 156–157, 159, 169–170, 173;
political asylum and, 157. *See also*
Mariel boatlift
Cuban Missile Crisis, 102, 106, 126, 142
Cuban Refugee Center, 75, 105, 127
Cuban Refugee Program, 103
Cuban Revolutionary Council, 91–92,
126, 142
Cuban Revolutionary Party, 90

Dade County: Black officials in,
179–180, 181; contracts with Black
firms, 179, 181; economically active
population of, 208–209; elected
officials in, 210–211; hurricane
preparedness of, 224; impact of
redistricting on, 212
Dahl, Robert A.: ethnic politics and,
215–216; pluralist theory and, 4, 215,
216, 217, 218
Dale, Bennett, 23
Daytona Beach, Fla., 97
"Definition of the situation": concept
defined, 9; varieties of, in Miami,
10–16
De Soto, Hernando, 64
Diaz-Balart, Lincoln, 225
Diaz-Oliver, Remedios, 130–131, 132
Dickson, Clarence, 46
Didion, Joan, 17
Discourse: of Anglo cultural
reaffirmation, 10; of anticommunism,
143; assimilationist, 149; of Black
double subordination, 10, 47, 50,
194–195, 197, 217; of Blacks, 49; of
Cuban conservatives, 143–144; of
Cuban liberals, 143; of Cuban success
story, 10, 149, 212, 226; defined, 9;
minority, 149; new Anglo, 213–214;
unification of, 225; varieties of, in
Miami, 9–17
"Disposal problem," 127
Dorsey, David A., 78
Due, Patricia, 177
Dulles, Allen, 126
Dunn, Marvin, 39, 48

Edison High School, 185, 189, 191
Electoral Council of the Nicaraguan
Exodus, 172

Employment: of Blacks, 39–46; of
Cuban immigrants, 39–46; of
Haitians, 56–58; of native whites,
39–46; of Nicaraguans, 152–156
Enforceable trust: among Cuban
immigrants, 136, 137; among Haitian
immigrants, 193
English Only movement: amendment to
Florida constitution and, 161;
campaign issues of, 161; in Miami, 11
Enterprise zone in Black neighborhoods,
180
Ethnicity: assimilation and, 5–8; in
Miami, 210–215. *See also specific
nationalities*
Ethnic politics, 215–216. *See also specific
nationalities*
Ethnics: defined, 5. *See also specific
nationalities*

Factor banking, 134
Facts about Cuban Exiles (FACE),
35
Fair, T. Willard, 184
Fascell, Dante, 162
Fauntroy, Walter, 54
Ferré, Maurice, 23, 24, 183
Fisher, Carl J., 73
Flagler, Henry M., 61, 62, 71–74
Florida: American conquest of, 67–70;
economic development of, 61–63,
71–76; English colonization of, 66;
French colonization of, 65; historical
connections to Cuba, 63–67, 90–101;
as independent republic, 70; Indians
in, 63–64, 65, 68–69, 70; legacy of
Civil War in, 70–71; proliferation of
local governments in, 80–81;
settlement pattern of, 74, 82; slaves
in, 67, 70; Spanish colonization of,
63–68; state politics in, 71, 82–83
Florida East Coast Railway, 62, 72, 81,
91
Florida International University (FIU),
13, 219
Florida Needletrade Association, 127,
128
Fonda, Jane, 137
Food and Drug Administration (FDA),
Haitian immigrants and, 188
Ford Foundation, 54
Fort Chaffee, Ark., 25
Fort Indiantown Gap, Pa., 25
Fort Lauderdale, Fla., 56, 69
Fort Myers, Fla., 69
Fort Pierce, Fla., 69

Frames, cognitive: defined, 9; in Miami, 10–16, 212
Free Cuba Committee, 148
"Freedom flights," 104, 106
Freedom Flotilla, 20, 22

Gálvez, Bernardo de, 66, 67
Garment industry: Blacks in, 40–41; Cuban immigrants in, 40–41, 127–128; Haitian immigrants in, 154; Jews in, 127–128; Nicaraguan immigrants in, 154; whites in, 40–41
Gary, Howard, 182
Geertz, Clifford, 136
Glazer, Nathan, 6
Graham, Bob, 24, 162
Graham, Ernest G., 85
Grambling, John, 79
Granma, 97
Greater Miami Negro Civic League, 79
Greeley, Andrew, 6
Greer, Tee S., 183

Haitian-American Community Agency of Dade (HACAD), 54
Haitian ethnic economy, 185, 192–193
Haitian immigrants: Black response to, 55–56; Carter administration policy toward, 54; characteristics of, 56–58; class divisions among, 193–194; discrimination against, 58; Haitian-owned businesses and, 193; middle class, 51, 54, 192–194; police violence against, 178, 181, 188–189; political divisions among, 193–194; in public schools, 191–192; relations with Blacks, 177–178, 185, 189–192; relations with Cuban immigrants, 177–178; residence patterns of, 56; white response to, 51, 55; working class, 51, 194
Haitian immigration: compared to Cuban immigration, 51–54, 188; phases of, 51; political asylum and, 53–54; Reagan administration policy toward, 52, 53; response of whites to, 51, 55
Haitian Refugee Center, 52, 54
Haitian Task Force, 54
Havana, Cuba, 18, 23, 100
Herald, El, 15, 175
Herald, El Nuevo, 15, 140, 175
Hialeah, Fla., 37, 39, 84
Hispanics. *See specific nationalities*
Home Rule Amendment, 86

Hotel industry: Blacks in, 40–41; Cuban immigrants in, 40–41
Hunter, Floyd, 4, 5
Hurricane Andrew: destruction by, 223–224; impact on social change, 224–227

Immigration Advisory Committee, 162
Immigration and Naturalization Service (INS): Cuban immigrants and, 158; Haitian immigrants and, 188; Mariel refugees and, 25; Nicaraguan immigrants and, 150, 157, 161, 163, 246 n. 33
Informal economy: casual work in, 155; Haitian immigrants in, 185; in Miami, 154; Nicaraguans in, 154, 155, 165, 171
Inter-American Transport Equipment Company, 131–132
Interethnic relations: changes in, 59–60; as problem in Miami, 13–14. *See also specific nationalities*
International Medical Centers (IMC), 123–126
International migration, theories of, 205–206

Jackson, Andrew, 67–68
Jackson, Jesse, 53
Jacksonville, Fla., 105
Jean-Juste, Gerard, 52, 193
Jews: community of, 73; Cuban immigrants and, 14; discrimination against, 73; English Only and, 161; in garment industry, 127–128; as residents, 84–85; as tourists, 84; visit of Mandela and, 141, 176–177

Kennedy, Edward, 54
Key West, Fla., 89–90, 93, 95
King, Martin Luther, Jr., 39
Knight-Ridder Corporation, 14, 34, 198, 200, 213. *See also Herald, El; Herald, El Nuevo; Miami Herald*
Ku Klux Klan, 39, 77–78, 79, 80

Labor unions, in construction, 133–134
Lamarche, François, 204
Lamm, Richard D., 216
Language: assimilation and, 6–7; as problem in Miami, 11–12, 59. *See also Bilingualism; English Only movement*
Latin Builders Association, 134
Lawrence, David, Jr., 214
Leland, Mickey, 54

Liberty City, Fla., 39, 55, 84, 86, 177, 184; enterprise zone in, 180; industrial park in, 180, 181; 1980 riot and, 47, 48, 49; origins of, 79
Lieberson, Stanley, 49
Little Haiti, 54, 55, 177, 185–188, 193
Little Havana, 39, 99; as model for Little Haiti, 54, 55; Nicaraguan immigrants in, 154
Lloyd, Clement, 2–3
Logan, John, 4
Los Ranchos Restaurant, 168, 169
Lozano, William, 2–3, 9
Lum, Henry B., 61

McDuffie, Arthur, 47, 48
Maceo, Antonio, 92
Machado, Gerardo, 95–96
Mack, Connie, 162, 172
McKinley, William, 92
McMillian, Johnnie, 184
Mahoney, Daniel J., 85
Maine, 92
Mandela, Nelson, visit to Miami, 141, 176–177
Mariátegui, Señor de, 92
Mariel boatlift: Carter administration policy toward, 22, 24, 26; Cuban government policy toward, 18–22, 26; origins of, 18–20
Mariel refugees: Black reaction to, 25, 38; Carter administration policy toward, 24, 25; criminals among, 20–21, 22–23, 24, 25, 26 30, 32, 59; Cuban-American response to, 21, 29, 30–37; homosexuals among, 26, 32; immigration status of, 25; INS and, 25; mental patients among, 22, 24, 26, 30, 59; official Cuban description of, 20–21; perceptions of discrimination of, 32–33; prison riots of, 1–2, 9; public opinion and, 30–31; public schools and, 25–26; white response to, 23, 27–30, 34
Martí, José, 89–90, 91
Martinez, Bob, 218
Martinez, Julio, 141
Mas Canosa, Jorge, 15, 218
Masvidal, Raul, 201
Meese, Edwin, 158, 246 n. 33
Menéndez de Avilés, Don Pedro, 65
Metro Charter, 82–87
Metropolis, 77, 79
Metrorail, construction of, 46
Miami, Fla.: air links to Havana, 100, 102, 104; boycott of, 141, 177, 184,

190; Calle Ocho, 15, 137, 168; as center for Cuban exiles, 63–67, 90–101, 104, 106–107; changes in 1980, 58–60; incorporation of, 72, 81; map of, 19; origins of, 61–63, 70, 204–205; origins of metropolitan government in, 85–87; political geography of, 205–210, 226; population of, 20, 186, 187, 210–211; social structure of, 8; as tourist center, 99–101, 144, 148, 207, 208
Miami Beach, Fla., 81, 84
Miami Coalition for a Free South Africa, 177
Miami-Dade Community College: Haitian students and, 185; Nicaraguan students and, 167
Miami Herald: Black views of, 16; boycott of Miami and, 184; conflict with Cuban immigrant community and, 15, 16, 27, 138, 173; creation of new Spanish edition of, 175; discrimination against Blacks and, 77; Mariel refugees and, 23–30; as object of discourse, 10, 14–16; position on Nicaraguan immigration, 173–175; as power broker, 85; Recarey case and, 125–126; Spanish edition of, 15. See also *Herald, El; Herald, El Nuevo;* Knight-Ridder Corporation
Miami-Managua Lions Club, 172
Miami News, 85, 183
Miami Pact, 98
Miami Theater Festival, 138
Miami Times, 79
Mills, C. Wright, 4–5
Mintz, Sidney W., 94
Miró Cardona, José, 142, 240 n. 24
Mohl, Raymond, 79
Molotch, Harvey, 4
Monroe, James, 68
Movement for Revolutionary Recuperation (MRR), 101
Moynihan, Daniel P., 6
Munroe, Ralph, 62

NAACP (National Association for the Advancement of Colored People), 38, 184; 1980 riot and, 49
Narváez, Pánfilo de, 64
National Council of Churches (NCC), Haitian immigrants and, 52
National Organization of Women (NOW), 177
Negro Uplift Association of Dade County, 79

Nelson, Alan, 165
Nicaragua, Contra war in, 150, 153, 156, 157, 159, 166
Nicaraguan-American Bankers Association, 153, 158, 169
Nicaraguan Business Council, 158
Nicaraguan Community Day, 170
Nicaraguan Democratic Youth, 172
Nicaraguan immigrants: in agriculture, 155; Black response to, 163; class divisions among, 172–173; cultural traditions of, 169, 171; middle class, 151, 152–153, 157, 168–169; political differences among, 171–172; residence patterns of, 167–168; response of Cuban-American community to, 163–167, 174–175; upper class, 151, 152, 157, 168; white response to, 161–163; working class, 152, 153–156, 170, 171
Nicaraguan immigration: compared to Cuban immigration, 151–152, 156–157, 159, 169–170, 173; phases of, 151–156; political asylum and, 157, 159, 160, 168; response of whites to, 161–163; U.S. government policy toward, 150–151, 156, 158–161, 165, 170
Nofziger, Lyn, 124

Obando y Bravo, Miguel, 167
Odio, Cesar, 163–165, 182
Oliveros, Gilda, 140
Opa-Locka, Fla., 81, 84, 177
Operation Save, 157
Osceola (Seminole chief), 69
Overtown, Fla., 2, 55, 163, 184; early history of, 70, 77, 70–80, 89, 93; enterprise zone in, 180; redevelopment in, 180, 181. See also "Colored Town"

Pennekamp, John, 85
Pensacola, Fla., 66, 67, 70
People's Revolutionary Movement (Movimiento Revolucionario del Pueblo, MRP), 142
Pepper, Claude, 123, 161
Philip II (King of Spain), 65, 236 n. 12
Pitts, Otis, 181
Plant, Henry M., 74
Platt, Orville H., 93
Platt Amendment, 93, 95, 96, 106
Police: Lozano case and, 2–3, 9; McDuffie case and, 47–48; violence against Blacks, 2–3, 80, 178, 179, 189;

violence against Haitians, 178, 181, 188–189
Ponce de León, Juan, 63–64, 71
Porter, Bruce, 39, 48
Prío Socarrás, Carlos, 97–99, 152
Public schools, Dade County: boycott of, 183, 184, 190; Haitian immigrants in, 185–186; Nicaraguan children in, 162

Quinlan, Michael J., 1–2

Race, assimilation and, 6–7
Racism: against Blacks, 195; in Cuba, 200; of Cuban immigrants, 183, 195, 197, 199; against Haitian immigrants, 189, 193; of whites, 195, 197
Radio, Miami Cuban: philantropy of, 248 n. 61; support for Nicaraguan immigrants, 164, 166–167; visit of Mandela and, 177. See also WQBA–La Cubanisima
Ray Rivero, Manuel, 142
Reactive ethnicity: among Blacks, 189, 217; among Cuban immigrants, 30–37; among Haitian immigrants, 188, 189
Reboredo, Pedro, Mandela visit and, 141
Recarey, Miguel, 123–126
Redford, Polly, 95
Reeves, Henry, 79
Reilly, Robert, 158
Religion, assimilation and, 6–7
Removal Act, 68–69
Rieff, David, 17, 34, 74
Riots in Miami: in 1968, 48; in 1980, 48–50, 59, 179
Rivero, José, 141
Rivkind, Perry, 158
Román, Agustin, 2, 9, 164
Rubén Darío Institute, 171

Saint Augustine, Fla., 65–66, 67, 71, 74
Sears, John, 124
Self-employment: of Blacks, 199; of Cuban immigrants, 40, 199
Seminoles: attacks against colonists by, 62; origin of name, 67; removal from Florida of, 68–69; rise and decline of, 70
Seminole War, 69, 71
Silverman, Arnold, 49
Small Business Administration (SBA): loans to Blacks, 46; loans to Cuban immigrants, 46, 133
Smith, H. T., 177, 184, 226
Social capital, among Cuban immigrants, 137, 140

Social networks, in Cuban ethnic economy, 135–137
Social structure, parallel, 8, 9, 16, 17
Somoza Debayle, Anastasio, 152
Southern Housing Corporation, 79
Soviet Union, Cuba and, 103, 140
Spanish-American League Against Discrimination (SALAD), 147
Spanish-American War, 93, 95
Spanish language, 36
Srole, Leo, 6–7
Suarez, Diego R., 131, 132
Suárez, Xavier, 177, 183, 201, 214; Mandela visit and, 141
Supreme Court, 92
Sweetwater, Fla., 81, 152, 154, 168, 169, 170

Tallahassee, Fla., 105
Tampa, Fla., 93
Thomas, Hugh, 95
Thomas, John, 103
Thomas, W. I., 9
Thornburgh, Richard, 162
Three Friends, 91–92
Treaty of Paris, 66
Treaty of Versailles, 67
Tuttle, Julia, 62
Twenty-sixth of July Movement, 98

Unemployment rates by race and origin, 45
United Nicaraguan Artists, 171
United States: relations with Caribbean, 206; relations with Cuba, 93–96, 106

University of Miami, 74
Urban League, 184; 1980 riot and, 49
Urban sociology, 3–4; theories of community power, 4–5; theories of ethnicity and assimilation, 5–9; theories of urbanization, 203–205
U.S. English, 161

Varona, Manuel Antonio de, 98
Visiedo, Osvaldo, 183
Voting Rights Act of 1990, 212

Walsh, Bryan D., 144
Warner, W. Lloyd, 5–7
Weber, Adna, 203
Weber, Max, 203
Welles, Sumner, 96
West Miami, Fla., 37
We Will Rebuild Committee, 224, 226
Whites: discourse of 10, 213–214; relations with Blacks, 14, 195–199; relations with Cuban immigrants, 17; response to Haitian immigration, 51, 55; response to Mariel refugees, 23, 27–30, 34; response to Nicaraguan immigration, 161–163
Wieland, William, 99
Woodlawn Cemetery, 96, 99, 152
WQBA–*La Cubanisima*, 139, 164

"Yankee City" (Newburyport, Mass.), 5–8
Young, Andrew, 53

Compositor:	Com-Com
Text:	11/13 Caledonia
Display:	Caledonia
Printer and Binder:	Haddon Craftsmen, Inc.